Red and Expert

A Conversation Between Chairman Mao and His Niece, Wang Hai-jung

WANG HAI-JUNG [in conversation with her uncle, Mao Tse-tung]: There is the son of a cadre [in her class at the Foreign Languages Institute] who doesn't do well. In class he doesn't listen attentively to the teacher's lecture and after class, he doesn't do homework. He likes to read fiction. Sometimes he dozes off in the dormitory and sometimes he doesn't attend the Saturday afternoon meeting. On Sunday he doesn't return to school on time. Sometimes on Sunday when our class and section hold a meeting, he doesn't show up. All of us have a bad impression of him.

CHAIRMAN MAO: Do your teachers allow the students to take a nap or read fiction in class? We should let the students read fiction and take a nap in class, and we should look after their health. Teachers should lecture less and make the students read more. I believe the student you referred to will be very capable in the future since he had the courage to be absent from the Saturday meeting and not to return to school on time on Sunday. When you return to school, you may tell him that it is too early to return to school even at eight or nine in the evening; he may delay it until eleven or twelve. Whose fault is it that you should hold a meeting Sunday night?

HAI-JUNG: When I studied at the Normal School, we usually had no meeting Sunday night. We were allowed to do whatever we liked that night. One day several cadres of the branch headquarters of the League (I was then a committee member of the branch headquarters) agreed to lead an organized life on Sunday night but many other League members did not favor the idea. Some of them even said to the political counselor that Sunday was a free day and if any meeting was called at night, it would be inconvenient for us to go home. The political counselor eventually bowed to their opinion and told us to change the date for the meeting.

CHAIRMAN MAO: This political counselor did the right thing.

HAI-JUNG: But now our school spends the whole Sunday night holding meetings—class meetings, branch headquarters committee meetings, or meetings of study groups for party lessons. According to my calculation, from the beginning of the current semester to date, there has not been one Sunday or Sunday night without any meetings.

CHAIRMAN MAO: When you return to school, you should take the lead to rebel. Don't return to school on Sunday and don't attend any meeting on that day.

HAI-JUNG: But I won't dare. This is the school system. All students are required to return to school on time. If I don't, people will say that I violate the school system.

CHAIRMAN MAO: Don't care about the system. Just don't return to school. Just say you want to violate the school system.

HAI-JUNG: I cannot do that. If I do, I will be criticized.

CHAIRMAN MAO: I don't think you will be very capable in the future. You are afraid of being accused of violating the school system, of criticism, of a bad record, of being expelled from school, of failing to get party membership. Why should you be afraid of so many things? The worst that can come to you is expulsion from school. The school should allow the students to rebel. Rebel when you return to school.

HAI-JUNG: People will say that as the Chairman's relative, I fail to follow his instructions and play a leading role in upsetting the school system. They will accuse me of arrogance and self-content, and of lack of organization and discipline.

CHAIRMAN MAO: Look at you! You are afraid of being criticized for arrogance and self-content, and for lack of organization and discipline. Why should you be afraid? You can say that just because you are Chairman Mao's relative, you should follow his instruction to rebel. I think the student you mentioned will be more capable than you for he dared to violate the school system. I think you people are all to metaphysical.

Red and Expert

Education in the People's Republic of China

Ruth Gamberg

Foreword by William Hinton

Schocken Books • New York

First published by SCHOCKEN BOOKS 1977

Copyright © 1977 by Schocken Books Inc.

Library of Congress Cataloging in Publication Data

    Gamberg, Ruth.
      Red and expert.

      Includes index.
      1. Education—China—History. I. Title.

    LA1131.82.G35   370'.951   75-34876

Manufactured in the United States of America

Frontispiece quotation from David Milton, Nancy Milton, and Franz Schurmann, eds., *People's China: Social Experimentation, Politics, Entry onto the World Scene, 1966 Through 1972* (New York: Vintage Books, 1974), pp. 241-43.

To the people of China
who are storming heaven.

CONTENTS

FOREWORD

The revolutionary struggle in China in the last two decades has demonstrated that socialist revolution is a protracted process. This process was initiated in China by massive changes in the system of ownership, which brought class exploitation to an end and almost, if not quite, abolished private production and trade. But these changes, sweeping as they have been, are not equivalent to a full socialist transformation of the system of ownership, not to mention other aspects of the economic base, such as the system of management and the system of distribution. Furthermore, transformation of the economic base represents, at best, only half of the task of the socialist revolution. There remain all the ramparts of the super-structure: the social institutions, the culture, and the consciousness of the people.

Massive changes have been brought about in these complex realms since 1949. In fact, each transformation of the economic base has been accompanied, if not preceded, by transformation in the super-structure. But viewed from the perspective of the total transition—the transition to communism—that is the goal, the changes in social relations, culture, and consciousness are no more complete than the changes in the economy.

As long as the transformation is not complete it is possible for the revolution to stagnate and even to slide into reverse. This may happen because large areas of capitalist economic relations—such as payment based on work performed, commodity production, and exchange by means of money—still exist side-by-side with a stubborn survival of feudal, semi-feudal, and bourgeois ideas that focus on self-interest and self-advancement. Soil thus persists for the polarization of income and the generation of privileged people who can crystallize out as a new elite content with the status quo that brought them their special position. As far as these people are concerned the revolution is over. They tend to link up with all the left-over, expropriated class forces—the original targets of revolutionary transformation—to resist further change and even turn the clock back.

For the majority of people, however, the revolution is far from over. The "Three Great Differences"—between city and country, between worker and peasant, and between mental and manual labor—persist. Despite major progress in the countryside, city life is still more abundant and stimulating than country life; workers generally dress better, eat better, and enjoy more security than peasants; those who work with their brains still earn more money and enjoy more respect than those who work with their hands. Since most of the people of China remain peasants who live in the countryside, and since the overwhelming majority of those who live in the cities continue to work with their hands, most Chinese live out their lives at the lower end of the difference gap. They are interested in continuing the revolution. They are interested in carrying it through to the end, to the point where all classes and class distinctions, all the relations of production that underlie these distinctions, all the social relations that arise from them, and all the ideas that reflect them are abolished.

Continued motion in the direction of these basic goals is much more important to laboring people in China than any immediate economic gains. The possibility of abolishing the wage system through changes in social relations that both stimulate and are made possible by the development of productive forces is a much more powerful incentive to hard work in a factory than higher earnings today or a bonus at the end of the week, the month, or the year. The possibility that community reorganization, both stimulating to and undergirded by rising levels of production, will enable the peasants to merge their collective property with that of the whole people (the state) and thus earn a share in the rising stable income of the nation instead of only a share in the fluctuating income of their own small community is a much more powerful incentive to plant and harvest diligently than any promise of high work points or subsidies for pig raising. This is the foundation, as I understand it, of the concept *politics in command* and consequently of the *red* in the title of this book. And it explains why *red* comes first.

Every opposition force that has come forward in China since 1949 has pushed the reverse idea—that the revolution is over, that the time has come to get on with production, period. Each, in turn, has been faced with acute problems of incentive and morale. Mao Tse-tung, on the other hand, offering primarily hard work and hard struggle to transform both society and nature, has repeatedly unleashed tremendous creative, productive energy. Over and over again it has been demonstrated that what the Chinese people really want is revolution—continued revolution.

In the context of this struggle education is both crucial and controversial. If politics in command is to mean anything, then hundreds of millions must seriously study philosophy and political economy. How to make this a living process rather than the rote memorization of dead dogma is a continuing problem. There is a powerful tradition of classical study in China that sweeps people toward a verbal mastery of revealed "truth." Replacing Confucian texts with Marxist texts does not in itself cause people's brains to come to grips with the real world. That is why Mao has stressed so often that knowledge comes from practice and has insisted that everyone take part in class struggle—that is, day-to-day political struggle—in order to master politics.

But politics in *command* is not equivalent to politics is *all*. Revolution in the production relations and in social relations releases creative forces—primarily untapped human potential. Liberated people, taking hold of technology and science, raise the level of production. Higher levels of production form a material base for further revolution. In this whole process, the step-by-step mastery of technology and science is vitally important. Hence the *expert* in the title of this book.

How to insure expanding expertise on a mass scale is a second continuing problem for Chinese education. Here again the classical tradition, the historical separation of theory and practice, poses a serious obstacle. Mastery of world science and technology by individual students, however brilliant, did not serve to overcome this separation in the past. Without a productive base in China where the lessons could be applied, the very precocity of those Chinese educated overseas tended to widen the gap between theory and practice. Since 1949, Mao, stressing practice, has insisted that everyone take part in production and if possible in scientific experiment. As the productive base expands, the gap between the real practice of the Chinese people and advanced world theory is reduced, but not the need to combine them continually in defiance of Confucian theory.

A third great problem facing Chinese education is implicit in the other two and lies at the heart of the controversy in the field that continues to this day. "The proletariat," says Mao Tse-tung, "seeks to transform the world according to its own world outlook. . . ." A proletarian outlook determines that both political study and study of technology and science should not only occur on a mass scale, but should promote equality and not privilege, should reduce and not expand differences. In China, education is called upon to negate that which in all hitherto existing societies it has been a major factor in calling into being: the distinction between mental and manual work. In China, education is called upon to reverse a trend that almost everywhere else it has been a major factor in accelerating: the development of urban society at the expense of rural. In China, education is called upon to help abolish that which it hitherto has been a major factor in generating and preserving: a privileged urban elite.

And for the present, at least, education in China is called upon to do all this with a very limited network of educational institutions and a very small pool of qualified teachers at all levels above that of the primary schools. Primary education, enormously expanded since 1949, is already available to almost all children, but secondary education, even though it has expanded ten times over in the same period is still many years away from universality. University education, also rapidly expanding, is probably decades short of levels already taken for granted in many American states. The sharp contradiction between the massive demand for education and the limited supply of formal educational opportunity generates constant experiment and struggle, both within the formal network of educational institutions and in the mushrooming informal network that the Chinese people are constantly creating.

Since only a select few can go on to regular higher study, who should be chosen to go? Who should do the choosing and according to what standards? What will the students be taught? How will they be taught? How will they be advanced from class to class and what will happen to slow learners? What will school graduates do with their knowledge? What will prevent their becoming a privileged elite? Will there be continuing education for those not chosen to go on to higher schools? What forms will it take?

How these questions are answered depends very much on the world outlook of the people involved. "The proletariat," says Mao Tse-tung, "seeks to transform the world according to its world outlook and so does the bourgeoisie. In this respect, the question of which will win out, socialism or capitalism, is not really settled.'' In no field is this more true than in education. But if this question has not really been settled, this does not mean that no strides have been made, no experiments undertaken, no new philosophy applied, and no victories won. On the contrary, education in China has been so transformed at every level that Ruth Gamberg can truthfully say, ''China's educational system is based on a completedly different set of assumptions that derive from a completely different world outlook from ours. The most basic questions, such as who are the students, the teachers, what are their objectives, what do they learn and teach, how is it handled—such questions yield new answers which not only shed light upon China's great experiment, but perhaps even give us cause to reflect upon our own system of education and the values that sustain it.''

Her study, a major effort to absorb and explain the results of decades of struggle and progress in Chinese education, cannot help but fascinate and challenge every Western reader. What can one say about a society that really takes seriously the idea that everyone has untapped potential, that everyone can be creative, that intelligence is not fixed, that human nature can be transformed? What can we make of the idea that creativity is not a private matter—a question of this or that individual genius doing his or her own thing—but arises from cooperation, from combining the intelligence and efforts of many? Or, for that matter, of the idea that education should teach people to think; that exams should test one's ability to think, or, even the collective ability of a group to think; that discipline is rooted in a voluntary commitment to decisions and rules that are comprehended and agreed upon? And how can we deal with the idea that education should be combined with productive labor while productive labor everywhere should generate education—every school a factory, every factory a school—with the further implication that education should never stop and that no one is too old to learn?

True, some of these ideas are not unknown to educators in the West. Various individuals have taken up the cudgels for one or another of them and applied them in experimental ways over the years. But that is about as far as it goes. Nowhere has there been any serious effort to apply them as a consistent set of interlocking ideas and methods that can provide an alternative to the elitist, careerist, track-plagued system of education that universally prevails among us in the West and both perpetuates and accelerates the polarization of society that most people have come to regard as inevitable.

xiv   RED AND EXPERT

That these ideas are applied seriously in China is demonstrated not only by the way in which most schools themselves have been transformed, but also by the fact that many millions of educated urban young people have gone off to the countryside to live and work permanently where their education can be of greatest service to the people, while at the same time committees of workers and peasants have been brought into the schools to supervise and transform them. For the present, higher education may still be selective, but it is no automatic stepping stone to a distinguished career, nor is it left to the direction of specialists.

Ruth Gamberg made it a point to talk about education with everyone she met while in China and with every type of person involved in education—educated youth in the countryside, peasants and workers on the revolutionary committees of schools, ordinary students in schools at all levels, teachers trained for their work, volunteers teaching what they know best, professors in institutions of higher learning, and administrators at all levels. It is one of the merits of her book that she is able to link what they are doing in teaching and learning with the reorganization and transformation of Chinese society as a whole, and explain, in language that any layman should be able to grasp, the key concepts of revolutionary Marxism as they are understood and applied in China. The picture emerges of an exciting, restless society embarked on momentous change where "life is education; all of society our classroom."

Ruth Gamberg concludes that "the curiosity and vitality of the Chinese people of all ages are a product of their profound and even joyous engagement with each other and their surroundings and of their direct, day-by-day participation in struggling with common problems as they discover together how to make decisions that will shape their collective destinies."

Socialist education is in the process of creation in China. It has in no sense been universally achieved. An unnamed teacher in a technical institute puts it very well: "The very nature of socialism makes this impossible. Wherever things are stagnant, revisionism must be strong. There have been many battles and many victories—over whether to study for marks or to learn how to analyze and solve problems, over how to integrate theory and practice, over developing new and meaningful methods and materials, and many, many other problems. But each of these battles must be fought today, tomorrow, and the next day in each school. Of course, with each victory that is won, it is easier to win new victories provided that we don't deceive ourselves into thinking that the victory was a once-and-for-all achievement. We must always be alert to problems; we must always guard against becoming uncritical of our work."

Obviously, for this teacher, the revolution is not over.

WILLIAM HINTON

Red and Expert

INTRODUCTION

In his informative series of films that so ably captures the lives and spirit of the Chinese people, Felix Greene, a long-time friend of China, reminds us that "three out of four people in the world have never been to China; the rest live there." This fact by itself is sufficient reason for us to learn more about this extraordinary country.

But there are other reasons, too. The Chinese people have embarked upon and are determined to complete the most momentous experiment of our times. They are molding a society where people have new goals and aspirations and new means of achieving them. Their experiment is based largely on a rejection of the economic, political, and social systems under which they used to live and under which much of the remaining three-quarters of humankind still lives. While many in the West may prefer to ignore or underestimate the significance of the Chinese experiment, the fact is that it is succeeding. And that success is drawing the interest of countless others elsewhere. China is becoming more and more a magnet attracting the attention of the still suppressed and frustrated millions who are searching for a viable model for development.

As important a reason as any for us to inform ourselves about China is that we have been so seriously misinformed. All too often Western observers and commentators have interpreted events in China from *their* own particular preconceptions and predispositions, which have necessarily precluded, or at least limited, our understanding of the realities of Chinese life. Two and one-half decades of anti-China bombardment from the Western media have impressed upon us a stock of ready-made negative images about the Chinese: bland, humorless, inscrutable, robotized products of militaristic thought control.

As it turns out, these all-too-facile impressions that often come to mind to explain, or, perhaps more accurately, explain away, everything Chinese are dead wrong. The China of the Chinese people could not be more different from what we have been led to imagine. Thus, whether we like or dislike their experiment, whether we appreciate or scorn their goals and achievements, whether we welcome or disapprove of their influence on others in the world—all are pretty much secondary considerations. We must first acknowledge reality.

Perhaps our best starting point is an honest appraisal of some of our own assumptions. Take "brainwashing" for example. North Americans are frequently aghast at the very idea of young children quoting Mao, "Chairman Mao teaches us that we should. . . . " To many it matters little how the sentence ends; it is bad enough to have "Chairman Mao" appealed to by little children, and our immediate response is often one of misplaced sympathy: "Poor kids; they haven't got a chance."

It is essential to look at China more dispassionately if we hope to comprehend this remarkable country. What *is* "brainwashing"? When we use this term we refer to a process that yields strong responses, positive or negative, based, not on knowledge and investigation, but on ignorance and coercion, however subtle or blatant. By this definition, one could quite convincingly argue that the response triggered off in some minds by the stimulus of the words "Chairman Mao"[1] is itself the result of brainwashing. We have all heard American adults, both schoolteachers and parents, invoke leaders from Washington to Lincoln to Kennedy, their deeds, and what can be learned from them. Yet we would never think of calling this brainwashing. It would seem, then, that it is not the technique of using models for children to emulate that is alarming. But neither is it the principles that Mao as a model personifies which are objectionable, since few in the West, paradoxically enough, know what principles and values are embodied in Mao's teachings.

Even after contact with some of Mao's basic ideas, some people still

---

1. Some Westerners are not aware that in Chinese names the surname appears first. When the Chinese say "Chairman Mao," it in no way partakes of the familiarity that the Cubans express toward their leader when they say "Commandante Fidel." "Chairman Mao" is simply an accurate title (Chairman of the Communist Party), neither more familiar nor more formal than "President Ford." It is the form always used by the Chinese.

remain suspicious of their real meaning. I recall a discussion between an American university student and two of his Chinese counterparts in which the Chinese students mentioned that they do exercises every day in line with Chairman Mao's teachings that the people should look after their health. "Do you *really* think that is the reason Mao says to do exercises, so that you can stay in good health?" the American asked. Who knows how far his own suspicions carried him from that comment: That exercises are really for the purpose of regimentation? That Mao fancies himself a wizard whose calling it is to mesmerize the people into a passive, submissive, puppetized stupor in order to better control them? Or even to prepare them to "take over the world"? Such a simple explanation as improving the health of the people struck this person as highly suspect, despite earlier discussion of such impressive, related facts as the successful combating of a multitude of diseases, the phenomenal decline in infant mortality, and the elimination of starvation. To him, exercising in China was to be construed as a kind of treachery, an Orwellian ruse to ensnare the innocent. After all, "Chairman Mao" had advocated it!

Even highly regarded Western scholars sometimes exhibit the same overweening skepticism about the simplest and most everyday occurrences in China. Reporting on his visit to the People's Republic, John Kenneth Galbraith, the noted economist, makes numerous misleading comments such as the following description of one of the things he saw during a boat ride.

"Fifty or so children of twelve or thereabouts are busy weeding a bank and making an ostentatious point of not being interrupted as we pass."[2] Surely he can't seriously be suggesting that the children were planted there when it became known that some foreigners would be passing by, or that they were given strict instructions to look busy!

It is a very sad commentary on our cultural myopia and the suspicion about China thrust upon us by our media that a case with supporting evidence has to be presented to *prove* that the Chinese do exercises for their health or that children are not distracted from their work because they are involved in it. Significantly, the first thing returning visitors from China are frequently asked to substantiate is that they

---

2. John Kenneth Galbraith, *A China Passage* (New York: New American Library, 1973), p. 82.

were not prohibited from taking pictures, roaming the streets unaccompanied, or talking to anyone they wanted to. It is an affront to the integrity and intelligence of the people of China that we on the other side of the globe suppose that we can see through to the "real" purposes of every detail of their lives while the 800 million who live there have been thoroughly taken in.

Of course, full responsibility for this state of affairs can't be placed solely on the media. While they have done a singularly efficient job of it, without some degree of receptiveness in our society as a whole, they would not have been so successful. Certainly the media can also be partially credited with helping to create that receptiveness in such ways, for example, as openly supporting or at best not actively challenging the virulent anti-communism of McCarthyism, the development of which coincided in history with the infancy of the People's Republic. There are undoubtedly a number of cultural elements that have provided the cushions into which the distortions about China could comfortably sink. I'll mention only two.

One of these is a deeply rooted cynicism in the West in general and perhaps in the United States in particular, a cynicism that prevents some people, even after having seen it with their own eyes, from accepting that the smiling and active children of China are not really happy at all; that the appearance of happiness is just camouflage disguising pathetic little machines.

A full-blown cynical outlook views everything as motivated by the most selfish considerations; high-sounding principles become just handy tactics to outmaneuver the naive. Such cynicism is projected onto others, and the world is seen as a place where everyone everywhere dupes or is duped, outwits or is outwitted, bamboozles or is bamboozled. In the words of H. L. Mencken: "No one ever went broke underestimating the intelligence of the American public." Such an outlook disallows the possibility of a society where people can be honest and yet not be "suckers" or "losers," where people can be successful and yet not cynical themselves. Such, however, is the very society that the Chinese are struggling to create. People do not expect to be lied to or misled. They generally trust and respect each other, but that doesn't make them fools. If they discover that a number of their leaders have been consistently self-seeking, they are apt to respond as they did during the late 1960s in what will be discussed later as the Great Proletarian Cultural Revolution.

A second aspect of our cultural heritage that provides fertile ground for distortions about China is an equally deeply rooted racism. Undoubtedly as a society, we are moving away from the crude "no tickee-no washee" variety of racism, but racism, usually in more subtle guises, has by no means been eliminated from our midst. The hero of "Kung Fu," a popular television series, couldn't be more kind or more concerned with justice. But the justice he metes out through the ancient Chinese martial arts couldn't be more brutal or frighteningly efficient. Perhaps he could be seen as a reminder of the continued threat of what in earlier, less euphemistic days was called the "yellow peril." At any rate, he by no means provides an alternative image. And what about the old man, his mentor, who is equally as kind and concerned about justice? Where do his unbelievably profound—though often unintelligible—succinct and unfailing insights and advice come from? His capsules of wisdom are as mysterious and unfathomable as those of his predecessors—Charlie Chan, and, before him, the mythical sages who file past our mind's eye in a long procession.

There is no end to the examples of such covert racism. Recently I read a report in a small town newspaper by a returned visitor to China. Much of it seemed in a way to be favorable, but it contained several very strange qualifiers which detracted from and actually threw into question the positive points. One such statement pointed out that the Chinese had practically eliminated crime "as we know it." What, I wondered, was that supposed to mean? Do they have other kinds, unknown and unspeakable, reminiscent of the supposed age-old tortures that defy Western comprehension and are indicative of the presumed Chinese lack of concern for human life? If so, is it because they're communists, or because they're Chinese, or both? Surely, in a society like ours, where crime is daily becoming more problematic, we should be prepared to give credit where it is due, if only to pay serious attention to a country that has almost eliminated crime on the chance that we have something to learn from it. But the racism that enshrouds even such a positive achievement as this gets in the way. We are advanced; they are backward.

The Chinese and others in the Third World would probably carry the racism interpretation being forwarded here a step further and see it as an ideological legacy of imperialism. Those who look upon whole peoples as incapable, under any circumstances, of teaching anyone anything useful have a center-of-the-universe mentality that comes from their long-term exploitative relationships with others. How else can one explain the statement on a broadcast by the Canadian Broadcasting Corporation, one of the most liberal networks on the continent, that Prime Minister Trudeau, on his 1973 trip to China, met with Rewi Alley, who was cavalierly described as "the man who probably knows more about China than any man alive"? As a perceptive New Zealander who has lived in China for over forty years, he perhaps does know as much about China as any other white man. One's first thought, however, is that there must be some Chinese who know even more. Worse still, there seems to be the subtle suggestion that the Chinese are not "men."

It seems to me, then, to be the responsibility of any Westerner who seeks a better understanding of China to examine his or her own conscious or unconscious resistance to entering an altogether different and new world—different from what we've been taught and new to our own experience. China can be neither understood nor appreciated unless we are prepared to plunge into this new world, and leave our own behind. To do this, we must ask and consider before judging. We must try to comprehend the philosophy of the Chinese and their political and economic perspectives. We even have to discover what their slogans and expressions actually mean. It would be easy, for example, to suppose that a phrase like "running dog agent" is just a propagandistic "communist" label meant to incite the uncomprehending common people. But it is rooted in Chinese history. It refers to mercenaries in the broadest sense, people with no scruples who, for a pay-off, will do the bidding of others. In old China, a rich landlord would sometimes raise dogs to accompany his assistants on their rounds of the peasants' homes to collect rent, taxes, and debts. The dogs, which were usually quite ferocious, were used to intimidate recalcitrant peasants and sniff out any concealed food they might have. The landlord's assistants played essentially the same role as his dogs, and it was but a natural connection for the peasants to refer to them as "running dogs."[3]

For this and many other reasons, to understand the China of today, we also have to know something about the China of yesterday. What happened to the Chinese people in the past, and what role was played by Mao, the man for whom they have so much admiration and whose teachings they study? For more than half a century, Mao and others

---

3. See Mrs. A. Tse, "Letter to the Editor," *China Now,* no. 39 (February 1974), p. 10.

have provided the leadership which has freed hundreds of millions from lifelong back-breaking toil for the enrichment of a few, and from the impoverishment that reduced many to scrounging for wild roots and tree bark for food, selling their children into servitude or prostitution, begging from the rich only to be cursed and spat upon, living out their lives in a misery of disease, ignorance, and superstition, convinced all the while of their own inferiority—a living hell culminating in an ignoble death in the shack or even the sidewalk or field that was home to them.

No one lives or dies like that in China any more. The Chinese say that the great transformation is due to "the wise leadership of Chairman Mao and the Communist Party" for it was they who provided an alternative to the heavy and seemingly endless centuries of feudal and later foreign oppression which dominated and enslaved most of the suffering Chinese people. Small wonder that the people of China trust those who have led them on their present path and are firmly convinced that they have much to learn from such leaders.

The wretchedness of the past is dead, and the Chinese are fashioning a new society, to be inhabited by a new breed of human beings. They are determined that it must be socialist.[4] They do not want the poverty and ignorance of their own feudal past. They do not want what they see as the inequalities and injustices of capitalism. Nor do they want what to them is the distorted revision of socialism as practiced in the Soviet Union.

The total picture of what they do want, however, cannot yet be fully viewed because it has not been fully painted. It is in the process of creation. The preliminary sketching has been done, certain contours are discernible and hues distinguishable, but the Chinese believe that much more work is necessary before the potential of the new socialist human being is fully realized. It is an evolutionary process, and like any other, develops slowly and unevenly with zigs and zags. It entails the freeing of the creative energies of China's hundreds of millions as they strive to refine each line and give just the right shape, color, and texture to each feature.

In China, the building of socialism is sometimes compared to a long journey of 10,000 li[5] of which they say they have taken but the first few

---

4. The word socialism is used by the Chinese to refer to the historical period that leads towards communism. For further elaboration of this point see pp. 87 ff.

5. One li equals about one-third of a mile.

steps. They are certain, however, that the steps they have taken and the path they have chosen are the right ones and with sufficient vigilance on their part will lead them to their destination. True to the spirit of ongoing revolution, the Chinese demonstrate a tenacious commitment to defeating every obstacle in that path. It has been said that Mao's favorite saying is, "The tree may prefer calm, but the wind will not subside." The revolution continues; the Chinese people are meeting the challenges. Everything in China is open to question, to debate, and to change except the one decision—which path to travel.

This book grew out of my visit to China in June of 1973. The last thing I had in mind then was to write a book, but upon returning home, I discovered much interest in China.[6] The frustration of supplying people with only brief and partial answers to their many good questions made it evident that more was required.

The subject of education seemed to provide a good vehicle for helping to inform people about China for a number of reasons. To identify the values and the forms of their expression in any society, it is always instructive to look at the educational system, for it is in the education and training of the young that we can discover what the dominant forces of a society deem important enough to keep alive in coming generations. In the case of China more specifically, because education is so pervasive, affecting in a very central way the lives of adults as well as children, and because the activities that go on inside of school buildings are linked directly with those outside, a look at education can teach us a great deal about how the society as a whole operates. Moreover, China's educational system is based on a completely different set of assumptions that derive from a completely different world outlook from ours. The most basic questions, such as who are the students, the teachers, what are their objectives, what do they learn and teach, how is it handled—such questions yield new answers which not only shed light upon China's great experiment, but perhaps even give us cause to reflect upon our own system of education and the values that

---

6. I visited China with a group of Americans, and the book is written from that perspective. As a U. S. citizen living and working in Canada, however, I have found the interest in China equally strong in both countries. Since there are numerous similarities in the educational system and the value training of children in Canada and the U. S., there are frequent references in the book to North America rather than just the United States or Canada.

sustain it. Not insignificant also is the fact that about 40 percent of China's huge population is under sixteen years of age.

The book has several limitations, however. One is that I do not speak Chinese. Thus, all discussions, except for those with our guides, a few English-speaking Chinese whom I encountered in China, and some Chinese students at universities abroad, were conducted through interpreters. While there is every reason to believe that they did their jobs as faithfully and as efficiently as possible, it is also likely that certain subtleties and nuances of the discussions simply couldn't be conveyed.

Another limitation of the book has to do with the speed of change in China. Revolution means change, and China's revolution continues every day. Thus, before observations can be recorded, there is the possibility that they will, in some respects, be out of date. This became evident to me when I had the good fortune to return to China in the summer of 1975. While the basic thrust and direction of education were essentially the same, many of the details of its workings had been further refined and developed. Nevertheless, despite the fact that the Chinese have gone beyond some of what appears in the pages that follow, a fact not to be overlooked or underestimated, we can still learn from the China that was in 1973 much about what it is now and even something about what it might become. As with any monumental experiment, there are things to be learned at any point while it is in progress. We need not wait for "all the facts to be in." Indeed, by the current Chinese way of looking at things, the facts might never all be in; if they continue on their present course, the experiment will never be complete, because for them human progress knows no end.

A third limitation is that during both of my visits to China, I was in cities a good deal of the time, which is not where most Chinese live and are educated. Although I visited some rural schools where I spoke with teachers and students, more of my information comes from urban schools. Because the cities are in advance of the countryside in most respects, including education, much of what I saw could not be considered strictly typical or average. But that doesn't necessarily make it unrepresentative. If anything, it perhaps gives a sharper picture of the direction of change. By looking at the more advanced elements of a society where everyone is moving together, we can better see the path that the less advanced will travel.

It is now almost customary to say that an undertaking like writing a book is not possible without the tangible and intangible help and encouragement of many people who, unfortunately, must remain unnamed. The unquantifiable nature of debts and gratitudes that I owe to all of them in preparing this work is nevertheless real. The mention of a mere handful should in no way suggest that the contributions of the unnamed are any less valuable. In any case, those to whom the greatest possible gratitude is due are the countless Chinese friends and acquaintances who so willingly gave of their time and energy in providing much of the information which has made this book possible.

Special thanks are due to Herb Gamberg, for the unselfish and enduring assistance given to me in all aspects of this undertaking. I am likewise indebted to Don Cornelius for his close reading of the manuscript and his perceptive suggestions throughout.

Also helpful in many significant ways have been Jim Stolzman, Hagos Gebre-Yesus, Isabel Crook, and David Crook. For their painstaking secretarial assistance, I especially thank Mary McGinn, Hazel Waters, and Bridget Trim. I am also grateful to Sharon Stolzman, Cheryl Gamberg, and Wendy Katz for help in proofreading and editorial work.

Chris Kuppig of Schocken Books has provided uncommonly valuable and expert advice.

Last, but not least, my thanks go to my son, Tony, who, despite the exuberance of youth, remained so cooperative.

For all this, it goes without saying that all shortcomings are solely my own.

I: AS BENDS THE TWIG

The world is yours as well as ours, but in the last analysis, it is yours. You young people, full of vigor and vitality, are in the bloom of life, like the sun at eight or nine in the morning. Our hope is placed on you.[1]

MAO TSE-TUNG

Four little girls wearing brightly colored dresses with ribbons and flowers in their hair; an equal number of boys wearing polo shirts and shorts—blue, yellow, white, red. In small groups they play with toys, sometimes exchanging them. All smile and sing.

In skips a girl and sings: "I'm a newcomer to the kindergarten." Looking around at the toys she appears delighted. "I see many toys and feel very happy. I like this airplane very much." Grabs it from another child.

Others stop playing, looking surprised and upset. Watching her fly the plane, shaking their index fingers at her in exhortation, they take turns singing: "That's wrong; she shouldn't have taken the toy from him."

"The toys of the kindergarten should be shared by all the children."

"She's a newcomer and doesn't know that, so she should be excused. But we have to help her see her mistake. We should remember Chairman Mao's teaching to care for and help each other."

All nod and sing: "Yes, we are all friends!"

Girl with plane stops, looks thoughtful, sings: "They've said the right thing; we *should* take care of each other. Now I have to think of Chairman Mao's teaching. What should I do?" Pause. "I should return the airplane." Gives it to boy, both smile, hold hands. He flies it for a few seconds, gives it back to her; they take turns.

---

1. Quoted in *Quotations from Chairman Mao Tse-tung* (Peking: Foreign Languages Press, 1966), p. 288.

11

All the children smile and sing: "We like to play with the toys. We are all friends. The toys of the kindergarten are shared by all the children."

The place was The East Is Red Kindergarten in Canton, and the occasion was a performance given by the preschoolers for us, their foreign guests.

To some, this may seem overly preachy for a kindergarten musical activity. A far cry from:

> There was an old woman who lived in a shoe,
> She had so many children, she didn't know what to do;
> She gave them some broth without any bread,
> And whipped them all soundly and sent them to bed.

In China such a rhyme would not be considered just light and harmless fun. Things aren't neutral; everything teaches something, even to young children, and that something either aids or hinders progress. The teachers at The East Is Red Kindergarten have consciously chosen to teach songs like "The Toys of the Kindergarten Should Be Shared by All the Children." To them it is not just a song, but represents the outlook and spirit that the Chinese think should pervade everything, including children's music.

In China, as in any other country, there are certain dominant values. China differs from most others, however, in at least one essential respect: the Chinese do not think they can afford to allow a haphazard or semi-conscious perpetuation of their values. Therefore, they meticulously select and discard as they go along. They insist that there be no ambiguity, no room to misinterpret the meaning and significance of their emerging values. Appearance and reality must be one and the same. These are to be made explicit. When children learn through song that "the toys of the kindergarten should be shared by all the children," the ideas of selflessness and consideration for others come across loud and clear.

Of greater significance is that this kind of little verbal moral lesson is, for the most part, not contradicted in the children's experience by the world around them. Instead, it is reinforced repeatedly as they and others achieve or are denied social rewards—the esteem of others—for practicing or failing to practice sharing and concern for others in their daily lives. They are told that these things are good, and indeed they are congratulated, pointed to as models, and admitted into youth organizations for attempting to live these values. The children of China are rarely put in the position of having to be and do one thing while others around them are being and doing something quite different. They are spared the hypocrisy of being urged to share while painfully learning that real success—wealth, power, fame, and privilege—attaches to those who amass, a process which in so many societies breeds at first confusion and eventually cynicism or romantic idealism. Rather, they are in the position of being able to take things at face value, and to have them simply deepen—rather than be contradicted—with time. It is in the kindergartens of China that the seeds of the new values are being planted. Let us return to the children's performance at The East Is Red Kindergarten in Canton.

It starts off with a greeting by about a dozen of the older children, the five and six-year-olds. As we approach the room where they will give the performance, one girl excitedly tells the others: "Here they are; the uncles and aunts are coming!" This sets everyone in motion. Before we are even seated, two children set the tempo by banging a bass drum and clashing cymbals, while the others, standing in pairs with arms around each other, waving red, pink, and white flowers, chant in bold, resounding voices:

> Welcome to you.
> Greetings to you, friends!
> The east wind is blowing,
> Red flags are fluttering.
> Our country has many friends
> All over the world!

A teacher plays an introduction on the piano which will accompany the song they are leading into. Without break, the drum and cymbals continue their beat, while one boy skillfully waves a very large red flag in time to the music. The others have produced small flags with long silk streamers of many brilliant colors which they ripple through the air in beautiful smooth patterns. The excitement mounts as the stage becomes a dazzle of color, sound, and movement; bright red, orange, pink, yellow; flowers, flags, streamers. In clear, confident tones, the children—now dancing, always smiling—sing:

Beating the drums and gongs
We are welcoming friends,
Who for many nights
Have travelled thousands of miles
To visit China.

A child shouts: "A warm welcome to our friends!"
Another: "With warmth we greet our friends!"
A third: "Let's give them a performance!"
All: "Yes!"

They are overwhelming. But there is no time to be overwhelmed because they are already singing the next song. It is difficult to be attentive; my mind is full of thoughts of China's supposed xenophobia. Most of what I had previously heard about China had conveyed the impression of a continuation of the ancient Middle Kingdom mentality with its pervasive insularity and sense of superiority over everyone else. The Chinese have supposedly always hated foreigners. But we are foreigners—and from a country that is not an ally. We are *American* foreigners, yet the children had apparently been taught to welcome us enthusiastically, to offer us their friendship. It seems that no one had told them that we were "foreign devils."

Is this just a façade, I wondered, part of a grand show being staged to delude outsiders? After all, the stereotype of the Chinese as crafty and inscrutable has still not disappeared. But then I think back to my encounter of a few days before. Pausing on a street in Shanghai to look in a shop window, I saw a very old woman standing beside me. Shrunken with age, she was leaning on her cane to secure the balance that her tiny feet were incapable of providing. As an inheritance from old China, her feet had been bound when she was a child, and were no more than four to five inches long. This torturous indignity is no longer inflicted on the young girls of China. The woman stared at me with curiosity. I wondered: what experiences might she have suffered at the hands of foreigners? Had she ever been barred from parts of her own city because they were the exclusive domain of foreigners and bore signs announcing "no dogs or Chinese allowed"? Had she worked in a factory (most of them used to be foreign-owned) for fourteen or sixteen hours a day, been beaten for slowing her pace, been paid so little that she couldn't feed her children? Had her husband been addicted like so many others to the opium brought into China by foreign powers to enable them to more easily and fully plunder the country? Thinking these thoughts, I would not have been surprised if she had spit at me when I smiled. Instead, she smiled back, a broad toothless grin, and extended her hand in friendship. I clasped it—moved and gratified.

This was not an isolated incident. Such things happened to us over and over again wherever we went, in the cities or the countryside, among the old or the young. For sure, we were stared at plenty. There have not been many foreigners in China in recent years, and to them most foreigners appear as real oddities with all that hair on all sides of their heads—it hangs dishevelled down their backs or is piled in layers on top; with some of the men it covers their faces so that only two eyes and a nose are distinguishable. And some of those noses are so big to Chinese eyes. Some foreigners are so tall, some so fat, and they wear such peculiar clothes—some so immodest. Yes, we are a veritable zoo, and it is difficult for them not to gawk in wonder and curiosity. But as soon as any of us offered any gesture of friendship it was immediately grasped and reciprocated by smiles, nods, appreciative comments, even applause. The Chinese do not appear to ask much of foreigners before they trust our good intentions.

None of this struck me as inscrutable. Very little scrutinizing seemed to be required to comprehend. These were undisguised, manifest, and infinitely human expressions of friendship and hospitality. While it is unlikely that traditional chauvinism has been completely eliminated in China, the old xenophobia has been considerably attenuated. Thus I felt no reason to remain aloof from the enthusiastic welcome that the children at The East Is Red Kindergarten extended. I trusted them.

My wandering thoughts return to the stage as a little girl with long pigtails, pink hair ribbons, and matching shiny pink plastic shoes is announcing other numbers in a loud distinct voice—dances native to the cultures of China's national minority groups, a song entitled "The Railway Workers Are Busy with Their Transport Tasks," a violin solo by a six-year-old girl. Then one of their favorites, "Let's Come Together for Exercises."

The piano music is light and gay as the children move into formation and begin calisthenic movements. One child looks around puzzled, stops exercising, and asks: "Where is Xiao Ming?"

The others also stop to look for him. "Why isn't Xiao Ming here?"

The audience can see why Xiao Ming is not there; he is wandering around the stage, mindless of the others, looking hot and uncomfortable (which is not hard to do in Canton during the summer).

"Look, there is Xiao Ming. Xiao Ming, come on!"

"I'm coming!" he yells, in a voice obviously intended to be raucous and unpleasant, but which for some reason evokes much laughter from all of us in the audience (especially the Chinese).

"Let's do exercises," say the children as they resume the calisthenics.

Xiao Ming would apparently much rather fan. "It's too hot," he grumbles. "Why should I do exercises?"

By now all the others are busily bending and stretching to the music, so he joins them, but halfheartedly. With one hand he continues to fan himself while with the other hand he feigns exercises. All the children are vigorous and enthusiastic in their gestures, except Xiao Ming who, through minimum effort, creates maximum laughter. The others smile, but Xiao Ming looks crabby. He is so uninvolved with their efforts and so wrapped up in his own discomfort that he forgets his charade and absentmindedly wanders off, fanning himself. Xiao Ming is a slacker!

This is too much for the others. Once more they interrupt their exercises. "Xiao Ming, what's the matter with you today?" asks one little girl, her five-year-old face showing great concern.

"It's too hot!" he snaps. "I can't carry on in this heat!"

"But Chairman Mao says we should all promote physical culture to build up people's health. Should we follow Chairman Mao's teaching or not?"

"Yes!" the others all answer, and each, by turn, comes forward to offer Xiao Ming advice punctuated by profuse gestures.

"You should do exercises, Xiao Ming!"

"We should learn from the uncles and aunts of the PLA![2] They don't worry about heat or cold or any other kind of hardship."

"Don't be afraid of anything, even if it's difficult!"

"Since I've done exercises, my health has been improving!" pipes one robust little boy who hardly looks as though his health had ever been a problem.

Xiao Ming listens carefully, considering all their points. At first somewhat tentative, but then more certain, he affirms, "Yes, we *should* learn from the PLA. You are right!" This is called self-criticism. Now he can do the right thing with conviction, bolstered by their applause for his change of heart.

---

2. People's Liberation Army

He asks: "Should we do it again?"

"Yes!" they all shout happily, and the audience shares in their delight.

They regroup into formation, the music starts and they continue the exercises, this time with Xiao Ming as vigorous and active as the rest. The fan, which he still clutches, gets in his way, so he places it on a nearby chair to be able to do the exercises properly. All jump, skip, hop, march, and stretch energetically in unison. For Xiao Ming, who previously had been inclined toward a softer life, this is hard work. But he sticks with it, wiping the sweat from his brow with a man-sized gesture. He glances at the boy behind him who nods encouragement.

The exercises are over and Xiao Ming reports: "It's really good to do exercises!" One look at that high-spirited, smiling face confirms the fact beyond doubt.

Another child announces: "The exercise period is over. Let's go outside and play." They skip and run off hand in hand in two's and three's.

An instant later, a tired but pleased Xiao Ming rushes back in and shouts: "I left my fan!" which he promptly retrieves before running out to rejoin his friends.

The lesson of this little play—that hard work and diligence make for self-discipline and allow people to triumph over their shortcomings—is a common theme in China. The advice to Xiao Ming—"Don't be afraid of anything, even if it's difficult"—finds many other expressions. People are told to be bold. "Dare to struggle, dare to win" is a maxim urged repeatedly, and it is directed to adults as well as to children.

At the Industrial Exhibition Hall in Shanghai our guides were as amused as we were when shipbuilders related how they had dared to struggle. They had built a 10,000-ton cargo ship on a slipway that was judged inadequate to the task because at high tide its far end was under water. Applying one of Mao's guerrilla warfare tactics—"When the enemy advances, we retreat; when the enemy retreats, we pursue"— they retreated and worked on the higher end when the tide advanced, then pursued the "enemy" and worked on the lower end when the tide retreated, thus outwitting the "foe" and achieving victory.

The same virtues of boldness and persistence are encapsulated in a phrase directed at schoolchildren: "Study hard, make progress every day." This is an important guideline for their daily behavior. All this emphasis on diligence, hard work, tenacity, and selflessness may, however, sound burdensome and ponderous to unaccustomed ears, even downright oppressive when applied to five-year-olds. The old images of robots and blue ants, humorless and dutiful, can easily take over. Don't they do anything but work and struggle? Don't they relax, laugh, have fun?

The Chinese do not seem to see seriousness and enjoyment as an either-or proposition. The two often occur at the same time. The seriousness of "Let's Come Together for Exercises" is not to be underrated, but it was far from ponderous. Xiao Ming's involvement with his fan and his grouchiness over his discomfort were hilarious, not just to us but to the Chinese teachers and children in the audience as well. Of course it would not have been funny if he had refused to change. His self-indulgence was funny only because it was obvious that eventually he would triumph over it. To view someone as static and to peg him as a dolt or buffoon, the butt of jokes—and inevitably scorn—does not seem to constitute humor for the Chinese. Instead, they prefer to see themselves as developing, progressing, becoming. Certain behavior, even if unacceptable, can at times be funny, but not as a definition of a person, only as a passing weakness. Also, "Let's Come Together for Exercises" and the other skits were musical activities, alive with singing, dancing, exercising, and acting—all of them enjoyable and far from the typical Sunday-school setting that is so often chosen for the moral education of children in a number of other countries. The integration of value training into pleasurable activities characterizes much of the early education of children in China and was evident in many of their playground games, such as the tug-of-war we saw.

Before giving the signal to pull, the teacher asked mixed teams of girls and boys what they should think of during a competition. Shouting back in unison they responded: "Friendship first, competition second!" (This was the same phrase I had heard repeated some weeks earlier by their adult counterparts before they began their gymnastic competition with an American team in New York's Madison Square Garden.)

As soon as the whistle blew, the children pulled and strained, urged on by a group of young spectators cheering: "Pull harder! Pull harder! Pull harder!" Who to watch, the contestants or their onlookers? Both were fascinating. The cheering squad because they did not appear to be championing one team or the other, but shouted encouragement to all. They showed friendship by insisting that everyone pull harder. Regardless of the outcome, only two things seemed to be important—to be friends and to exert maximum effort. Those pulling were fascinating

With typical high-spiritedness, children learn "friendship first, competition second."

because their energies were totally concentrated on pulling their hardest; yet, even after one team succeeded in pulling the other over the line, not a single child on the losing side showed any overt disappointment—no scowls, muttering, accusations, or excuses. Nor was there any gloating, strutting, jeers, or boasting on the winning side. Instead, all retained their good cheer as the defeated team shouted, "Learn from the other kids!" who called back, "Learn from you!"

It was a thoroughly enjoyable activity for everyone, with some very pointed moral lessons. We saw a new conception of competition wherein the winners are shown not only to have perfected greater skill or extended more effort, but are also expected, in the spirit of friendship, to teach their opponents how to improve, even to the point of perhaps being able to win another time.

"We don't compete to win or lose, but to learn," one teacher told us.

The real lesson these children appeared to be learning was that in the new China there is room for everyone to succeed, that there is no longer any need for losers.

The idea of teaching young children serious value content has taken some time to emerge in China. The Cultural Revolution which began in 1966 shook people's thinking and brought about a re-evaluation of this question along with many others. Before then, while not always consciously articulated, there apparently was some implicit consensus that childhood was a time simply to be carefree, a time when children should be protected from the strenuous demands of adolescence and adulthood. The teachers at the kindergarten told us that they used to see their responsibility as fulfilled when the children were healthy, well fed, and had plenty of time to play. Stories and songs often centered on fanciful tales whose leading characters were talking animals, mythical creatures, and all those familiar others who populate the pretend world that adults so often choose for children over the real one.

Now more preschool teachers judge this point of view as "bourgeois" and leading in the direction of "counterrevolution," a danger which they fear could threaten their accumulated achievements. How, they ask, can the young generations grow into adults with the new socialist values if these values are neglected while the children are most impressionable? To postpone this early education would only bring a diminished and partial commitment to socialism in later years.

"Now we have a clearer orientation," explained a teacher at The East Is Red Kindergarten. "By introducing socialist ideology in the kindergarten, we have made great changes in the content of our work. Now we pay attention to *educating* the children, and this has brought basic changes in their outlooks."

The new content can be seen not only in stories, music, and games but in the "academic" work as well. We observed what was called a picture-reading class, a form of reading readiness. As we entered the classroom, the five-year-old children greeted us with the chant that by now had become quite familiar— "Shu-shu ai-yi hao." ("Welcome uncles and aunts.") After a brief wait while the excitement caused by our presence subsided, a little girl at the front of the classroom continued where she had left off. She pointed first to one and then another of the colorful and attractive pictures arranged sequentially on a large chart, telling and half-enacting the episode they depicted. Using her hands and facial expressions to convey the action, she said: "The boy is getting the room ready because some friends will come to visit him. He gets enough chairs for all his friends, but he sees that one of them is broken. He repairs the chair so that his friends can come to his home. The friends come in, and one of them sees that there is a chair that had been broken. So he says that he will sit on it. But the boy will not give the chair that was broken to his friend, and he takes it for himself.''

Afterwards, when asked to enlarge upon the story from their own experiences, nearly every child had something to say. The first one to talk said that the other day he had seen one of the boys in the classroom give a toy to a friend. After the friend had played with it for a while he offered to return it, but the first boy told him to keep using it because he had others.

The next incident to be related was even more directly stimulated by the picture-reading story. It was about the plight of one of the children at school who did not have a chair. A classmate noticed this and got him one from another room. And so on.

There was no question that the children got the point of the lesson. In addition, however, certain features of their stories stood out as unusual for their age. For one thing, each experience recounted exemplified one or another of the same values highlighted by the broken chair story. Not once did a child veer off into an irrelevant direction as young children so commonly do when a phrase or picture conjures up unrelated images and incidents. They showed as great a measure of mental discipline as many children I have encountered who are nearly twice their age.

What was even more striking was that in the experiences they reported, only infrequently did they make themselves the central figures. One after another they told about good deeds performed by other children. This was quite unlike my own previous teaching encounters with young children who almost always begin their narratives with ''I.'' It's not unusual in North American classrooms for the teacher to end up playing referee as one half-heard, half-completed ''I'' story is interrupted by another and another, each telling becoming more urgent as the children vie for notice and approval.

Among the Chinese children we observed, the place of ''I'' was noticeable by its comparative absence. They seemed able to relax and enjoy each other's stories; their feelings of self-worth did not appear to be threatened by their not having constant individual attention. Even at this early age, the importance of others and what can be learned from them is obviously already becoming part of these children. That this seems acceptable to them, that there was no evidence of jealousy but only appreciation for their peers' accomplishments is testimony to their own self-confidence. They give the impression that they are genuinely comfortable with themselves and each other, genuinely secure, that they don't worry about making mistakes or shy away from taking risks. They seem to be free of the burden of having to size everyone up and of using tricks and playing games to get around people. They seem to be clear about what is expected of them and where they stand. By the same token, adults do not appear to be prodding them all the time or over-praising them for every little act.

Perhaps most instructive of all was to watch the children in less formally structured situations, because here too the same values came across, indicating that they were, in fact, being internalized. For example, we saw some of the six-year-olds at the kindergarten off by themselves playing a musical circle game of the type in which a few children in the center skip around to the singing and clapping of the others, and at a given point in the music each picks another child, they do a brief dance together, the second set replaces the first, and the game is repeated over and over. Every time, the choice of partners was made simply and without hesitation. The selectors apparently did not see it as a weighty decision requiring careful reflection or causing embarrassed pauses. Among those who could potentially be selected, there was no grunting, gesticulating, or any other ploys to gain attention. To be picked or not picked for the center of the circle was neither a source of great joy nor disappointment; not a special favor and not rejection. There did not seem to be anything *personal* about the process. Their status in relation to the center of the circle appeared to have no bearing on their enjoyment of the game or their sense of self-esteem.

Not only at the kindergarten, but wherever I went in China, never did I see children fighting, physically or verbally. In schools, on playgrounds, and in their neighborhoods they always conducted their activities together without quibbling, bullying, or whining. I had heard and read similar observations from other visitors to China, so I watched very closely for any signs of these things, especially when children were on their own, away from teachers and parents. Everything I saw confirmed what others had said, with only one qualification. Several times I observed what appeared to be a mild form of teasing or jostling—what could be called "horsing around." Interestingly, it always seemed to be confined to boys who appeared to be more or less between ten and fourteen. But it was invariably done smilingly and good-naturedly, and usually with lots of boisterous laughter on all sides. Not once did I see thoughtless, nasty, or downright cruel behavior or hear the grating, irritated, and abusive sounds that emanate from children who are competitive, tense, resentful, and often so unhappy. Of course, it cannot be said that children in China are never unkind to each other, but the fact that so many visitors have been impressed by the unusual extent to which they are pleasant and cooperative leads me to conclude that unkindness is not common.

The cornerstone of the new socialist values that Chinese children are learning is summed up in the slogan heard as often as any in China—"Serve the people." This is not to be confused with "doing good works"—the charitable acts of the well-off toward the poor, the sick, and the neglected—a kind of service which is intended, at best, to achieve only limited gains. "Serving the people" can be much more successful and rewarding all around, because it is done in the context of building toward equality. Serving others is seen to be for the purposes of creating good every bit as much as for removing bad. All are expected to serve as well as be served; service is to be infused with a new spirit in which both servers and served see themselves as building together. This, of course, can be realized only if people are respected, and it is always easier to respect others if respect is mutual. All those groups which were formally oppressed in old China—the workers, peasants, women, and national minorities—are presented as the new heroes and heroines. The children learn that it is through the efforts of these groups, the great majority of the population, that the new society is being constructed, and it is they whom the children are being taught to respect, identify with, and serve.

As a fundamental guide to thought and action, a great many other values are subsumed by the Chinese under the principle of "serve the people." To serve well, the children must learn concern for others, selflessness, and cooperation; they must learn to accept responsibility for themselves and others through self-discipline, self-reliance, fearlessness in taking initiative and working hard; they must learn to be willing to learn from others, to be open, friendly, and outgoing.

Beginning when they are very young and continuing through the years, virtually all children in China are taught these values through their daily activities both in and out of school. While the practice of teaching all children essentially the same outlook may run counter to the Western ideal of variety as "the spice of life," the Chinese eschewing of variety for its own sake is indicative of their belief that many pursuits

Preschoolers learn to "serve the people" through musical activities. Here, "barefoot doctors" give acupuncture to an ailing "grandmother."

in life require unity. They say that they have been able to overthrow an exploitative and oppressive system and to begin building a new socialist society only because they have been and remain unified on certain basic socialist principles.

Unity based on consensus is an essential component of their socialist idea of democracy. A young worker from Shanghai likened a smooth-running society to a machine.

"When you go to a factory, you may notice how well the workers coordinate their work, just like the parts of a machine. If they don't work together, the factory will stop and no goods will be produced. The whole society should work together like a machine. In this way the people can march forward. If someone wants to go forward and some-one else wants to go back, if one person wants to turn left and another wants to turn right, how can the people march forward? How can the society develop?" (We should resist reading our view of the machine into his analogy. While some of us might think of machines as the symbol of mind-dulling sameness and bland routine, to the Chinese, so long without them, machines represent liberation from harsh, relentless drudgery; freedom from want; the freedom to have time and energy to pursue more than just the bare essentials of life. They symbolize a new and rational organization of society.)

In this connection the Chinese would draw a distinction between individualism and individuality. Individualism, freedom of the individual in the sense most commonly used in the West—the idea that each person should have the freedom to choose socialism or capitalism, to choose to serve the people or not—is rejected out of hand in China as "bourgeois thinking." The same worker explained what is meant by bourgeois.

"We see the bourgeois way of life—bourgeois ideology—as teaching people to be selfish, to always think only of themselves, not of others. We should have a proletarian outlook of helping each other. We must be selfless and serve others, not just ourselves."

In China, socialism and service to others and all the values they imply are not negotiable. The pursuit of self-interests to the possible detriment of collective interests may be a right by the bourgeois standard of freedom but not by the socialist one. Laissez-faire individualism, the condoning of almost any direction an individual may choose for himself, is seen by the Chinese as disruptive of the unity necessary for progress, as selfish, and therefore as unresponsive to collective needs. Their position claims that to allow all influences to thrive regardless of where they may lead is to sanction selfishness and, hence, counterrevolution and reaction over revolution and progress. In its place, they believe that the more unified they become on their fundamental socialist principles, the more rapid and complete their forward movement will be.

Individuality, on the other hand, is far from discouraged. While everyone is urged to serve the people, they obviously cannot, nor are they expected to do it in the same ways. Here variety, diversity, individuality, and freedom are actively encouraged as long as they are aimed toward the betterment of the people. In factory after factory, in commune after commune, the workers or peasants regularly get together to discuss a whole range of problems. What are the needs of the country? How can we increase productivity? How can we make our work more efficient and easier? Can we innovate machinery to simplify a particular process? What people should we select as our leaders at this factory, at this commune? They also discuss issues related to their own welfare. What facilities should we provide for the workers (peasants) here: a nursery so the mothers can continue to work; a basketball court for relaxation; a part-time school for the workers (peasants) to improve their literacy and technical skills? How can we improve our medical benefits?

In the neighborhoods, the same process goes on. The residents meet and select their leaders and, through numerous and ongoing discussions, devise plans for running neighborhood clinics, preschools, and elementary schools; programs of recreation for youth, adults, and the aged. Block by block, courtyard by courtyard, neighbors talk about how to provide lunch for schoolchildren whose parents both work, what sanitation problems need attention, how to improve neighborhood services for repairing radios, laundering clothes, mending shoes, etc.

In every sphere of life in China, including education, wherever people are together pursuing common goals, there is a good likelihood that the same enthusiastic involvement will be found. Who can better decide how to serve the people than the people themselves? This massive grass roots participation in determining how to serve others and then doing it is the Chinese expression of individuality; this is what constitutes freedom in China.

Recently, in Canada, I spoke to a young Chinese about his idea of freedom. He was a peasant from a village near Sian who had just arrived to study English. He said, "I think we must look at the definition of freedom. What is freedom? The question is very complicated because it is defined in different ways according to the ideology in different societies. Some people think that freedom is doing anything they want, but I think maybe that is not freedom. Suppose, for example, that you work in a production team. The peasants must work collectively in the fields. Let's say that you don't want to work. Of course if you have something special to do, you can get a leave. But if you don't have any reason, you just don't want to work, that would be very bad. It means that you want other people to do things for you, only for you. That is selfishness, and in China, we do not think that selfishness is freedom."

"What if someone did something harmful to the interests of the collective?" I asked.

"Then the people would stop that person and discuss it with him. They would try to convince him to change. I think this is the *people's* freedom."

"Do you feel that you have freedom?"

"Me? I have tremendous freedom! I can do *anything* I want for the people!"

As we were about to leave The East Is Red Kindergarten, several children ran off to pick flowers for us which they delivered with gracious and spontaneous farewells.

"We hope you come back again."

"We are all friends."

One boy gave me a flower, took my hand, and said, "If you get a chance to visit us again, we will welcome you." I told him that I hoped he would be able to visit my country when he got bigger, and he replied: "Thank you, aunt." With children on all sides, two or three holding each of our hands, we moved reluctantly toward our waiting bus. To shouts of delight from the children we paused to demonstrate the frisbee we had given them. Next to where I stood was a bulletin board with a large colorful picture of adults and children of many nationalities, smiling and offering each other flowers. Across the top in large red letters was the ever-present reminder, "SERVE THE PEOPLE."

II: NO MORE THE SPECIAL FEW

The great only seem great to us
Because we are on our knees.
Let us rise![1]

He had a black gauze cap and green silk gown,
A jasper ring on his cap and a purple belt;
His socks were white as snow,
His shoes like rosy clouds;
He's a lordly look and a natural dignity.
A man like that, if not a god,
Must be at least a high official or ruler of men.[2]

Such was the scholar of old China. For over three millenia education was confined to a small group of scholars who commanded political power far beyond their numbers. As early as the second century B. C. their right to administer the many offices of government was legitimized by an examination system which became a regular feature of life in China from the seventh century A. D. down to the twentieth. Through this examination system scholars were selected to man the imperial bureaucracy.

Some historians praise the justice of that system claiming that opportunity to become a scholar-administrator was equal, that the ranks were open to all who showed intellectual promise. There was some truth to this claim as the rare peasant did occasionally rise to prominence. Opportunity, however, was far from equal. Scholarship was restricted exclusively to males, automatically cancelling out any opportunity whatsoever for half the population. Most of the other half was, for all intents and purposes, also out of the running. To qualify for an examination required years and years of study; a potential candidate had to pore over the classics, reading and re-reading them until they were committed to memory. Becoming a scholar was a full-time job, and success was not assured. It was not a vocation to attempt halfheartedly. Competition was

---

1. Motto of *Révolutions de Paris,* a weekly publication that appeared in Paris from 1789 to 1794. Quoted in V. I. Lenin, *Collected Works,* 45 vols. (Moscow: Foreign Languages Publishing House, 1961–70), vol. 38, p. 32.
2. Quoted in Hilda Hookham, *A Short History of China* (London: Longmans, Green and Co., 1969), p. 85.

tremendous and a scholar's entire future depended on the outcome of the examinations. Few peasant families could afford to maintain a non-productive member or to pay the steep education fees for the many years required to study for the examinations. At any rate, the peasants, by force of their situation, were extremely practical people, and being able to recite the classics was hardly of immediate value in filling their stomachs.

Therefore the sons of landlords and officials, who had the wealth and leisure necessary for the long period of study, became the scholars. Upon successful completion of the examinations, they too would become officials, putting them in positions to bestow favors on their families, thus assuring the continuation of their privilege and power. Essentially, then, the educated of China formed a small ruling elite which perpetuated itself century after century.

Modernization of Chinese education began early in the 1900s as China attempted to stave off domination by foreign powers. The traditional educational system was simply inadequate to meet the changing social and technological demands of the country. The imperial examination system was abolished. Emphasis on the Confucian classics was lessened, being supplanted by an infusion of subjects more suitable to the needs of the day—such as world history, geography, science.

Largely at the instigation of the urban intellectuals, many of whom had returned from studying abroad, a literacy campaign was set in motion. Many more people than in the past were able to attain some schooling in the new elementary schools and evening classes that were established. Despite this impetus, however, education still fell far short of reaching large numbers of the illiterate peasants and workers, or of addressing itself to their practical needs. Although over 80 percent of the population lived in rural areas, the cities, as in earlier days, remained the centers of intellectual activity. A good many of the country people who had gained some literacy skills soon lapsed back into illiteracy for lack of anything to read.

By 1949, the year the Communist Party came to power, the year referred to as liberation by the Chinese people, an estimated 85 percent of the total population was still illiterate, with the rate of illiteracy reaching 95 percent in the rural areas.[3] The people, their energies having been siphoned for a hundred or more generations into the single funnel of unrelieved toil for sheer survival, were mired in ignorance and supersti-

---

3. There were only 125,000 college-educated people in the entire country, and many of them had been trained overseas.

tion. Their vision met its horizon at the edge of their native village. Their minds were enslaved to the rituals and ideals that kept everyone in his or her place—moderation in all things, and obedience of the young to the old, woman to man, servant to master, inferior to superior, even the living to the dead.

PAST BITTERNESS

The educational problems inherited by the new revolutionary government were staggering; the economic problems were overwhelming. First priority had to be keeping people alive and at some minimal level of comfort. Most of China's huge population had been denied a sufficient supply of life's basic physical necessities since time immemorial. A quick résumé of conditions before 1949 will provide an idea of what the new government was up against and how much it has since accomplished.

Water was the constant enemy of the Chinese people—either too much or not enough. China was plagued by endless cycles of floods and droughts which brought famine and starvation to hundreds of millions. In the early 1930s, one author stated about famine in China that "if the meaning of the word is a shortage of food on a scale sufficient to cause widespread starvation, then there are parts of the country from which famine is rarely absent. . . . There are districts in which the position of the rural population is that of a man standing permanently up to the neck in water, so that even a ripple is sufficient to drown him."[4]

It is not easy to comprehend the magnitude of the fact that up to 1949 the Chinese had suffered on average one major famine a year in one or another part of the country for the preceding 2,000 years. What is the meaning of such proportions of suffering?

> There was a crop failure in the Taihang and Taiyueh mountains, a flood in southern Hopei and locusts in Honan which soon began to sweep over all four provinces. . . .
> In Honan, the roads to the Taihang Mountains were soon filled with corpses. In the spring of 1942, the buds of all trees were eaten. The bark was stripped from every tree so that the trunks presented a strange white

---

4. R. H. Tawney, *Land and Labor in China* (New York: Harcourt, Brace & Co., 1932), pp. 76–77.

appearance like people stripped of clothes. In some places, people ate the feces of silkworms; in other places, they ate a queer white earth. But such food could only stave off starvation for a few days and the victims quickly died.

Women exchanged their babies, saying: "You eat mine, I'll eat yours." When a man was going to die, he dug a pit and sat inside and asked neighbors to fill in the earth when he was dead. Afterwards, however, no one could be found to fill in the pits for all were either dead or too weak to shovel earth. Men sold their children first, then their wives. Those who survived were getting weaker and even in those areas where there was rain, they were too weak to plant or plow....

One could not find a cat, dog, pig or chicken, so there was no breeding. Many times whole families committed suicide. The head of the family would bury his father, mother, wife and children alive and then commit suicide himself....

An invasion of locusts magnified the famine almost beyond human endurance. For days on end, for the first two years of the famine, great clouds of these bugs swarmed over the four provinces, blotting out the sun and consuming almost all plant life in their path.[5]

In less disastrous circumstances, the peasants were victimized by burdensome taxes often as imaginative as they were cruel, which made their lives not much more secure than in times of famine. During Chiang Kai-shek's regime,

taxes consisted of land rent in kind, fifty per cent of the harvest crops, and after that a multitude of other taxes of a range and variety almost unbelievable, which remained in force in one form or another till 1949. There were, among others, a general tax, tobacco tax, wine tax, transport extra tax, education tax, commercial tax, rent tax, festivity tax, mining tax, equalization tax, winter protection tax, ammunition tax, monthly tax, street number tax, New Year pig tax, tooth tax, head tax, winepot tax, market inspection tax, road tax, stricken people tax, red lantern tax, banquet tax, cleaning village tax, police tax, sugar tax, paper tax, rice tax, extra salt tax (there were five salt taxes), boat tax, getting away from conscription tax, getting let off from forced labor (corvée) tax, ticket tax, iron tax, coal tax, salt cellar and stove tax, rolling tobacco leaf tax, special lamp tax, embroidery and printing tax, northern expedition tax (collected since 1925), municipal tax, length of door tax, breadth of window tax, hair and blood tax, tax on weights and weighing machines,

5. Jack Belden, *China Shakes the World* (New York: Monthly Review Press, 1970), pp. 61–64.

bandit tax, bandit suppression congratulatory tax, suppression of communism tax, extra pacification tax. . . .[6]

In the early 1930s "there were, according to offical investigations, 188 different kinds of taxes to which the Chinese peasantry had to submit."[7] And if that were not bad enough, "taxes had been collected thirty-nine years in advance by 1935; after 1935 the collection of tax in advance accelerated and reached seventy years in advance. . . ."[8]

In these circumstances, it is easy to see why money lending was a lucrative operation. Every village had its usurers who were also often landlords and were merciless in their exactions.

A "good money-lender," described as a blessing to his village, has been known to charge only 25 per cent; but such self-restraint is exceptional. Interest at 40 to 80 per cent is said to be common; interest at 150 to 200 per cent to be not unknown. Goods pledged are taken at two-thirds of their true value. As far as the poorer peasants are concerned, permanent indebtedness is the rule rather than the exception. They pawn their crops in summer, their farm implements in winter, and their household belongings throughout the whole twelve months.[9]

Things were not much better in the cities. Describing his city's past, our guide in Nanking said, "Before liberation, this was a typical consumer city swollen with bureaucrats. In a population of some 700,000 there were about 200,000 servants, waiters, and singsong girls in the restaurants, opium dens, gambling houses, and drinking places, as well as prostitutes in the special service of the pleasure-seeking capitalists, the high-ranking Kuomintang[10] officials, and the foreign aggressors

---

6. Han Suyin, *Birdless Summer* (New York: Bantam Books, 1972), p. 125.

7. Belden, *China Shakes the World,* p. 99.

8. Han Suyin, *Birdless Summer,* p. 127.

9. Tawney, *Land and Labor,* p. 62.

10. The Kuomintang was the Nationalist Party which succeeded in overthrowing the last dynasty of China and establishing a republic in 1912. It was led by Sun Yat-sen. The Chinese still consider him to have been a progressive nationalist. Under his leadership the Kuomintang formed an alliance with the Communist Party in 1923, but he died soon after and the leadership of the Party went to Chiang Kai-shek. Under Chiang, the Kuomintang changed its progressive character and became the deadly enemy of the Communist Party. After two civil wars between them, which were interrupted from 1937 to 1945 when they formed a shaky alliance against the Japanese invaders, the Communists finally defeated the Kuomintang in 1949 and established the People's Republic of China. The Kuomintang fled to the Chinese island of Taiwan and proclaimed it the seat of government for the Republic of China. It still claims to be the sole legitimate government of all of China.

who ran amok in Nanking. So in this city there was little industry to speak of. Even matches and cigarettes couldn't be made here. People in Nanking called them 'foreign matches' and 'foreign cigarettes,' 'foreign clothes' and 'foreign nails.' Almost all daily necessities had to be imported. At that time Nanking had only 16,000 industrial workers. A quarter of the population was unemployed, and beggars could be found everywhere in the city.''

The corruption of the rich and the destitution of the poor continued in spite of the reforms set down on paper by the Chiang government. The paper reforms were often as useless as the paper on which the same government printed its money. As would be expected under these conditions soaring inflation rounded out the grim economic picture. *Peking Review* has since reported that between 1940 and 1949 the prices of grain, the most basic of all commodities,

> rose to over 200,000 times their former level. . . . In old China, with grain in the hands of the reactionary Kuomintang government and the landlords and capitalists, speculation and hoarding were rife. When grain was brought to market in autumn, the landlords and grain dealers did all they could to hold down the purchasing prices and hoarded it in large quantities. When there was a shortage of grain in spring, they raked in huge profits by raising grain prices.[11]

REVOLUTION IN THE ECONOMY

The natural and social calamities that had reduced China's people for so many centuries to a subhuman existence had to be brought under control. They were the first order of business for the new government in 1949. Land reform, aimed at eventually putting the richest landlord and the poorest peasant on an equal footing, was launched immediately; no longer would the few squeeze the life's blood from the many. In an attempt to give equal parcels to everyone the land was redistributed, but many peasants lacked even primitive tools and certainly draft animals to work the land. The willingness of neighbors to share what they had and to cooperate in their farming efforts was a widespread and in many places a largely spontaneous response.

11. "How China Solved Its Food Problem," *Peking Review* (November 9, 1973), pp. 10–11.

At first they formed mutual aid teams with neighboring peasants assisting each other in cultivating the land and sharing whatever farm implements they owned. But numerous problems developed. Some plots were less fertile than others. It was wasteful and inefficient for each family to try to save enough money to buy its own equipment. Since mutual aid included the idea that a family would receive as much aid from others as it contributed to them, the system worked to the disadvantage of those families with fewer able-bodied members. One result was that those who prospered were able to buy out small families or families with mostly old, very young, or infirm members. There were other problems such as whose fields would receive priority during the busiest periods.

The search for a solution to these problems led to the formation of cooperatives in which land was pooled and farmed jointly by large groupings of peasants. Productivity and cooperation increased. However, part of the return to the individual peasant, usually half, was based on capital shares (the amount of land contributed to the cooperative), the other part being labor shares (amount of labor contributed). Since the capital contributed was sometimes quite unequal, so too was the return—often regardless of how hard a person worked, thus generating new inequalities and sometimes resentments.

The struggle to resolve this difficulty eventuated in higher-stage (sometimes called socialist) cooperatives based on payment according to labor contributed. This development represented real progress as had the changes at earlier stages. Nonetheless, new problems continued to arise, problems such as how to evaluate each other's work. In addition, there were other needs besides basic farming that required attention. For one thing, water had to be controlled, and large numbers of people were required to build dams, dikes, and irrigation works.

To meet these challenges communes, which are composed of large groupings of peasants often numbering in the tens of thousands, were established in 1958, and they still remain the basic form of agricultural organization in China today. In addition to payment based on work every individual is guaranteed a basic supply of grain. The communes are divided into production brigades which are further subdivided into production teams (usually corresponding geographically to the villages). The size of the communes and the three-tiered structure allow for a significantly more advanced division of labor such that not only is farming more efficient but many peasants who had formerly been tied to the land have been freed to engage in a number of other economic pursuits, making possible a diversification and self-sufficiency undreamed of in the past. Most of the means of production used for agriculture are owned by the teams and brigades. Larger undertakings requiring more comprehensive and coordinated forms of organization, such as major water conservation and flood control programs and the new factories that dot the countryside, are usually organized and controlled by the commune. The commune–brigade–team arrangement has facilitated the development of other activities, not only economic, but also social and governmental. Responsibility for them likewise falls to one or another of these three levels, with the smaller projects such as lower level schools, clinics, and simple recreational facilities set up and run by the local units, and those requiring more sophisticated equipment and skills like secondary schools, hospitals, and more complex recreational facilities coming under the commune jurisdiction. Both the brigade and the commune have their own governmental organizations.[12]

These stages of increased cooperation, one flowing into the next, developed in less than a decade. They came not through fiat from above—although there was certainly direction and encouragement—but primarily in response to problems encountered by the peasants themselves and as a result of their new-found freedom to seek creative solutions to those very problems. So successful were the gains in agriculture that the age-old scourge of massive starvation was averted during 1959-61, a period of dire natural conditions that would have meant certain disaster a few years earlier.

Land reform, though vital, was only one of many revolutionary policies initiated by the government to reverse the old patterns of misery and corruption. The old taxes were abolished; usury was prohibited; trafficking in opium was outlawed; prostitution was forbidden—and these legal strictures have been successfully enforced.

Goods of all kinds had to be produced and made available to the people. Factories, large and small, were built in all parts of the country; a developing transportation network now facilitates distribution of prod-

---

12. For more on the fascinating subject of how the communes developed, see Anna Louise Strong, *The Rise of the People's Communes in China* (New York: Marzani and Munsell, 1960); Isabel Crook and David Crook, *The First Years of Yangyi Commune* (London: Routledge and Kegan Paul, 1966); and E. L. Wheelwright and Bruce McFarlane, *The Chinese Road to Socialism: Economics of the Cultural Revolution* (New York: Monthly Review Press, 1970).

ucts. Many villagers who less than a quarter of a century ago had never seen a machine of any kind are now producing and sometimes even inventing them.

In Nanking, as in all other cities, a totally different story can now be told—the beggars have completely disappeared; the former small industrial work force of 16,000 has grown to over 360,000; the city is no longer dependent and undeveloped but has even surpassed self-sufficiency and now produces enough surplus to export many of its goods to other countries. Even more remarkable, there is no unemployment in China. If anything, there is a shortage of labor for many projects.

Moreover, China, for over a century groaning under a massive and always increasing indebtedness to richer imperial powers, is now without external or internal debt. Unlike most countries, China owes not a farthing to any other nation or to private banks. A people weighted down for centuries by taxes of every description now pay no personal income tax, and nearly all other personal taxes are but so many legends of the past.[13]

The cost of basic necessities is well within everyone's means. While some Western countries subsidize farmers to limit their production in order to keep prices up, in China, the peasants—who at all times are urged to produce their maximum—are subsidized so that the prices of agricultural goods will be low to consumers. Prices for most agricultural and industrial products are set on a national level and cannot vary from one region to another by more than 1 percent. Thus, people are not

---

13. There are only three kinds of personal taxes presently levied in China. (1) License plate tax on bicycles. This form of taxation applies quite widely since there are many privately owned bicycles. (2) Housing tax on privately owned homes. This applies only to houses in the cities. Since all new urban residential construction is state-owned, the only houses involved are the old still privately owned ones that pre-date 1949. Home ownership by any individual is limited to the one dwelling in which he or she lives, since private rent collection is considered exploitative. Therefore, no one would ever pay tax on more than one house. In addition, most of the privately owned homes in China are in the rural areas which are not affected by this tax. For these reasons, the tax applies only to a relatively small and constantly diminishing segment of the population. (3) Slaughter tax. Since most animals are owned by a production brigade or commune, the slaughter tax is generally borne by the collective. However, individual peasants sometimes raise a very few of their own animals which they generally sell to the state, in which case they are also not affected by the tax. Nor does the tax apply to the slaughtering of small animals such as chickens and ducks which the peasants most commonly own. It covers only the fairly large animals such as pigs and applies only to those situations in which a peasant slaughters rather than sells it to the state. Therefore, this tax is not very widely applicable. Moreover, the amounts of money levied for all three types of taxes are low.

rewarded or penalized for their closeness or remoteness to production centers or for the level of development of their distribution facilities.

And prices are stable. Contrary to the claims of the Western press that there is "world-wide inflation," China, which contains nearly one-fourth of the world's population, is totally free of any inflation whatsoever. Increases in prices apply only to a very few imported items such as wristwatches, reflecting inflation elsewhere, but not in China. For internally produced goods, quite the reverse is true. Incredible as it may sound, the prices of many basic products such as medicines, chemical fertilizers, and farm machinery and implements have been dropping steadily as they become available in greater quantities.

Despite the real and continuing rise in the standard of living and the tremendous emphasis on increasing the sheer volume of goods and services, China is not, strangely enough, a "consumer society" in the usual sense. Working people not only actively produce together in a communal way; even their consuming habits are devoid of that alienation so common to profit-making societies. Distribution outlets in China seem more interested in assisting than in bilking people; they show concern about the desires of consumers for safe, well-made, durable goods by conscientiously eliciting consumer attitudes and opinions about their products.

There are no external obstacles to the reliability of the consumers' opinions, because they do not have to flounder through a sea of promotional gimmicks to get through to the actual product in order to make sound judgments. There is no advertising, or fancy packaging, "specials," "bonuses," "prizes," green stamps, and what have you. No one's job depends upon the rate of sales; there are no commissions. A product either suits a customer in its quality, serviceability, size, color, shape, taste, texture, etc. or it does not. If it doesn't, it will not be because he was misled by someone whose job hinges on selling him something regardless of his requirements. Consumers are thus allowed, even encouraged, to be rational in their buying habits. An American journalist living in China has observed that "there is neither a fetish made out of possession of material things, nor is there the feeling of man being pitted against man in a fight for survival. This is overwhelmingly a nonacquisitive society even while the standard of living slowly goes up."[14]

---

14. Julian Schuman, "Chinese Consumers," *Eastern Horizon* 12, no. 3 (1973), p. 41.

All these economic changes have taken place with a speed and thoroughness historically unprecedented. There are many reasons, but fundamental to them are, first of all, the strain to always try to pinpoint the precise nature of problems, and secondly, the great effort to maintain unswerving commitment to solving them. The solutions are seldom partial. The Chinese are proud of what they have achieved but not satisfied. Moreover, they appear to have a keen sense of priority, a focused view of the importance of attending to first things first without being distracted by less relevant side issues. And priority necessarily has gone to feeding, clothing, sheltering, and medicating their hundreds of millions who were so wretchedly poor. Their success has been astounding.[15] While still at a low standard of living compared with the affluent strata of society in the West, everyone in China now has an adequate supply of the material necessities of life. The living standard is improving not only steadily, but just as important to the Chinese, more and more equitably. No segment of society gets rich because others remain poor. They benefit together.

REVOLUTION IN EDUCATION

Education is important for any industrializing society if it is to train people in science and modern technology, but in China there is another equally important purpose for education. The ultimate objective is to eventually achieve a society without classes. The Chinese maintain that it has been the existence of classes which has allowed some to exploit, oppress, and dominate others, not only in China but everywhere in the world. Abuse meted out by one group to another will, they claim, cease

---

15. No one goes hungry in China today. Nor does the formerly well-deserved epithet—"the sick man of Asia"—any longer apply as a characterization of the country. Massive campaigns of innoculation and public health education, intensification of medical training, and widely distributed health services have virtually wiped out diseases that were rampant in the past—diphtheria, whooping cough, tetanus, smallpox, polio, cholera, tuberculosis—even syphilis. The Chinese, like ourselves, now most commonly die of cancer and heart disease, a sign of great progress since encounter with these killers generally comes in advanced years. A comparison of infant mortality rates in Shanghai and New York City shows lower rates in Shanghai, even when the comparison includes only white New Yorkers, who are obviously better off than their non-white counterparts. (See Victor W. Sidel and Ruth Sidel, *Serve the People: Observations on Medicine in the People's Republic of China* [New York: Josiah Macy, Jr. Foundation, 1973], pp. 255–66.) Robust health and freedom from disease are new to China and stand in stark contrast to the physical suffering of Third World humanity.

only when class society no longer exists. To develop the economy and distribute its goods and services on a more equal basis so that people are free from want is a necessary step in creating a classless society, but by itself insufficient. They must also develop a new ideology to match, and it must become fully part of the people.

The Chinese believe that a socialist economy without a socialist ideology would quickly degenerate into capitalism. It was only to be expected, for example, during the initial stage of land reform when peasants got their own piece of land, many for the first time, that some would have visions of becoming prosperous by following the only path to prosperity they knew—becoming landlords and moneylenders. These aspirations brought corresponding behavior. Even when they moved to the higher stages of cooperative farming, some formerly landless and land-poor peasants wanted to devote all their energies to tilling just their own plots, expanding just their own houses, planning for just their own futures. This kind of problem arises time and time again. People have had to be educated and to educate each other out of the old individualistic mentality and to the new community mentality, for with each new stage of development, with each new gain, there are some who wish to maintain the privileges of the most recent stage, who often proclaim that the revolution has gone far enough and are therefore inclined to oppose further changes. Thus the process of re-education must continue apace.

Education and re-education, then, are as important in China as is economic development. It is through education that the gains in other spheres of activity can become consolidated and the foundations of socialism be made secure. Education for everyone, not just some; it doesn't take many people with the old ideology to corrode the building materials of the new society. Through schools, part-time study programs, evening classes, political study groups, the mass media, and the popular arts, children and adults are all being taught the new ideology.

The first step in equalizing people through education is to make them literate. To obtain a basic level of literacy in Chinese, however, is not easy. It entails learning 3,000 or more characters. While some are formed from combinations of other words, they must all nevertheless be learned separately. Many of the characters have been simplified in recent years, but a large number still contain many strokes, in some cases twenty or more. There are few shortcuts in learning to read and write Chinese, yet huge numbers of people have become literate.

A literacy campaign was inaugurated soon after liberation. Its suc-

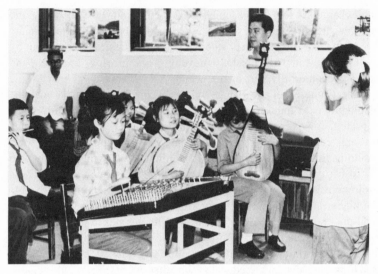

Children are no longer denied education. Their activities are varied and enjoyable.

cess has overwhelmingly outstripped the efforts to universalize literacy started earlier in the century. This time the benefits of being able to read and write are clearly evident. With literacy, a person can take a more active part in the many decisions and tasks that are of direct consequence to himself, his community, and, by extension, the society as a whole.

Now, once learned, literacy skills are less likely to be forgotten. Even in remote areas, there are opportunities to read, and the material is usually relevant to people's lives. Printed information on matters of vital concern—how-to booklets on increasing crop yield, improving sanitation, administering first aid—are widely disseminated. Political essays, daily newspapers, posters, and notice boards announcing local events and reporting national and international news are available throughout China. There are conscientious efforts to find new techniques for increasing and retaining literacy, and some can be quite creative. For example, at a musical performance I attended in Canton, the words to the music were flashed on two long vertical screens on either side of the stage in large characters as the performers sang them.

While the main purpose was to enable members of the audience, particularly those who spoke a different dialect, to understand the words, it was also hoped that by these means, some of the less literate people might pick up a few characters.

The extent of literacy has swelled in the span of just one generation from a low of about 15 percent in 1949 to an estimated 80 to 90 percent today, the remaining illiteracy being concentrated primarily among those who matured before liberation. Whereas approximately 5 percent of the children in rural China received a full elementary education or its equivalent during the 1940s, today, over 90 percent of elementary school age children, in the country as a whole, are in school.

The growth of secondary education is also spectacular. Take Lin-ching County, a rural area in Shantung Province, as an example: in 1945 there was only one secondary school with a capacity for about 250 students to service a total population of 300,000. By 1973, the population had grown to approximately 500,000, but there were 118 secondary schools with 19,484 students. Even accounting for the population growth, this represents a more than 4,600 percent increase in students.

Compared to the relative availability of elementary education, however, there is considerably more variation in the extent of secondary schooling from one locality to the next. Typical of nearly all else in China, the educational system inherited uneven conditions—the urban areas had more teachers and schools than the countryside; more men than women were literate; some locales had always had more hospitable natural conditions and therefore had been able to produce and afford more for social services than others, and so on. This unevenness can be equalized only gradually, so there are still regional variations. Estimated percentages of students from rural areas who go on to middle schools[16] generally range from 60 to 75 percent; in the cities, from 80 to 90 percent or more (100 percent in Nanking and some other cities), with the percentages always rising.[17] Although not all those who begin mid-

---

16. Middle schools are equivalent to our secondary schools. In many places, they are divided into junior and senior middle schools, and approximate North American junior and senior high schools. In others, there are general middle schools which encompass a full secondary education. Students enter middle school at age twelve or thirteen. What are called elementary schools in North America are referred to as primary schools in China and begin at age seven.

17. Such estimates are always general approximations when there are few concrete statistics available. In the case of China, where such high priority is placed on education, there is added unreliability of statistics due to the fact that they are quickly out of date.

dle school receive a full secondary education (completion of junior middle school being the most common break-off point), the national objective for the future is to achieve universal secondary education.

Most schools we visited had large classes by North American standards. In a Shanghai general middle school, where there were forty-five to fifty-five students to a class, we commented on the size.

"We agree," explained one of the teachers, "that smaller classes would be more efficient. Every year more new schools are being built and more new teachers are being trained so that eventually our classes will be smaller. In the meantime, however, although we encounter difficulties in running large classes, we teachers are clear in our minds that our primary aim now is universal middle school education. So, even though we have many students, we are happy to run big classes."

With characteristic directness, she briefly outlined the two alternatives: on the one hand, small classes would make it easier for the teachers but would run the risk of producing people who could come to look upon themselves as an elite; on the other hand, if the teachers accommodated more students, the dangers of elitism would be lessened and the country could move more rapidly toward universal secondary education. To make immediate sacrifices to serve immediate needs seems to be a principle that is not uncommon in China. So many things need doing and so many services are required. The question is, should scarce resources be expended on training a relatively small group of people to become highly expert or should they be spread around so that a great many develop minimal competencies? The latter is chosen as the main thrust, without completely sacrificing the former.

The training of doctors, for example, presented the same dilemma. In the past, the small number of doctors was concentrated in the large cities where they primarily tended the rich. The huge rural population could not wait the many years necessary for sufficient numbers of people to become fully trained doctors. They were needed right away, and, with the ingenuity typical of present-day China, "barefoot doctors" were created. The name (which is misleading—they do wear shoes) derives from the fact that they have been selected from among the peasantry and they continue to be peasants, working in the fields part of

---

Both in 1973 and 1975 when I was in China, I asked about the extent of universal education in each city and commune I visited. While there were variations from one locality to the next, in every instance, the grade levels at which universal education had been achieved were higher in 1975 than in 1973.

the time and attending to the medical needs of the people the other part. An initial medical training generally lasting from three to six months enables them to start practicing immediately. They conduct health education programs, do preventive work, and take care of simple ailments, freeing the more experienced doctors to handle more complicated cases. As they practice, their medical education continues. They might participate in hospital consultations on difficult cases; they have get-togethers among themselves to exchange experiences; they attend classes that are given periodically by more fully trained doctors-in-residence on the communes, and by doctors from the cities, who travel the countryside in mobile medical teams; or they might attend special short-term courses offered by medical colleges. More than one million barefoot doctors have been trained since the end of the 1960s.

They do not replace fully trained doctors. Full medical training is still given in the medical colleges. Both kinds of doctors are needed; they support and complement each other. This kind of rational planning is an example of what is called "walking on two legs."

> [China] does not emphasize one to the neglect of the other but develops both simultaneously in such a way that they coordinate with and promote each other.
>
> The relations between [them] are like that between the two legs of a person. When both legs coordinate well, the person is able to walk steadier and faster.[18]

This approach to medical problems is representative of the ways in which education serves to equalize the population. It provides the opportunity for more people to learn new skills. In addition to the relatively few for whom a full premedical and medical education can currently be supplied, a great many others can also learn doctoring on a lesser scale. Thus, and even more importantly, the entire population becomes the beneficiary of this burgeoning and creative educational program. Everybody gains greater equality through all receiving good medical care. This method has also helped to diminish the status distinction between doctors and non-doctors. Medical knowledge no longer need be sanctified; doctors need not be worshipped as high priests with semi-magical healing powers. They are no longer a small group which

---

18. "The Policy of 'Walking on Two Legs'," *China Reconstructs* 22, no. 8 (August 1973), p. 21.

holds a monopoly on the mysteries of the body. Medicine in China is coming to be regarded as is any other kind of work, as a body of knowledge and skills requiring study and practice that anyone—including ordinary peasants—can acquire through diligence and hard work. The same is true of farming, factory work, or any other occupation, and because workers and peasants perform essential and valuable services, attitudes are engendered which are making them as highly respected as doctors.

This view was articulated on our first day in China during a discussion with our guides. We noticed that they always addressed each other as "comrade." We asked if it signified membership in the Communist Party. One of them, a serious man in his mid-forties, with the appearance of an intellectual, answered, "Oh no, not necessarily. In China, all people are comrades. We have a common goal. We are all working for socialist construction, so it does not matter what kind of job a person does. Since each job is an important contribution toward building socialism, we are all equal. Whether a person does the most menial physical work or holds the highest administrative post, we see it as simply a division of labor. We don't think that some people are superior and others inferior. We are working toward equality among all workers in China, so we call each other comrades." This attitude appeared to be borne out over and over in people's actions towards each other everywhere we visited. It is probable that older status distinctions, involving subtleties not easily recognizable to a foreigner, still exist, but the clear-cut thrust of Chinese society is undoubtedly in the direction of eliminating them.

HALF THE SKY

In the past women were even more harshly oppressed than other Chinese. Women owed total and unquestioning obedience to their fathers and their husbands. A women was denied the right to own property, to choose a husband, to divorce, to remarry if her husband died. She might be one of several wives; she might be married before puberty; she might be sold into slavery, concubinage, or prostitution; she might have her feet bound in childhood; she might even be drowned as an infant. She had no voice whatsoever in any of the crucial matters that affected her life. She was economically dependent and politically powerless.

The world was seen by ancient China as made up of two opposing and complementary forces—yin and yang—that formed a dynamic and synthesized into one. Yin was darkness and decay; it represented weakness and passivity, all that was seen to be female. Yang was its counterpart—light, growth, strength, activity—in short, maleness. This ancient philosophy was deeply ingrained in the elaborate code of conduct toward women. The wisdom of the sages was thought to be proof of woman's total and immutable inferiority. *"There are only two categories of inferior beings: the nobodies and women,"* said Confucius 2,500 years ago. Such "wisdom" found endless plain-spoken expressions through the centuries. *"A women married is like a pony bought. I'll ride her and whip her as I like"* states a familiar proverb.

Parents would look for a suitable groom while their daughter was still a child. Without consulting her, they would sell her to another family, the brideprice depending on her family's status and her looks. The groom might well be much older or younger than herself and was quite likely someone she had never seen. Once married, she moved in with her husband's family who were often total strangers and for whom she was a servant. She had to submit to all demands from both her husband and mother-in-law. She ate their food scraps and wore their cast-off clothes. Even if she complied with all their demands and was uncomplaining and unrebellious, she could expect to be beaten regularly: *"When a woman is angry, her husband beats her; when he is angry, he also beats her."*

There was no place to turn for protection; she was her husband's property. Divorce, escape from this intolerable situation, was out of the question: *"When you marry a chicken, stick with the chicken; when you marry a dog, stick with the dog."* She was forbidden to go anywhere: *"Men go to the county town, but a woman's place is in the home."* And she was expected to bear her husband many sons:

> Sons shall be born to him—
> They will be put to sleep on couches;
> They will be clothed in robes . . . .
> Daughters shall be born to him—
> They will be put to sleep on the ground;
> They will be clothed with wrappers.

If a woman was unfortunate enough to bear many daughters, she might be forced to sell or kill some of them, but she could not hope to quell her husband's wrath at having so betrayed him.

Although often the work of a peasant woman in tilling the fields was economically indispensable to her family, she was looked down upon as nonproductive and useless: *"Man's labor produces everywhere; women can only make water soup."* It was unthinkable for her to expect any help from men in the housework: *"If a man does housework, he will get poorer and poorer."* Her activities were bound exclusively to her family. She required no education. *"The state of being uncultured is a virtue in women"* and *"Heaven is man; earth is woman"* spoke the proverbs.

It is not surprising that women often ran away or committed suicide. What is surprising is how quickly and completely women's circumstances have been changing since liberation. Women can now choose their husbands, divorce, remarry, own property, receive education, and participate in community and political affairs. Footbinding, concubinage, prostitution, slavery, and infanticide are illegal and have been virtually eliminated. When we asked some doctors at Sun Yat-sen Medical College in Canton if female victims of physical abuse are treated in the city's hospitals, the question was met with surprise.

"We don't have that kind of problem. Before liberation, there were many such cases, but not now. That was a social problem, and it has been cured."

Couples now receive free birth control information and devices to limit the size of their families. I asked a woman doctor at the College how many children she considered to be the right number for a family, and she said,

"One's okay; two's fine," and after a pause she added, smiling, "three is beginning to be more than enough." Parents or grandparents who express disappointment at the birth of a girl can expect to be criticized by their neighbors for still retaining "remnants of the oppressive feudal ideology."

A woman about fifty-five years old, who had been selected by her neighbors as one of the leaders of their Peking neighborhood of over 52,000 people, knew what being a woman meant in both the old China and the new China. She described women's progress: "Before liberation, we were treated as if we were not human beings. We were looked upon just like straw, but now we are considered as a treasure."

Today's slogans reflect women's new position just as faithfully as the old ones reflected their position in the past. Now people say,

One of China's young liberated women teaching others who will some day "hold up half the sky."

"Whatever men comrades can accomplish women comrades can too. Women hold up half the sky!"

Basic to women's emancipation is their new role as a vital force in the economy. At first there was male resistance to women going outside the home to work. Paraphrasing the slogan of their growing liberation, women, when confronted with resistance, would angrily assert, "We can do everything men can do!" Some men who hung on to the old ideas would mockingly shoot back, "Fine! If you can do everything we can do, then do everything!"

Many women took up this challenge. During the Great Leap Forward initiated in 1958 by Chairman Mao—who urged acceleration of production, fuller utilization of the labor power of the people, and reliance on Chinese efforts rather than foreign assistance—people all over the country, women as well as men, were mobilized. Communes emerged from the cooperatives, the policy of "walking on two legs" was formulated, and innumerable small-scale, labor-intensive industries were started.

Many of the new industries were set up by small groups of women who had never held jobs outside the home; often the women were illiterate, and most of them had absolutely no knowledge of industrial techniques. Motivated by their desire to contribute to socialist construction and to prove their capabilities, and egged on by the jeers of resentful men, they persisted, learned skills, innovated, cooperated, and in a great many cases succeeded. A number of these small factories have become large state enterprises manufacturing sophisticated equipment with the original founders still working in them. Others remain as smaller neighborhood industries, sometimes called "housewives' factories." They turn out simple products but make an important contribution to the overall economy.

Today there are not many women in China who could be called traditional housewives. By most calculations, well over 90 percent of the women work in occupations outside their homes. Their families do not appear to suffer as a result. Young children attend preschools or are looked after by grandparents or by that small percentage of housewives who do not go out to work. Preschools on a large scale are new in China having been set up since 1949 in response to the great demand to free women for work in society.[19] Accordingly, where possible, these are organized to suit the convenience of the mothers. There are nurseries for infants and children from the age of fifty-six days to generally around two-and-a-half years. Many are attached to workplaces, thus allowing mothers to bring babies to work with them and leave them in the care of trained personnel for the day. The mothers get paid breaks from work to nurse the infants.

From the ages of two or three to seven, children might attend kindergartens which are most often set up by the neighborhoods in the cities and the production teams or brigades in the countryside, and therefore are in the vicinity of their homes. The great majority of the centers provides daycare only, but there are also some boarding facilities for children whose parents work either odd shifts or too far from home to return each day. While the development of preschools has been

---

19. In the city of Peking, for example, prior to 1949 there were only fifteen preschools, all of which catered exclusively to the children of the rich. Today there are 4,500 kindergartens and nurseries accommodating nearly 200,000 children and babies.

very rapid, there are still not enough for all of China's tens of millions of tots. The cities, which in so many respects are in advance over the countryside, generally have more and better facilities, but there, too, there is sometimes a shortage of preschools. In such cases priority is given to children who have no retired grandparents living with them, the idea being to avoid holding back any able woman who wants to work outside the home.

Women's welfare is a matter of special concern. In addition to the growing network of preschool facilities, there are several other benefits specifically for women. During pregnancy, women factory workers have a decreased work load without decrease of pay; they are allowed fifty-six days paid maternity leave (seventy for twins); women with menstrual difficulties are not penalized, being given lighter work loads if necessary and in special cases, time off without loss of wages. Other than these special considerations, women workers also receive the same regular work and retirement benefits as men.

To ease the burden of the household chores that would ordinarily fall on housewives, many neighborhoods, especially in cities, have service centers that attend to such things as washing, mending clothes, and repairing shoes—all done cheaply and quickly. In factory after factory, I asked women about who did the housework in their families. The answer was invariably along the same lines: "Whoever gets home first starts; then the other one joins," or, "My husband, children, and I have a division of labor; we all share in the housework." Numerous people also emphasized, however, that this situation often does not exist in the rural areas and that "more education is necessary."

Women are justifiably happy about their new position in society. Freed from intolerable feudal restrictions, they have a new sense of usefulness and power. In one factory where the majority of the work force was female, one worker, her face beaming, pointed out: "As you can see, in this factory women hold up more than half the sky."

The same pride can be observed among older retired women. We visited the home of an ex-hospital worker. Women—and men—who lived the life of preliberation China tend to look much older than their years, and this woman was no exception; but her vitality belied her wrinkles. Her days were spent helping to keep the neighborhood clean, doing the marketing for younger neighbors who were away at work, preparing lunch for their children, giving acupuncture treatments, doing preventive hygiene work, conducting education in family planning, reading newspapers to the other older people, and helping to improve the literacy skills of less literate retired workers. Reflecting on the changes in her life, she said: "In the past, I served just my own family. Now I can serve the whole country. Since liberation my life has been good, and I want to do more for the people. Even though I am a retired worker, my mind will never retire."

While economic independence is basic to women's liberation from family, social, and political strictures, it is the continued education of both women and men that solidifies this liberation. Like the other injustices from old China, the uneducated state of women is being attacked frontally. The Chinese do not seem to go in for timid solutions. If women have been denied education, no amount of tokenism will change their subordinate position. To behave and think equally, and to be viewed as equals by men, they must *become* equal.

Whereas before 1949 only a fraction of the small literate population were women, today there is much less disparity along sex lines. There is none among the children. In the primary grades, virtually all girls accompany their brothers to school. In the middle schools, if there is sexual imbalance, it is not immediately apparent to the casual observer. It is likely, however, that there is a slight discrepancy in some rural areas because it is there where the old ideas and outlooks die more slowly; consequently, there are probably still parents who are not fully convinced that their daughters need to spend as many years in school as their sons. But education in the new ideology is ongoing among adults as well through study groups, informal discussions, and the mass media, making it difficult for such outmoded attitudes to persist with the same force. These are diminishing, and with their decline there is a concomitant rise in educational opportunities for females.

This is evident at the higher levels of education which, in the past, admitted only a very small proportion of women students. At the medical college in Canton, where students receive a full medical education, we discovered that 40 percent of the students were women. Only seven years before, the figure had been 30 percent. In the library at Peking University, I had a lengthy discussion with a female student dressed in the green jacket and trousers of the People's Liberation Army. On this question, she said, "Among the students who come from the PLA there are quite a lot more men because there are more men in the army, but it is much closer to being equal for the other students."

As for the professors, the older ones are almost all men because they were educated in the old society, but among the younger professors there are many women. In all fields, including those requiring a high level of technical and scientific knowledge, there are growing numbers of women. In many, the numbers are not yet equal, and in some they are still far from equal.

The important point, however, is that the hideous nightmare of the past is now but a bitter memory, and it is plain to the visitor that the Chinese, especially the women, will not be satisfied until the past is dead once and for all. Women have accomplished wonders in a mere quarter of a century, and, with each passing year, they are moving ever closer to full equality with men.

BROTHERS AND SISTERS

China's national minorities are another segment of the population that was super-oppressed in the past. Contrary to a popular Western notion, not all Chinese have the same culture. There are fifty-five nationalities in China with different languages, cultures, and histories. The Hans are numerically preponderant. Although the other fifty-four nationalities constitute only about 6 percent of the population, in China that comes to some fifty million people. Comparing the minorities to women, the specifics of their oppression differed, but not the severity. At the National Minorities Institute in Peking we were told that the people of the minority groups were often oppressed by contending feudal rulers, including their own. Some nationalities lived in areas with severe geographic and climatic conditions. Some were isolated and had extremely undeveloped economies. Some had no written languages and no schools.

The revolutionary government has taken upon itself the very difficult and delicate task of trying to unify all of China's nationalities without destroying their indigenous cultures. Special governmental districts have been set up in areas with a high proportion of minority peoples. Called autonomous regions, they are equivalent to provinces and function somewhat similarly. A professor at the Institute who had studied anthropology at Harvard in the late 1930s explained some of the differences.

"With the agreement of the central government, the autonomous regions can make their own laws consistent with their cultures. They print newspapers, documents, laws, and so forth in their own languages. The purpose is to help them develop and to ensure their political equality while always respecting their cultures. Reform has taken a long time among some minorities. It has depended upon the concrete conditions in the area and the consciousness of the people. The central government didn't carry out reforms among all the minorities immediately after liberation. They did a lot of educational work and waited until the people *wanted* reform. For example, I was in Tibet in 1951 and saw the situation with my own eyes. A few local people wanted reform but not the majority. There was no reform until 1959 when the great majority of Tibetans rose up against the Dalai Lama."[20]

This approach is consistent with the view expressed by Chairman Mao in 1944:

> All work done for the masses must start from their needs and not from the desire of any individual, however well-intentioned. It often happens that objectively the masses need a certain change, but subjectively they are not yet conscious of the need, not yet willing or determined to make the change. In such cases, we should wait patiently. We should not make the change until, through our work, most of the masses have become conscious of the need and are willing and determined to carry it out. Otherwise we shall isolate ourselves from the masses. Unless they are conscious and willing, any kind of work that requires their participation will turn out to be a mere formality and will fail. . . . There are two principles here: one is the actual needs of the masses rather than what we fancy they need, and the other is the wishes of the masses, who must make up their own minds instead of our making up their minds for them.[21]

Because of the national minorities' extremely backward state, the drive to educate them has been intense. Teacher training institutes and schools at all levels have had to start almost from scratch in some places. To compensate for the great imbalance, the central government contributes a larger share of finances than usual to these areas. In some of the sparsely populated regions, the expense has been even greater to

---

20. The reader is referred to Stuart and Roma Gelder, *The Timely Rain: Travels in New Tibet* (New York: Monthly Review Press, 1965), for a vivid account of conditions and events in Tibet during that period.

21. Mao Tse-tung, "The United Front in Cultural Work," *Selected Works of Mao Tse-tung,* 4 vols. (Peking: Foreign Languages Press, 1961–65), vol. 3, pp. 236–37.

Children of national minority in South China now receive education.

provide schools and teachers for relatively small numbers of students. Initially, in a number of cases, most of the teachers were Hans. This was true of leaders in all spheres—economic, social, and political. With more universities and institutes being built in the minority areas, members of national minorities are becoming increasingly able to supply their own cadres (leaders), and in several instances they now hold leadership positions proportional to their numbers in their local populations. One of the main purposes of the nationality institutes like the one we visited in Peking is to train such cadres so that the minorities can run their own affairs. Success in this endeavor has extended beyond their own local areas: 14 percent of the representatives of the Second and Third National People's Congresses, the highest governing body in the country, came from minority groups, more than double the percentage of their combined total populations.

Previously looked down upon as inferior barbarians, and at many periods in their histories prevented from speaking their own languages, celebrating their holidays, wearing their national clothing, and practicing their customs, some of the minority peoples had suffered great loss of self-respect. To reverse this, the institutes have special arts programs where young people study the music, art, lore, crafts, and customs of their own culture, rediscovering and adding to its richness.

Damaged self-images are being rebuilt and strengthened not just among the relatively small layers of students at the institutes but among the minority populations as a whole. Written languages have been created for ten of the nationalities that formerly had none. Radio programs, films, plays, books, newspapers, and magazines are produced in minority languages. Where there are written languages, schoolchildren become literate in their native tongues.

One danger would appear to be that all these measures would serve to fragment the country, further splitting off each national group from the others. It is here that the ingenuity of the policy relating to nationalities is striking. The Chinese are doing two seemingly opposite things at the same time—and apparently succeeding. While on the one hand strengthening native cultures and local pride, they are also on the other hand building unity on a countrywide scale. For people to learn to genuinely respect those traditionally held to be inferior, they must stop regarding them as "strange." Unfamiliarity is what breeds contempt; familiarity, demystification, and knowledge of a people and what they have been through breed respect.

Each nationality is immersed in its own culture but at the same time is exposed to the others. Minority cultures are being popularized, especially among the 94 percent who are Hans. Every song and dance performance we attended, whether staged by children in schools or adults in theaters, had several numbers from or about one or another minority done in their native dress. A typical evening of television includes a documentary, a news report, or a play about the achievements of some minority group. Posters, films, literature in various ways extol the minorities. They appear to be extremely effective in combatting centuries-old Han chauvinism.

Another unifying element is the gradual spread of a standard language throughout the country. This is not easy in China, because, in addition to the many languages, there are regional differences in dialect among the Han majority, some mutually unintelligible. What the Chinese call common or ordinary Chinese is now taught throughout the country. Among the national minorities, especially the educated youth, bilingualism is increasing.

Undoubtedly the most effective way the Chinese are building unity is through common socialist ideology. While the particular conditions, problems, and needs might vary considerably from one national group to the next, the overall objectives of building socialism and of all peoples serving each other are forwarded in every corner of this immense country. The stories, songs, examples, and other particulars may differ, but in classroom after classroom, in both minority and majority areas, the children are learning essentially the same values as at The East Is Red Kindergarten in Canton. Said one student at the Institute who was of Korean nationality, "All of us from all the nationalities are brothers and sisters—many in one big family."

This attitude exemplifies the emerging socialist morality. Minorities as well as women now figure prominently as heroes and heroines in China; those previously despised are now portrayed as equal partners in building the new society. It is not just a new image that is being conveyed; the people of China are genuinely deepening their respect for each other as they become more unified in their strivings toward common ideals.

III: ONE STEP BACKWARD, TWO STEPS FORWARD

There's no Jade Emperor in heaven,
No Dragon King on earth.
We are the Jade Emperor,
We are the Dragon King.
We order the three mountains and five peaks:
"Make way! Here we come!"

CHINESE FOLKSONG

A NEW KIND OF REVOLUTION

Liberation marked the first phase in transforming the educational system of the whole country; the Cultural Revolution marked the second. The huge numbers of people who started to receive education after liberation in 1949, most for the first time in their lives, were making gains in learning to think of others first, to "fight self." But changes of revolutionary proportions never proceed without a hitch. The old outlooks had a life span of tens of hundreds of years. Ideas of right and wrong, attitudes, behaviors take a long time to form; they cause people to respond in automatic ways that are taken to be "natural" simply because they have become automatic. Changing them requires in the first place intense dissatisfaction with what went before—not a problem for most Chinese at the time of liberation. It also means, however, embracing what might be. This is a problem for anybody, because "what might be" cannot be fully known until after it has become something. It is even more problematic when this "might be" has to be newly created. Only once had it ever been tried on a large scale before—by the Soviet Union. Only one example to learn from and this one, as it turned out, proved to be abortive. For the rest, it has had to be figured out step by step as it unfolds. It has been and continues to be one gigantic experiment.

Such an experiment entails the unleashing of the imaginations, energies, and courage of an ever-increasing number of people. There is little room for the laxity that can eventuate either in stagnation or regression. The successful bringing into being of a wholly new society demands the destruction of the reactionary old through focused attention on the construction of the revolutionary new. Even then, smooth forward movement is not assured. Necessary changes in one arena can be bypassed for a time, causing reverses on other fronts. Problems can be poorly understood or understood by some but not others. Individuals and groups can grab advantages for themselves, thereby thwarting the progress of others. So many things can go wrong in so many different ways, and they can be so subtle, yet so disastrous. Things have gone wrong; there has been backsliding and sidetracking in just about every area of activity at one time or another. The brilliance of the Chinese Revolution, however, has been the sensitivity of its leaders and of the people to these reverses on the one hand, and to their own potential strengths on the other. This has enabled them to redirect mistaken courses before it was too late as well as to carry their transformation forward.

The field of education presents numerous examples of the kind of problem that was coming to be widely recognized by the 1960s. Selection to university continued to be done by standardized examinations which were becoming more rather than less difficult, favoring the sons and daughters (especially the sons) of intellectuals, cadres, and formerly privileged classes. Once admitted, large numbers of students failed and were expelled, the great majority of these being of worker-peasant origin. The schools at the higher levels were not serving the common people in numbers proportionate to the total population. At some of the major universities, less than 40 percent of the students came from worker and peasant families. Worse yet, this represented a reversal from just a few years before. The socialist values of cooperating with each other and exerting efforts for the collective good were being ploughed under. Students were learning to compete, to think "me first," to strive through their education for the individualistic rewards of fame and prestige. The feudal outlook that placed such a high premium on intellectual activity while disdaining manual work, and by extension, those who performed it, was being revitalized.

Many teachers had been trained in the old society and it had never occurred to some of them to see learning as a process of acquiring intellectual skills for the purpose of better serving the people. To them, education had always been a means to narrowly self-interested ends, and that's what they taught. In some cases, of course, it was deliberate;

there were unquestionably some who wanted to sabotage the socialist revolution. In far more instances, however, it was not intended. What was socialist ideology supposed to be? How can you transform education so that it is consistent with an ideology that is just being born? How can you help this ideology to emerge and blossom when you don't know what it is? Teachers taught the only ideology they knew—and all too often it was a backward one.

Had such tendencies been allowed to go unchecked, the consequences would have been catastrophic for socialism in China. Similar problems, equally serious, were being experienced not only in the schools but practically everywhere else as well. The practice of criticism and self-criticism, which has become a built-in feature of the Chinese Revolution since the formation of the Communist Party in the early 1920s, has been an effective tool in combatting antisocialist tendencies. It bases itself on a principle known in China as "unity-criticism-unity." Starting from a position of unity in their efforts and objectives, people are encouraged to criticize their own and other people's mistakes. Mistakes are seen as any actions or outlooks that impede the progress toward a new society and which, if serious enough and if not corrected, can lead to what the Chinese consider counterrevolution. Criticism is a much-used method for defining and solving problems, removing obstacles, recognizing strengths, and rechanneling energies. It is a difficult exercise and must be carefully conducted. In 1957, Mao cautioned:

> All erroneous ideas, all poisonous weeds, all ghosts and monsters must be subjected to criticism; in no circumstances should they be allowed to spread unchecked. However, the criticism should be fully reasoned, analytical, and convincing, and not rough, bureaucratic, metaphysical, or dogmatic.[1]

Successful criticism leads again to unity, this time at a higher and more advanced level. As long as progress is unending, which it is to the Chinese, the process of unity-criticism-unity is also without end.[2]

---

1. Mao Tse-tung, "Speech at the Chinese Communist Party's National Conference on Propaganda Work," *Selected Readings from the Works of Mao Tse-tung* (Peking: Foreign Languages Press, 1971), p. 496.

2. The method of unity-criticism-unity is not deemed suitable for dealing with all problems. Mao identifies two kinds of contradictions: contradictions between the people (those who support progressive movement) and the enemy (those who oppose it); and contradictions among the people. He characterizes the former type of contradiction as

Ongoing political study is another means used in China to develop people's awareness of their conditions and their ability to better analyze and solve problems. The practices of criticism and self-criticism and of political study are conducted by people throughout the society, including the grass roots level. But the strength of the old ideology, even in some of its newer manifestations, is too great to be totally broken by these means alone. It has been necessary at times to focus people's attention both on mistakes and deficiencies and on new possibilities in a more concentrated fashion, accelerating the intensity of criticism and the pace of developing socialist consciousness. At such times special campaigns have been launched nationwide. Sometimes the emphasis has been primarily economic and has centered on such problems as residual capitalist or exploitative practices; sometimes it has been political with the primary target, for example, corruption or bureaucratic tendencies among officials; at other times the stress has been mainly ideological as with certain attacks on elitist ideas among intellectuals or cadres.

The nature of the campaigns has depended upon the nature of the problems confronted, but all of them have had basic points in common. All have been struggles involving many people, and all of them have made a significant impact on their participants. As responses either to mistakes or deficiencies, and as methods for bringing to light new forms and outlooks, their overall objective has been to strike out at counter-revolutionary ideas and practices, and by so doing to further develop socialism.

The Cultural Revolution should be seen as another stage in the continuing struggle toward this objective. The difference is in its scale, scope, and intensity. It was, after all, a revolution. But it was a new kind of revolution. The problem: "Every counterrevolutionary restoration starts in the realm of the mind—including ideology, the superstructure, theoretical and academic work, literature, and art—so as to win over public opinion."[3] The solution had to hit the nub of the problem; it

---

antagonistic and the latter as non-antagonistic, maintaining that most fall within the category of contradictions among the people. They are therefore non-antagonistic and should be resolved through non-antagonistic means. It is this type of contradiction which lends itself to the method of unity-criticism-unity. See Mao's essays, "On the Correct Handling of Contradictions Among the People," *Selected Readings,* pp. 432–79, and "On Contradiction," ibid., pp. 85–133 for his full analysis.

3. *Liberation Army Daily,* May 4, 1966. Quoted in Peter Mauger et al., *Education in China,* Modern China Series, no. 5 (London: Anglo-Chinese Educational Institute, 1974), p. 23.

had to be, as its name indicates, a revolution in culture, a revolution that would transform attitudes, ideas, outlooks, and their expression.

By 1966, it was judged by many that there had been such considerable backsliding on so many fronts that nothing short of a full-scale mobilization of the people—a revolution—could reverse the trend. China had not fully recovered from the effects of the sudden withdrawal in 1960 of all Soviet aid, technicians, and teachers that it had become quite dependent upon, or from the three years (1959–61) of natural catastrophies. Solutions to these and many other problems had largely and perhaps inevitably become imbued with a Soviet cast of mind, since the U.S.S.R. had been the sole model for development.

However, by the early 1960s, many Chinese were becoming highly critical of the Soviet Union. When they looked northward, they saw a revision of socialist principles, a moving away from socialism toward capitalism. Worse yet, some saw the same potentially disastrous tendencies developing at home. Large numbers of people in high government and Party positions in China were "taking the capitalist road." These "capitalist-roaders" were wielding considerable influence in spreading "revisionist" ideas. They were said to have willing followers at all levels of government and Party who were poisoning the ranks of the people through subtle and devious means. The schools and all other institutional spheres were being infected by their influence. Such leaders had to be exposed and criticized. The call by Mao in August, 1966, to "Bombard the Headquarters!" fully inaugurated the revolution that would make possible this exposure and criticism. It also marks the Cultural Revolution as historically unprecedented. Never before in world history had a full-scale revolution against leadership been set in motion by the highest political figure in a country.[4]

---

4. A careful distinction was drawn by Mao between those who were consciously advocating revisionism (the "handful of capitalist-roaders") and the much larger group that was being led, or as the Chinese see it—misled—by them. The first group was to be "fully exposed, refuted, overthrown and completely discredited and their influence eliminated. At the same time, they should be given a chance to turn over a new leaf." (Decision of the Central Committee of the Chinese Communist Party Concerning the Great Proletarian Cultural Revolution [Peking: Foreign Languages Press, 1966], p. 8. This document served as the guideline for the Cultural Revolution.) The others should be shown the error of their ways through discussion, debate, persuasion, criticism: "Contention between different views is unavoidable, necessary and beneficial....The method to be used in debates is to present the facts, reason things out, and persuade through reasoning." (Ibid., p. 6.)

The timing of a revolution, however, is determined not only by the severity of the problems faced but also by the potential of the people to make an historical leap into the future. The Chinese had accumulated sufficient revolutionary experience and socialist consciousness to be armed for yet another revolution. The Cultural Revolution thus must be seen not simply as a holding action which prevented the entrenchment of revisionism in China. Equally as important, it was a surge forward into a deeper consciousness of proletarian ideology.

What the Chinese say about the Cultural Revolution is much different from what has commonly been communicated in the West.[5] While we have been told that violence and bloodshed are synonymous with the Cultural Revolution, the Chinese contend that such was not at all what the Cultural Revolution was about. Yes, there was violence. There were excesses as at Tsinghua University.[6] But they are seen as unacceptable, and they were never sanctioned by the revolutionary leadership. A professor at Peking University told us, "Discussion and persuasion were the weapons of the Cultural Revolution." An ex-student, now a factory worker who had actively participated as a Red Guard, said, "It was a revolution by words, not by guns." The objective was to root out bourgeois ideology and implant socialist ideology.

Technically, the Chinese date late 1965 as the start of the Cultural Revolution. However, since the momentum did not really pick up until

---

5. During the late 1960s, the purposes and methods of the Cultural Revolution were thoroughly maligned, particularly in the United States. Through the mass media we got just about no information but a whole lot of interpretation from the "China-watchers" who "watched" not from China but from Hong Kong. A cursory look through the pages of *Time* magazine, for example, reveals an incessant barrage of titles proclaiming "Nightmare Across the Land," "The Red Guards: Today China, Tomorrow the World," "Dance of the Scorpion," "Muzzling the Dragons," "The Edge of Chaos," "Lurid Tales from Canton," "An Act of Barbarism," "More Violent than Imagined," etc. The articles told monstrous stories about "unbridled fury and frenzy," "destructive nonsense," "hysteria," "contortions," "indiscriminate beatings," "sharp and bloody clashes," "lawlessness and violence," "Mao's mobs," "shock troops of Mao's purge," "teenage, slogan-drunk students," "Mao-think," "fanatical followers," "weird rampages," "running riot," "breaking heads," "Maoist magic," "hotheaded radicals," and the like. Describing Mao, we got phrases like "the Red Emperor of China," "dying dictator," "inflexibility," "puritanism and self-hypnosis," "obsessions"; even his wife did not escape unscathed—"the vindictive Dragon Lady out for personal revenge," she was described as the Red Guard's "chief cheerleader, den mother, and Joan of Arc." Sensational writing all right, but not very enlightening. No wonder that the mere mention of the Cultural Revolution still conjures up vivid impressions of horror and disgust in so many of us.

6. See William Hinton, *Hundred Day War: The Cultural Revolution at Tsinghua University* (New York: Monthly Review Press, 1972).

the next year, it is generally said to have started in 1966. As for its conclusion, there is even more uncertainty. In the West, it is generally said to have ended in 1969, and if one considers only its more turbulent period, this is true. Basing their calculation on the same reasoning, some Chinese cite 1970 as the year that marks the termination of the Cultural Revolution, but there does not seem to be clear agreement on this point. According to the original plan for the Cultural Revolution, it was to consist of three stages: struggle, criticism, and transformation. During my visit in 1973, the emphasis was on transformation. People commonly talked about how they were making use of what they had learned by translating those lessons into their daily lives.[7]

Arguments can be forwarded to connect the movement during 1974–1975 to criticize Lin Piao and Confucius[8] either to the ongoing Cultural Revolution or to see it as a separate phenomenon. One might also view the Fourth National People's Congress of early 1975, at which a new Constitution was adopted as indicating a fairly clear termination of the Cultural Revolution. Although by mid-1975 the Cultural Revolution was generally referred to in the past tense, there still remained some question of interpretation. The stress then was on stabilization and unity—stabilizing the good leadership that had been developing during the preceding years of the Cultural Revolution and correcting mistakes

---

7. For a substantial period during the height of the Cultural Revolution, schools and universities were closed down while students participated in the movement. While schools at the lower and middle levels were all reopened several years ago and there has been a significant expansion of them, higher level education is still not operating at full strength. As of 1973, the university system was running, on average, at about half its 1965 capacity. At Peking University, for example, while there were over 2,200 faculty members, the student enrollment was only 4,300, far from the 10,000 that it was before the Cultural Revolution and that it is expected to eventually reach again. The number of students in each department was low; some departments, like law and psychology, had not yet resumed classes; certain areas of specialization were still to be added in others. This is seen as only temporary. "Our educational transformation is at an experimental stage," it was explained. "We think that subjects like law and psychology are very important, but what we taught in the past was transplanted from Western countries. We must figure out how to change the curriculum to meet our socialist needs."

8. Though Confucius died many, many centuries ago, strong traces of his ideas have persisted. The "Doctrine of the Mean," for example, thwarts rebellion by advocating quiet moderation and passive acceptance of one's fate— hardly consistent with a revolutionary philosophy. Chinese revolutionaries consider such ideas pernicious and akin to the political maneuverings of Lin Piao who was a major leader in the Communist Party and in the military apparatus until he was discovered in 1971 to be planning a coup d'etat. He was killed in a plane crash while attempting a hasty escape to the Soviet Union. His thought and action have since been linked to those of Confucius in a massive campaign against the deleterious and elitist influences of the Confucian tradition.

as a sounder basis for unity. This too can be seen as part of the stage of transformation.

It is not always easy to distinguish the end of one great movement from the beginning of another. Perhaps the most important lesson here is that societies cannot be approached with a static conception that interprets upheavals as intermittent and inexplicable interruptions occurring within a situation of presumed harmony and stability. Rather there is movement all the time, with events evolving more or less noisily from and into each other. This is particularly evident in China where change for something better is actively and rationally sought on a continuing basis by so many people.

The Chinese I met do not seem to be utopian in their view of the Cultural Revolution. They do not consider that they have settled things for good and that from here on in it will be all unity with no more need for criticism or struggle. They say that feudal and bourgeois ideologies are stubborn, that elements of them still exist, some quite strongly, and that they expect them to persist for some time to come. The more highly politicized Chinese observe that some inequalities are inevitable and cannot be completely eliminated until full communism is achieved. Thus when new inequalities arise, though they may be less severe than others that have been combatted, they nonetheless serve to generate a self-seeking, or, as the Chinese put it, a bourgeois outlook. Therefore, not only vestigial bourgeois and feudal ideologies but also newly generated bourgeois outlooks will continue to be objects of struggle. Since the Chinese foresee the inevitability of a number of intense struggles yet to come, they anticipate many more cultural revolutions beyond the horizon.

Whatever China's future holds, it can safely be said that at this point, the first Cultural Revolution has had a profound impact on just about everything and everyone. It is only to be expected that the schools, whose job it is to transmit ideas and values, have been at least as intensely affected as perhaps any other institution in society, if not more so. In any discussion on education, the Cultural Revolution is looked to as the reference point of change.

NEW REFORMS

A number of measures designed to curb elitist tendencies in the schools have grown out of the Cultural Revolution. Students are no longer admitted to postsecondary institutions on the basis of competitive examinations. It is said of intellectuals that before the Cultural Revolution, they passed through three doors—from the door of the house to the door of the college to the door of the office. But now, everyone must pass through the door of the job (and it usually isn't an office) before approaching the door of the college. After middle school, students must go to work for a minimum of two years before they can be considered for selection to higher education.

The Chinese don't want simply to understand their world; they want to change it. They are convinced that it can be neither well understood nor changed in any way beneficial to the people by anyone who lives a cloistered existence cut off from that world and its people. Therefore, prospective students are no longer granted the special privilege of an ivory tower existence. They have to get out and actually experience and become part of the real world of the workers and peasants. This has made a tremendous difference in their outlooks. They are less likely now to see themselves as superior to those who do manual work. How can they have contempt for workers and peasants when they themselves are workers and peasants?

After having worked for two or more years, anyone who wants to attend a university or institute may apply. This is perhaps the most unusual reform of all, because prospective students apply for admission not to the university authorities but to their fellow workmates. The Chinese say that it is a form of bourgeois elitism to select people for advanced study purely on the basis of academic achievements. "We do not want to train bookworms but people who can play a useful part in socialist revolution and construction."[9] To leave selection completely in the hands of university administrators and professors who are far removed from the applicants and have no direct knowledge of them is to court and even create bookworms. Workers and peasants, on the other hand, will choose differently, especially since those they select are likely to return to the same place of work where they will apply their new skills and quite probably teach them to others. The workers and peasants, rather than university authorities, can more reliably be counted on to choose people who will make a good job of it and be of practical usefulness to all of them later.

---

9. Chu Yen, "Revolution in Education: Why the University Enrolling System Should Be Reformed," *Peking Review* (September 21, 1973), p. 21.

The professors we spoke to did not appear to be at all resentful about their loss of total power in student selection. One of them at Peking University explained the advantages of the new system.

"Ours is a socialist country, so we must train students who can serve the people best. If students work just for their own benefit, their own personal fame, that means our education is a failure. We don't admit students only by academic standards. The workers and peasants who work with them can give a good all-round assessment. In technical fields, for example, they can judge which people have good techniques at their places of work. The students they select have experience; they know the parts of machines and how to produce. They have the visual side, and so when they study in the university, it is easier for them to understand theories they will come across in books and discussions. The workers and peasants select students according to the needs of practice. They also know a person's ideological outlooks and attitudes toward the people. They select those who are most dedicated to building socialism. And then too they take into consideration whether the person loves to study or not so that they can recommend the most serious and hardworking."

Another professor, this one from the medical college in Canton, showed just how much he appreciated their judgment when he said, "When the peasants deliver the agricultural tax,[10] they always deliver the best grain; when they choose people to go to university, they always select the best saplings."

After the applicant's workmates reach a decision, they pass their recommendation on to the leaders at the workplace. The leaders are likely to approve the recommendation since they tend to have similar views, having themselves been selected to leadership positions on essentially the same ground as the students are to be chosen—dedication to serving the people. Therefore, the interests of leaders and led are

---

10. "Part of each production team's income goes to the state as agricultural tax. This was set by the people's government at 5 to 7 percent of each team's gross income. But the policy is not to change the amount of tax when production rises. Thus, though the actual sum paid has stayed the same, the rate has dropped." ("How Chiaoli Production Team Distributes Its Income," *China Reconstructs* 21, no. 9 [September 1972], p. 9.) In one rural area we visited, the agricultural tax amounted to only 2 percent of actual income; in another, less than 1 percent. There are not a few peasants who actually take pride in delivering the tax grain since they see it as a contribution to the development of their country. In some places, "it is made the occasion of a festival, with drums and flags." (Joan Robinson, *Economic Management: China 1972,* Modern China Series, no. 4 [London: Anglo-Chinese Educational Institute, 1973], p. 12.)

often likely to be closely tied. At every level, decisions of this type are, as far as possible, made on a consensus basis. The idea is to reach genuine agreement, to decide for or against a course of action because people really see eye to eye on it rather than because more people happen, for whatever reasons, to vote one way instead of another.

The final step is approval by the university. This takes the form of what is called a cultural test. Wondering if this test might in fact be just a somewhat modified version of basically the same entrance examination as was administered before the Cultural Revolution, I questioned several professors and administrators at Peking University about its form and content and discovered that the term is really something of a misnomer. Its aim, I was told, is to check on "the cultural level, political consciousness, and ideological understanding" of prospective students. It is to be an "all-rounded assessment." This assessment consists primarily of examining the candidate's entire file and discussing it at length with him or her. Thus the "cultural test" is actually an extensive oral interview.

The materials that are scrutinized and discussed with the applicant include his self-assessment, a document which was initially written to help him clarify his own views on the suitability of his candidacy and which figures into the deliberations at every stage in the selection process. The same treatment is given the other materials—the detailed summatory statements outlining school and work experience, ideological development, and strengths and weaknesses. These have been provided by former teachers, workmates, and leaders at workplaces. Sometimes the deciding body at the university supplements the information in the file and the interview with the applicant by meeting directly with such people. The precise steps taken by the university authorities vary somewhat depending on what they think is required in any particular case to supply them with sufficient information to make a sound decision.

Still curious about what precisely was meant by checking on the candidate's "cultural level," I questioned further. The concern is to discover the extent of the prospective student's general knowledge, the emphasis being on his problem-solving abilities. This is generally determined through the various assessments that are being weighed and discussed, including the candidate's assessment of himself. In addition, he might also be given specific problems to solve. But even though the cultural level is a factor, my talks with the university authorities left me with the distinct impression that the final decision is based at least as much on political considerations as on strictly academic ones.

This impression was further substantiated when I found out that those selected to attend university are not necessarily the ones with the most prior schooling. In fact, about half the students at Peking University had only a junior middle school education. As the university officials see it, the lack of a full secondary education does not necessarily constitute a deficiency.

One of them explained: "A large number of the students had settled down in the countryside for three or even five years and during this period they learned very much from the peasants. So in spite of the fact that they have never attended senior middle school, their experience in the countryside has greatly increased their actual cultural level."

As university work is demanding, to relieve those students with a somewhat lower cultural level from any undue burden and to compensate for their shortcomings, a special half-year course is provided before they begin the regular program. This is most commonly necessary for students in scientific and technical fields.

My concern about the equality of their new system led me to ask what happens to the applicants who are rejected. With typical patience, one of the professors reiterated a fundamental premise on which education in China is based.

"The purpose in going to university is not for private gain. The students always say, 'The people sent me to the university and so I study for the people.' But attending university is just one method of study. There are many ways for people to raise their cultural level."

He mentioned political study groups and night school as examples. I later found out that the university itself is more active in stimulating and providing broader educational opportunities than was immediately apparent. The very large faculty at Peking University may teach a relatively small regular student body, but that is only part of the job. "We 'walk on two legs'," said one professor. Numerous short-term courses ranging from weather forecasting to the study of Marxism-Leninism are offered to a combined enrollment of 30,000 people. The faculty also assists workers in factories and peasants in communes in setting up and running their own colleges and spare-time classes.

Besides the new university selection procedure, other safeguards have been built into the educational system to reverse the earlier unequal practices. High on the list is the reduction or elimination of fees.

In the primary and middle schools, a minimal fee plus the cost of some few supplies amounts to approximately two to five dollars a year. In the institutions of higher education, tuition, rooms, books, and medical care are free. Students with less than five years work experience are given an allowance for food and pocket money. In order to prevent unnecessary hardships from falling on older students who might have family members dependent on them, all those with five or more years work experience continue to receive the full wages they were getting when they left their jobs—this support in addition to no education fees. In the nurseries and kindergartens, there are some fees, generally from one to three dollars a month plus a small charge for food. These facilities are heavily subsidized by the workplace or level of government that sets them up. But at every level from preschool onward, special subsidies are provided when necessary, the result being that no one is denied education for lack of money.

Also helping to ensure greater educational equality for the population as a whole are the special arrangements which are provided where regular full-time schools are not feasible. In sparsely populated regions, there may be traveling teachers who move from one small village to the next, giving classes in rotation. On the grasslands, they sometimes travel on horseback to reach their students and set up what are called "mobile schools for herdsmen." There are even "floating schools" for students in fishing communities, with classes being held on the boats during work breaks and in the evenings. For others in remote areas, there are correspondence and radio courses. Where youth are needed during the busy farming seasons, the rhythm of the school year may be adjusted so that school vacations conform to agricultural cycles. The idea at all times is to universalize and hence equalize education by devising forms suitable to local conditions.

WHO CONTROLS EDUCATION?

It is in the control of education that we see several other practices which serve to erode elitism—practices that act as checks on what direction the schools will take—socialist or revisionist. For one thing, there is an attempt to provide grass roots supervision over education through the implementation of what is called a three-in-one combination, which makes education the joint responsibility of the school, the family, and society. The three are expected to combine their efforts in educating the young, each branch of this unit taking on a number of tasks which it is to coordinate with the efforts of the other two.

Most of the schools have a number of after-class activities which range anywhere from barbering to fine arts, but the society also takes on a large responsibility for organizing such things. At the neighborhood level, residents set up facilities and programs in sports and the arts. Larger jurisdictions, especially in the cities, can be even more ambitious; they can provide parks, playing fields, libraries, museums, theaters, and the like.

In Shanghai, we went to an extraordinary place, an after-school activity center for children from seven to fourteen called a Children's Palace. Set up by a district of the municipality it is one of several in the city and consists of a huge sprawling building with lovely expansive grounds. Before touring the building we went into a large meeting room where several children served us tea. A ten-year-old girl stood up, welcomed us and then delivered a twenty-minute introduction to the Children's Palace—what kinds of activities were conducted there, their purpose, and the children's response to the activities. This was done with a self-confidence that I had never before seen in a child that age—a big smile, no notes, no nervousness, and in the presence of twenty-two foreign guests, an equal number of her peers, and about ten Chinese adults who were our guides and translators.

Despite the size of the Children's Palace, it is still insufficient to accommodate all the schoolchildren in the district every day and so there are two types of programs which together serve 1,500 children daily. The "mass activities" are for all the children who come once a month in rotation and more often during the summer. "Training activities" are for children who are selected by their schools to attend a specific activity two or three times a week for a period ranging from three months to a year. It was said that after the training program the children are encouraged to teach the others in their schools what they have learned.

The range of the program is most impressive. Physical activities consist of basketball, soccer, ping pong, track and field skills, traditional Chinese exercises, acrobatics, and others. There are art, craft, and hobby classes, including singing, dancing, playing musical instru-

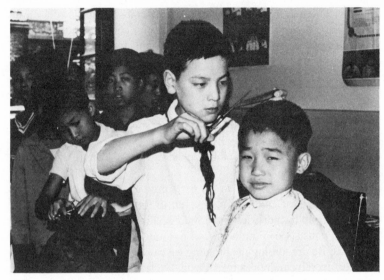

After-school programs. Boys practice cutting each other's hair (above).

Primary school pupils make puppets for a puppet show (below).

ments—both traditional Chinese (they also make Chinese instruments) and Western, drama, puppetry, magic, drawing, painting, calligraphy, paper cutting, creative writing, embroidery, printing, and model airplane, rocket, and ship building. Programs are arranged in which children study and discuss current events and international affairs; they also visit factories and communes.

While the activities are primarily recreational, they are also important for the skills the children are learning which they can apply to serving others. An instructor, praising the advantages of the three-in-one combination, told us about some students who were being trained in the use of acupuncture by an old doctor of traditional Chinese medicine. One of the children, a girl of thirteen, was doing so well that she was able to give acupuncture treatments to her neighbors for common ailments.

Residents in the immediate neighborhoods where the children live also attend to educational and recreational matters. They might conduct after-school homework and study groups to enable the students to help each other with their schoolwork, giving assistance themselves as needed. In one neighborhood we visited, the residents had established what they called a children's home, a place where such diverse activities as ping pong, fishing, political study, painting, storytelling, productive work, musical performances, and field trips to historic sites were organized. More unexpected, perhaps, is that oftentimes neighborhood groups handle squabbles and conflicts among the children, attempting to teach them the importance and value of cooperation. One resident explained, "If something happens among the students that is not conducive to unity, we have discussions and help them ideologically." She related an incident about two neighborhood children who had had a disagreement about a toy. Both had complained to their parents, each accusing the other. Not only the parents but some neighbors entered into the dispute, checked out the facts, and gave the children "ideological education."

As she spoke, it occurred to me how different this was from my own experience, which was that parents are usually left to themselves to try to solve such problems; we receive little or no outside support in getting our own children to do their homework or not to fight with the other kids on the block. Consequently, we often end up nagging and battling our children who, in the interest of survival, learn not to hear us, to turn us off. Small issues can develop into family problems, sometimes with serious consequences, whereas in China, such matters are more likely to be not just family but also community concerns that only rarely mushroom out of proportion.

At first it was not easy for me to understand how neighbors could succeed in achieving a high degree of "ideological unity" among the children. Upon reflection, however, it became evident that with essentially the same standards and expectations being held for everyone by virtually all the adults in the neighborhood and in school, children can learn appropriate behavior very early. Under these conditions fulfilling their responsibilities and cooperating with each other become natural responses; after a time the children themselves begin to reinforce this behavior among each other. When children are remiss, the chances are that both peers and adults (their parents and others) will show them the error of their ways. With everybody helping them, it is quite easy for children to behave well. Maybe that is one of the reasons why I never saw them fighting or in any way abusing each other.

The family, however, as one of the branches in the three-in-one combination, does have an important role to play in its own right. That the community helps parents rear their children does not imply that society has taken over their job and destroyed the family unit. While it's true that a great many children spend a lot of time in institutions, outside observers of China must be careful not to associate these places with stereotyped images of cold lonely orphanages or grim "institutions" for neglected children. The institutions for children in China, be they nurseries, neighborhood children's homes, kindergartens, children's palaces, or any of the others where children are to be found, are in every respect healthy places where children receive good care, where warm relationships surround them, and where parents can have a direct say in how they are run.

At the same time, to assert that preschools or other organized outside-the-family activities for children have not eroded family ties is not to suggest that family relationships in China are as they have always been. The mutual dependency for physical and psychological protection from an inhospitable environment that of necessity characterized so much of the basis for family unity in the past is rapidly being replaced by connection based on mutual respect for each other's achievements and potentialities. Family members can now realize a relationship of greater comradeship—equality—with each other as they can with those outside the family. Unlike many other societies, it appears that the Chinese family is becoming less of an inward-looking sentimental unit and more of an outward-looking active one, in which members are more and more likely to engage in common pursuits that link directly to the goals of the wider society.

Although parents take a major responsibility for their children, the increasingly cooperative relationship among neighbors is often sufficiently strong to undercut the outlook which sees children as the private property of their parents. In a very real sense, children "belong" to the community. In a large neighborhood in Peking we visited the home of an old woman who would have been left alone for several months while her grown daughter was working on a commune had a child in the neighborhood not moved in to keep her company.

When I heard about this I wondered about the opposite situation of children without parents and asked if there were any orphans. In this neighborhood of more than 52,000 people the answer was that they had never had any. One of the residents explained: "If a child's parents die and there are no grandparents, he will live with a neighbor. Sometimes it happens that parents have several children and they give one to others who don't have any, but we never have the situation where there is a child who has no parents."

It seems to be as simple as that. This doesn't mean that children are loved any less—nor just by their own mothers and fathers, but apparently by most everyone around. It is because the family is not a purely private domain, because its members are not each other's property, that adults and children, though not actually related, need not remain without each other for long.

Within the family child rearing and education quite often echo what is being taught in the schools and communities. For example, we visited the apartment of Han Ju-ying, a working woman in Shanghai and discussed how she and her husband help to educate their two sons, aged twelve and fourteen. Ordinarily Han would have been at work, a twenty-minute bicycle ride away, but this was her day off. The three-room apartment had a flush toilet, a rare convenience usually found in new buildings like the ones in that neighborhood. It was lunch hour, and the boys were present when we discussed the subject of housework.

"We all help," she said. "We are on an equal footing. My husband is the strongest, so he does the heavy jobs. On our day off, the two of us do more housework, but on the other days most of the chores are done by the children. They prepare the meals for themselves because we go to work and have no time. When we are at work, they become the housekeepers. But it has required a long process to educate them to do this work. At the beginning, they didn't do the jobs well, and when we came back it was quite dirty in the kitchen and sometimes the rice was burned. The younger brother always went out to play games, and when I got back home the older one would complain to me about him. At first I told him, 'Well, you are older so you should do more.' But he wasn't convinced, and the problem still wasn't solved. Then I thought this might be due to a lack of division of labor between them, so I assigned jobs for them. I said, 'You prepare the meals because you are older, and your younger brother will be in charge of keeping the rooms clean—sweeping the floors and dusting the furniture.' But the younger one was somewhat narrow-minded. He said, 'All right, I'll do my job well,' but he only cleaned the rooms and corridor, not the kitchen. He didn't sweep the kitchen floor. He said, 'That's my brother's job because he is in charge of cooking.'

"When I discovered this, I realized it was not good; it was not beneficial to the boys. I consulted with my husband about how to educate the children, and we arrived at an agreement. On our holiday we held a family meeting and discussed the problem together. We told the boys that they should follow Chairman Mao's teachings, and we all agreed that we should achieve unity in the family, that we should cooperate. In the past I always excused my younger son because I thought he was too young, but I realized that was not correct. We should cultivate children to love labor while they are still young. So by this educational work they have now become better, and sometimes when the younger brother comes home earlier than the elder one, he will also prepare the meals. Then when I get home he tells me, 'Mummy, today I prepared the meal. I did the jobs for my elder brother.' And I encourage him."

There are several obvious beneficial consequences of the cooperative three-in-one combination. One is consistency. Children are rarely put in the position of being taught in school something that contradicts what they are taught in the movies that contradicts what their parents tell them that contradicts their own experience. They are unlikely to suffer from burdensome feelings of confusion, conflicting loyalties, frustration, resentment, and alienation. Schools, families, and communities are organizing themselves to work together to serve the children and youth and to teach them how to serve others.

Another consequence of this arrangement is the absence of a generation gap. Old and young are likely to recognize that they value the same things and have the same goals. The experience of the old and the energy of the young are seen as attributes that nourish each other and strengthen common efforts.

Still another beneficial result of the three-in-one combination is that the false barriers between school experience and life experience are being lifted. Education is something that happens to virtually everyone, whether in or out of school; it is continuous. What might elsewhere be considered an extracurricular activity becomes more of an extension of the curriculum in China.

The growing community control of education is the most important result of the three-in-one combination. It is not only in the out-of-school activities, however, that the community holds a significant measure of power in educational matters. Such activities are only one area of concern. The family and society are able to influence the schools' activities through a variety of methods.

In many places groups of residents from the neighborhoods and brigades visit the schools regularly to keep themselves informed and to give suggestions to the teachers for improving their work. They in turn receive recommendations on ways in which the community can extend and coordinate its educational efforts with those of the schools.

In one of the schools I visited, every class had an ''educational committee'' composed of parents, teachers, students, and cadres. The committee met regularly to discuss school and classroom issues. In another school, a kind of log was maintained on each child, containing comments on his progress. The log was passed back and forth between the child's home and school; comments and replies were entered by both parents and teachers. Where feasible, teachers make home visits to the families of their students, not always an easy job considering the large size of many of their classes. At the lower levels of education, where the schools are usually in the neighborhoods they serve, this task is less cumbersome since the teachers often reside nearby and are part of the community life. Through such means as these, there is likely to be a smooth flow of information and a consistent basis for cooperation among the three parties responsible for education—the school, the family, and society—which, from all appearances, are quite successful in functioning as one.

These developments represent a significant democratization of the educational system. Additionally, an even more fundamental form which affects not only education, but also all other matters of general concern, has been adopted countrywide. Governmental powers used to be confined to relatively small concentrations of people, an arrangement that was challenged and abolished during the Cultural Revolution. In its place revolutionary committees, incorporating broad representation, were established at all levels except the national.[11] These governmental units directly represent the people in their jurisdictions and organize many social and economic activities.

It is at the local level that we can see real grass roots democracy in action. Residents in an urban neighborhood or a rural production brigade get together and decide who among them are the best qualified and able to lead them and administer their affairs. These, along with a few others who are appointed, will be the members of their revolutionary committee. The people, however, have the power to recall a member at any time who is doing a poor job or is using the position to further his own selfish interests. I was told that it is rarely necessary for this power to be exercised because criticisms and suggestions are frequently offered by the people and even solicited by the leaders. Said the vice-chairman of one brigade revolutionary committee, "The masses are our supervisors."

The grass roots revolutionary committee takes on tasks directly affecting the residents, including supervising the work of certain production units in the area, operating clinics and pharmacies, setting up service centers that look after many household jobs previously done by housewives, attending to neighborhood sanitation, arranging adult study programs, assisting in the organization of mutual help activities among neighbors, and many more.

Education is one of the revolutionary committee's principal areas of responsibility. The revolutionary committee establishes and runs the schools that are required by the residents living within its jurisdiction. Thus, immediate neighborhoods in the cities and brigades in the countryside set up, finance (with the assistance of higher government levels as required), and take charge of their own preschools and primary schools. Because the middle schools are fewer in number, they are more centralized and are usually run by higher levels—the district or municipal revolutionary committee in the cities and the commune or county revolutionary committee in the rural areas. Through the revolutionary committees the people themselves now have a direct voice in setting up

---

11. The national equivalent of a revolutionary committee is the State Council which is selected by the National People's Congress.

schools according to their needs, and in maintaining close contact with them once they are established.

Schools, factories, hospitals, and other institutions also have their own governing bodies which are also called revolutionary committees.[12]

"It is a question of who holds power," one teacher observed. "Chairman Mao has said, 'The domination of our schools by bourgeois intellectuals should by no means be allowed to continue.' And it was true that before the Cultural Revolution such people ran our school, but in 1968 we formed a revolutionary committee. Now the working class exercises leadership here."

School revolutionary committees undercut the former domination by "bourgeois intellectuals" by adhering to the following guidelines designed to guarantee broad representation. Members should include both women and men; the young, middle-aged, and old (another type of three-in-one combination); teachers and students, the public, and members of a workers' propaganda team and the PLA (yet another three-in-one combination).[13] The revolutionary committee in one of the schools I visited was composed of seven teachers, four students, three neighborhood people (a retired worker, a street cleaner, and a cadre), one PLA man, and four workers' propaganda team members. Eight were women; eleven were men. The old had four representatives, the

---

12. Exceptions are to be found where these institutions are run by larger organizations. So, for example, a factory might have a nursery-kindergarten and a workers' college, but it would have only one revolutionary committee which would take responsibility for all the activities in the factory. The factory revolutionary committee would have several sections or departments to administer different aspects, such as production, workers' welfare, education, etc. In such a case, the nursery-kindergarten and the workers' college would have their own leading groups with representation on the factory revolutionary committee.

13. The workers' propaganda teams were formed during the Cultural Revolution when they entered the schools to help students and teachers resolve their differences and unite. With their assistance, school revolutionary committees were formed and the drive to "revolutionize education" was undertaken. While their role and that of the PLA was more prominent in the early years of the formation of the school revolutionary committees, they still retain membership on many of them.

It should further be noted that for the Chinese, the word propaganda carries no connotation of deception or manipulation. It is a commonly used word that conveys only a positive sense of education or the dissemination of information. (People talk about "doing propaganda work for birth control" or "conducting propaganda on disease prevention," and so on.) This corresponds with the earlier meaning of the term in English where to propagate meant to educate, transmit, or publicize.

Teachers, students, and peasants get together to discuss the work of the school.

middle-aged six, and the young nine. Some would hold their positions for a term of two years, others for three.

The participation of those who in many countries would be considered nonprofessionals is real in every respect. It is quite possible for visitors to be escorted around a school and have their questions about curriculum, examinations, and teaching methods answered by a member of the revolutionary committee who turns out to be a student in the school, or a worker, or a peasant from the community. Such people are, from what I could judge, well informed and highly regarded. It is they who are in charge; there is no such thing as an externally imposed executive administrator, an "expert" from outside the school and its locality who runs the school and whose qualifications rest on academic degrees in educational administration.[14]

Another significant practice has been developed in China's schools as a means of preventing the control of education from slipping out of the hands of those it is meant to serve. It is the same self-corrective process of criticism and self-criticism that is widely practiced all across the country. Like their adult counterparts in work and community activities, students in school are expected to air their grievances and articulate their suggestions to teachers and fellow students in an open and straightforward manner. The teachers are expected to do the same. In the past, the teachers' position, especially at the higher levels of education, was sanctified. No one, least of all students, would have dreamed of criticizing them, but now criticism is actually encouraged as the Chinese work toward the goal of eliminating abuses of authority.

Since criticism as practiced in China is so foreign to many outsiders, it requires examination in order to grasp its dynamics. When most of us talk about criticizing, we usually mean "getting something off our chests" by "telling someone off." While some of us may feel free to say a great many things to each other about someone else, we would also more often than not go to some lengths to avoid criticizing a person directly. There are not a few among us who would likewise go pretty far to avoid being criticized. How many of us have ever given or received criticism without there being a trace of anger, vindictiveness, or resentment on either side?

Yet this is what the Chinese apparently attempt to do. To them criticism is an exercise in evaluation, a way of discovering weaknesses and strengths. They maintain that through criticism people can help each other to distinguish between right and wrong. This is not to say that in actual practice criticism is never misused or turned against people unjustly. That does happen, especially during the more intense political campaigns. By and large, however, criticism is used as a

---

14. While education is largely decentralized and the main emphasis is on grass roots control, there is also administrative coordination from one level of government to the next. Such coordination has existed for some time, but it was not until the Fourth National People's Congress was held in January 1975 that a single national Ministry of Education was formed. The Ministry, which also maintains departments at lower levels of government, takes overall responsibility for education in all spheres, setting policy guidelines and organizing conferences. It often shares leadership with the education department of other ministries that also provide educational programs such as the industrial ministries.

means of improvement of others and oneself and is therefore generally considered to be constructive and useful.

I had my doubts that it was possible to criticize and be criticized without any feelings of anger, vindictiveness, or resentment until I met an American journalist and translator in Peking who had been living and working there for sixteen years. He said that he had sat in on numerous criticism sessions and that they were handled in such a way that people did not seem wounded or insulted even though the talk was serious and direct. He worked every day with cadres who had been severely criticized during the height of the Cultural Revolution. At that time, the criticism wasn't always gentle, and sometimes not even justifiable. Yet these same cadres are back at their old jobs working side by side with many of their former critics. I wanted to know, "Don't they carry a grudge?"

He simply shrugged his shoulders, raised his eyebrows, and said, "No. Amazingly enough, they don't."

To find out why not, I spoke to a number of people. One, a young worker, explained quite clearly: "We must not worry about small things, because if we talked about every detail, it would be too many things for people to handle. We must have a noble spirit and overlook the minor things. You know, when we criticize people, we do it out of feelings of good will toward them. We all have weaknesses, and so if we criticize a person, it is only to help him improve. He understands that, and when others criticize him, he would not think of being offended; he will be touched by other people's attitude toward him."

He further pointed out that criticism can be looked upon as a sign of respect only because of the way in which it is done. Two principles are followed; they are summed up as "leaving a way out" and "curing the disease to save the patient." To "leave a way out" means to criticize constructively, to attack the mistaken behavior or viewpoint, but not the person himself. "We must spare him embarrassment," the same young man said, and he went on to explain that the person's dignity and sense of worth should not be destroyed. Here it helps to recall Mao's advice that criticism not be "rough, bureaucratic, metaphysical, or dogmatic."

About "curing the disease to save the patient" the worker continued, "Practice proves that many people will be cured by criticism, just like a patient who has been treated. If a person is sick, the doctor will help him by giving him medicine or performing an operation to cure the disease so that he will get well again. But if he insists that he doesn't want the doctor to treat him, then his health will get worse. So this is how criticism works. If you reject correct criticism, then your mistakes will become more and more serious. But if you allow others to criticize you and you recognize your mistakes, you will try hard to correct them. The criticism will help you to become a better person.''

I asked him if people generally agree with the criticisms right away and he replied, ''We try not to bully each other. If someone is criticized, he must have a chance to think about it. 'Is it true? Do I do those things?' he must ask himself. You know, if someone always says he agrees with every criticism right away, then maybe he doesn't really agree. Maybe he is just pretending and being falsely humble. That will not cure the disease.''[15]

In China, antisocial acts are not usually considered problems limited to offended and offender; serious character weaknesses are not only personal concerns. They are matters to be set right with the help of the collectivity since everyone might be either directly or indirectly affected. The revolutionary view is that anyone is entitled to criticize anyone else. Students and teachers are no exception. To grant them this opportunity, some schools have set aside special times at regular intervals when they get together for sessions sometimes called ''teaching democracy'' or ''equal evaluation'' meetings. The purpose of these meetings is to openly and critically discuss ''the teachers' teaching and the students' studying.''

During a discussion with some students and teachers at Chen Hsien Street Primary School in Nanking, they stressed the point that, apart from this formal channel, students may raise criticisms of the teachers whenever they think necessary. A young teacher said,

''We think it is important to learn from the opinions of the students, so we encourage them to give us their criticisms at any time and under any circumstances. In the classroom, the teacher is just like a performer; the pupils watch the teacher very closely, so they know what we say and if it is clear and accurate. We can learn from what they say about our teaching ability. An inexperienced teacher like me gets more criticism from the pupils. I would like to become more experienced and be a better teacher. According to Chairman Mao, teachers must be educated first; then we can become better teachers. So I try to base myself on this

---

15. For a fascinating view of the dynamics of criticism and self-criticism as practiced under very difficult conditions, see Allyn and Adele Rickett, *Prisoners of Liberation: Four Years in a Chinese Communist Prison* (New York: Anchor Books, 1973). The authors, both Americans, present a unique account of their experiences when they were imprisoned for espionage in China during the early 1950s.

principle. I should not only listen to the opinions of the pupils, but I must also put them into practice."

"The pupils criticize not only the young teachers, but also veteran teachers like myself. All of us have heart-to-heart talks with the pupils to get to know their opinions better," added an older teacher.

So that we would realize that the students don't concentrate only on the teachers' weaknesses, a boy of about eleven added, "Sometimes the teachers have very good attitudes toward teaching and give very good lessons. We praise them immediately to encourage them to do still better."

"Yes, we must learn about our strengths as well as our weaknesses," the older teacher said. "We must all feel free to express our opinions fully at all times because we can all learn from each other, including old teachers like me. It is one of the embodiments of Chairman Mao's teachings that 'Officers teach soldiers; soldiers teach officers; and the soldiers teach each other.' We must pay careful attention to students' criticisms. How can we judge their opinions and suggestions? We must always judge from the angle of the suggestions themselves. Are they reasonable or not? That is what matters, not the age of the students."

Criticism is part and parcel of everyday life. Just as a person can expect to be praised for doing a job well, he can anticipate criticism for doing it badly. There are times, however, when other measures are required. Mao has let youth know that rebellion is sometimes called for. Just before the Cultural Revolution, he suggested a fairly mild form of rebellion when he said,

> There are teachers who ramble on and on when they lecture; they should let their students doze off. If your lecture is no good, why insist on others listening to you? Rather than keeping your eyes open and listening to boring lectures, it is better to get some refreshing sleep. You don't have to listen to nonsense, you can rest your brain instead.[16]

This is a calculated statement aimed at arousing young people against the centuries-old Confucian ethic of the blind acquiescence of the young to the old. It is up to those who are being maltreated to take the initiative in righting wrongs committed against them. It would be

---

16. Quoted in Stuart Schram, ed., John Chinnery and Tieyun, trans., *Mao Tse-tung Unrehearsed, Talks and Letters: 1956–71* (Harmondsworth, Middlesex: Penguin Books, 1974), p. 205.

unrealistic for anyone to expect the perpetrators of injustices to correct themselves of their own accord if the victims remain passive and accepting. Changes do not evolve "on their own." They must be initiated and engineered by the dissatisfied and then carefully implemented and elaborated. Therefore, if youths are expected to sit through boring lectures, they must rebel. How else will things ever change? Mao's advice to the new generations is heard all over China: "Young people should dare to think, dare to speak, and dare to act, should be boldly creative, and must not be intimidated by big names and authorities." This advice is based on his belief that "young people are the most active and vital force in society. They are the most eager to learn and the least conservative in their thinking."[17] It is the young who are relied on heavily as initiators and engineers precisely because they are the least conservative, the most pliable. Established patterns have less of a grip on young people than on their elders. They are the least wedded to old habits and outlooks. They are "the most active and vital force," because they have very little to lose and so much to gain by challenging traditions that still persist even though they do not serve their interests.[18]

But rebellion need not be restricted by age. As early as 1939, Mao said to all the dispossessed of China, old as well as young:

> Marxism consists of thousands of truths, but they all boil down to one sentence, "It is right to rebel." For thousands of years, it had been said that it was right to oppress, it was right to exploit, and it was wrong to rebel. This old verdict was only reversed with the appearance of Marxism.... From this truth there follows resistance, struggle, the fight for socialism.[19]

---

17. Introductory note to "A Youth Shock Brigade of the No. 9 Agricultural Producers' Co-operative in Hsinping Township, Chungshan County," *The Socialist Upsurge in China's Countryside*, Chinese ed., vol. 3. Quoted in *Quotations from Chairman Mao Tse-tung*. (Peking: Foreign Languages Press, 1966), p. 290.

18. The Chinese would be quick to clarify that this view does not apply to all youth regardless of outlook. A careerist, whether young or old, for whom events are unfolding according to plan would have no reason to opt for change. Such a person would be counted as an element that impedes progress. Tender age alone is not enough; only in combination with an ideology that puts the interests of the working people in the forefront are youth regarded as "the most active and vital force."

19. Mao Tse-tung, From a "Speech at the Rally of People of All Walks of Life in Yenan to Celebrate the Sixtieth Birthday of Stalin." Quoted in David Milton, Nancy Milton, and Franz Schurmann, eds., *People's China: Social Experimentation, Politics, Entry onto the World Scene, 1966 through 1972* (New York: Vintage Books, 1974), p. 239.

By rebellion, Mao is not referring to wild striking out at any target, the kind of rebellion that is motivated by unanalyzed frustration, blind resentment, or mindless "self-expression," but rebellion based on "daring to think," to call into question, and to break through unjust impositions.

Perhaps people can agree with Mao that it is right to rebel, but against what, against whom? Mao also answered this question when he wrote a letter to middle school students telling them that it is right to rebel against reactionaries.

To determine who and what are reactionary entails a discovery of who and what are progressive. In the realm of education, people should struggle for an educational system that fulfills the basic goal of all-rounded development for everyone. They must "revolutionize education," which demands an analysis of the forces that retard that revolution. In this way, each new wave of students and teachers can disinter "the dead weight of the past," what is seen by the Chinese as the dangerous malignancy of outmoded feudal and bourgeois ideas and attitudes that remains rooted in the school system and that can potentially infect anyone and paralyze forward movement.

Obviously, however, not everyone is so bold. In some circumstances it can be a huge and even frightening responsibility to think, speak, and act in accordance with what one believes to be right. Some people may be timid about taking such initiative. Others are satisfied with small victories and relax their enthusiasm for change. Some have difficulty deciding what is reactionary or how to rebel against it. Others might use rebellion as an instrument for the pursuit of self-interest and the acquisition of power.

The point is that struggle against retrogressive outlooks and practices and abusive power has been condoned in China, by no less an authority than Chairman Mao. Youths (and adults) need not feel powerless or feel themselves in opposition to an impersonal, remote, awesome, seemingly immutable "system." China's youth are expected to be in the vanguard of social change. Rebellion is the ultimate instrument of people's control over their lives. Whenever and wherever education takes an elitist turn, it is the obligation of ordinary young people and adults to criticize those responsible and, if necessary, rebel against them. This is grass roots control.

FRONT DOOR ONLY

There is no question that education today goes far in equalizing those who were formerly so unequal. The composition of student bodies in universities and institutes has changed significantly from what it was before the Cultural Revolution. Now it more closely resembles the class composition of the whole society. This change, along with students' work experience, changes in curriculum and teaching methods, and the educational work of groups outside the school, makes a big difference in the outlook of the student population. It appears to be the general feeling that far fewer students now see education as a ladder to individual success. A student at Peking University said, "We know that we have been selected by the workers and peasants, so we take our studies seriously." This seriousness was confirmed by the fact that between 1970, when the new enrollment policy was adopted by the University, and the time when I was there three years later, there had not been a single student drop-out.

A well-publicized incident reflects the new perspective of many students. It seems that a political science student in his second year applied to leave university because he was conscience stricken about having "gone in by the back door." His father held a high position and had pulled strings to bypass the new university entrance procedures and get his son admitted directly. After seeing the revolutionary commitment of his classmates, the young man began to feel uncomfortable about his yearnings for personal position and glory. During his first year, he and the other students spent some time working in factories and communes. There his discomfort grew into shame as he saw the diligence of the workers and peasants and how earnest they were in helping the students with any problems they had. He began to tell himself that all these people—his fellow students, the workers, the peasants—were dedicated to serving the people while he seemed to care only about serving himself. Things got worse for him when he visited some relatives during his summer vacation and heard stories about how his grandfather and two uncles had been killed in the 1920s and 1930s fighting for the revolution.

He returned to the university with great reluctance, but he could not forget what he had seen and heard. Compared to all those others he seemed so selfish. Finally, he decided that he had to correct his mistake. He had entered the university without recommendation, and the only honorable thing to do would be to leave and go to work. Along with his application for withdrawal, he included a self-criticism which said in part, " 'Going in by the back door' involves the question of whom we are to serve.'' He asserted that it is everyone's duty, regardless of position, to serve the people, that his way of getting into university had been selfish in the extreme because it had prevented someone else, someone selfless and worthy, from entering, that his way was dangerous because it opted for a privileged elite. ''Is this lovely land our parents and other revolutionary forbears won through so much sacrifice to come to an end with us? No! Never! . . . We must continue the cause they have pursued and carry on the proletarian revolution they have not finished through to the end.''[20]

The young man spoke to his parents and convinced them that he and they had been wrong. The parents then wrote to the university to criticize themselves and support their son's application to leave school. An editorial in *People's Daily*[21] told the whole story and praised their self-criticism: ''The brave correction of their error by the parents of Chung Chih-min is an expression of the new style of thinking and doing things in our socialist society.''[22] Chung left school and is now working. He and his parents have become models to emulate. In the Chinese view, to err is human, to correct commendable.

---

20. ''An Application to Withdraw from University,'' *Peking Review* (February 22, 1974), pp. 11–12.

21. *People's Daily* is the major newspaper and has nationwide circulation.

22. Quoted in ''An Application to Withdraw from University,'' p. 19.

IV: EVERY SCHOOL A FACTORY

Not in theory but in practice
Miracles are wrought with axes
And the age of miracles is not past.[1]
BERTOLT BRECHT

CLASS STRUGGLE

According to Marxism-Leninism,[2] socialism is a long transitional period between capitalism and communism. There is a Communist Party in China, but that does not mean that there is communism in China. The purpose of the Party is to lead the people to communism, the communism of the future in which there will be no classes.

However, the Chinese believe that classes still exist in China and everywhere else and that, so long as they do exist, there will be antagonism between them because they have conflicting interests. This point of view holds that in a capitalist society, for example, it is in the interests of the owning class—the capitalists—to maximize its profits, and that this is accomplished by minimizing its expenses, in other words, paying workers as little as possible, which obviously clashes with the interests of the working class. This view also purports that exploitation of the workers is unavoidable because profit is intrinsic to

---

1. Bertolt Brecht, "The Caucasian Chalk Circle," in *Parables for the Theatre,* rev. English version by Eric Bentley and Maja Apelman (New York: Grove Press, 1963), p. 170.

2. Marxism-Leninism refers to the economic, political, social, and historical analysis that began with Marx and Engels in the middle of the nineteenth century. It has been further developed by a number of other revolutionary theorists and activists, most notably Lenin in the Russian Revolution and Mao in the Chinese Revolution, and has grown into a comprehensive body of thought. To the Chinese, Marxism-Leninism provides both the tool for a scientific understanding of the dynamics of societies and the guide for action to bring about thoroughgoing social change.

the very essence of the capitalist class. Without profits there is no capitalism.

It is this clash of interests that the Chinese as Marxist-Leninists call class struggle. The oft-quoted opening line of *The Communist Manifesto* written over 125 years ago remains the linchpin of Chinese political thought and action: "The history of all hitherto existing society is the history of class struggles."[3] Class struggle, in this view, can and does take many forms—at one time violent, at another not, at one time overt, at another hidden—but, regardless of its form, it goes on unceasingly and will continue until communism is achieved. A socialist society is no exception.

One or another class or alliance of classes always holds economic and political power. This "ruling class" is so called because it possesses the power to see that its interests are served and those of other classes are suppressed. Accordingly, in a capitalist society, the capitalists are the ruling class; in a socialist society, the workers are the ruling class (though the latter statement is often met with skepticism in the West). Marxist-Leninists maintain that for one class successfully to take power from another it must seize it, because no ruling class will give up power voluntarily; it will fight to hold on to it, consequently impelling the powerless class to fight to gain it. At that point, the class struggle is violent and overt. This corresponds with events in China for much of the first half of this century when the proletarian-peasant alliance (wage workers and the poorer sections of the peasantry) struggled to liberate the nation from foreign domination and to seize power from the ruling class (the feudal landowners and the comprador bourgeoisie).[4] Its success in 1949 is called liberation not only because foreign domination was brought to an end, but also because the working classes were emancipated from this earlier class rule and themselves assumed power.

Marxist-Leninists say that socialism is an advance over capitalism because proletarian class rule serves the interests of the great majority of

---

3. Karl Marx and Frederick Engels, *Manifesto of the Communist Party* (New York: International Publishers, 1948), p. 9.

4. By comprador bourgeoisie the Chinese refer to those native capitalists who served their own interests by acting as agents in the interests of the foreign capitalist powers which had made major inroads into China. The analysis of classes in the Chinese countryside made by Mao sums up the way the Chinese view the alignment of class forces in their country during most of this century. In brief, the *hired laborers* were those who owned none of the means of production (land, tools, animals). They therefore had to sell their labor power to rich peasants and landlords. The *poor peasants* owned some of the

people—the working people—whereas in capitalist society the ruling class represents only a small fraction of the population. They further assert that the exaction of profits in capitalist society means, in effect, that one small class benefits at the expense of the others, a situation that is eliminated when the proletariat is in power, since no one is allowed to profit from anyone else's labor. Therefore, socialism is seen as a big step in the direction of the full equality that will be realized when there is communism.

But the seizing of class power is only a first step, though an essential one for reaching communism. The new class must consolidate its power or there will be a reversal to the old class rule, since the unseated classes will not take kindly to this new state of affairs. Perhaps Chou En-lai, China's premier for many years, expressed it best when he said in an interview in 1971:

> It was a most difficult task to take over the government on the basis of the old society twenty-two years ago. . . .
>
> At the early years after Liberation, there were still shops and enterprises owned privately, by private merchants. As for those of the countryside, the landlords and rich peasants had land divided up among the peasants. But they still remained in the countryside, and they too were given a share of the land, and they remained in the countryside and some of them may have even joined the commune.

---

means of production but not enough to be self-sufficient. They had to work for others as well as farm their own land. *Middle peasants* owned sufficient land, tools, and animals to not have to hire themselves out to others. They farmed the land themselves and were not considered exploiters because they either did not hire others or did so only to a slight degree. These classes, the hired laborers, the poor peasants, and the middle peasants, constituted the vast majority in the countryside. They were the main revolutionary allies of the proletariat (industrial workers), which was and still is the class considered by the Chinese to be the revolutionary vanguard. However, the peasantry, especially its middle stratum, had "petty bourgeois tendencies," that is, aspirations towards individual prosperity, and hence were not always reliable revolutionary allies. *Rich peasants* were those who owned and worked their own means of production but also hired others to work for them. The rich peasants therefore appropriated the labor of others and realized a surplus from it. The *landlord* class is seen as having been purely parasitic in that they owned the means of production but did not work. Landlords' wealth came solely from the exploitation of other people's labor. The rich peasants and landlords of course wanted to hold onto and increase their wealth, and as such were seen as counterrevolutionaries. While no class in present-day China makes its livelihood off the labor of others, these terms are still widely used to express people's class backgrounds and, to an extent, explain surviving class outlooks. (See Mao Tse-tung, "Analysis of the Classes in Chinese Society," *Selected Works of Mao Tse-tung,* 4 vols. [Peking: Foreign Languages Press, 1961–65], vol. 1, pp. 13–21.)

So if you add up the landlords, rich peasants, bourgeoisie, and also the bourgeois intellectuals, they amount to tens of millions, several tens of millions. In fact, including family members, over fifty million.

We couldn't send all these fifty million abroad. Whom would we give them to? You don't want them over there.

We couldn't wipe them all out. We're opposed to that. . . .

Even the last emperor of the Ching Dynasty . . . was left in Peking, transformed by us. We looked after him until his death three years ago.

And a lot of former Chiang Kai-shek high-ranking officers, including some generals—hundreds in fact—the overwhelming majority have been pardoned and are living well on the mainland.

But I just say this to show that the old remnants are to be found everywhere in China. So our socialist revolution is not a revolution which can be completed upon the declaration or formation of our government. Nor is it solved by changing the lease of ownership.[5]

So the class struggle continues. It has never stopped in China; and the Cultural Revolution has been the major high point to date.

In launching the Cultural Revolution, the Central Committee of the Communist Party published guidelines outlining the nature of the struggle and how it should be conducted, which say in part:

Although the bourgeoisie has been overthrown, it is still trying to use the old ideas, culture, customs, and habits of the exploiting classes to corrupt the masses, capture their minds, and endeavour to stage a comeback. The proletariat must do the exact opposite: it must meet head-on every challenge of the bourgeoisie in the ideological field and use the new ideas, culture, customs, and habits of the proletariat to change the mental outlook of the whole of society.[6]

While the schools are a main vehicle for transmitting "the new ideas, culture, customs, and habits of the proletariat," it is not just the youth who need to learn them. The entire population must be re-educated if "the mental outlook of the whole of society" is to change.

Thus the difference between the class struggle as waged by the proletariat in China today compared to before 1949 is that it no longer

---

5. Quoted in Collins Associates, *Quotations from Premier Chou En-lai* (New York: Thomas Y. Crowell, 1973), pp. 86–88.

6. *Decision of the Central Committee of the Chinese Communist Party Concerning the Great Proletarian Cultural Revolution* (Peking: Foreign Languages Press, 1966), p. 1.

needs to rely on violent methods. That was necessary to gain power. To hold power it turns primarily to education in its many forms—persuasion, discussion, propaganda and criticism and self-criticism.

The Chinese usually refer to the class struggle as "the struggle between two lines." One line favors and struggles for the further development of socialism and eventually communism; its upholders are the proletariat, the revolutionaries. The other line seeks a restoration of feudalism or the installation of capitalism; its upholders come from among the ex-landowners, former comprador capitalists, and the new potentially privileged strata unavoidably generated by the conditions of scarcity in a developing country. They are the "revisionists," the "capitalist-roaders." Since those who would consciously and willfully subvert the revolution constitute a very small minority, in order for them to gain support their methods are necessarily indirect and covert. The struggle between these two lines— "revolutionary" and "revisionist"—forms the heart of the analysis of any educational issue. Problems are most commonly discussed in these terms.

Tse Shu, a teacher at Chen Hsien Street Primary School in Nanking, vividly described part of the two-line struggle in education. "The school is a place where young people are trained, so the question of what we teach is a big problem which will determine the future, even the destiny of our country. The problem has been very acute in this primary school. Before the Cultural Revolution, Liu Shao-ch'i[7] pushed a revisionist line in education in his attempt to lead students astray. He and his like worked hard to put intellectual knowledge first, to put marks in command, and to convince students to study just for themselves. Many teachers were influenced by this revisionist line. They encouraged students just to bury their heads in books and not be concerned with anything else. The teachers used to cultivate land and operate machines only on the blackboard, so the students were completely ignorant about how the workers worked and how the peasants farmed. If a student is learning about agricultural science but only learns from books, he might think he knows the difference between grass and

---

7. Liu Shao-ch'i was the President of the People's Republic and is seen to have been the main leader of the antisocialist forces. As the chief advocate of revisionism, it was against him and his followers that the Cultural Revolution was waged. He is considered a traitor to the socialist cause who "wormed his way in" to high Party and Government posts where he "hid his true colors" by posing as a revolutionary. In 1969, he was expelled from the Communist Party and barred from any further participation in politics.

rice, but when he actually sees them he can't distinguish. This is a separation between theory and practice. At the same time, because they were separated from the workers and peasants, the children learned to look down on the working people. They thought that intellectual work was superior to physical work.

"We call this the three divorces in education. The divorce from politics—because the students just read books, they didn't know why they should be concerned about politics, about affairs outside the classroom. Divorce from the masses—they had no connection to the workers and peasants and so they thought they were superior. Divorce from production—they didn't have opportunities to apply their theoretical knowledge to developing the country. If we had adopted the Liu Shaoch'i line, we would have traveled the same path as the Soviet Union. That means we would have fostered an elite class, a spiritual elite.

"The revisionist line in education was smashed in the course of the Proletarian Cultural Revolution.[8] Teachers and pupils of the whole school have repudiated and criticized its remaining poison."

CHILDREN PRODUCE   *classroom*

Smashed, repudiated, poison are strong words when applied to children's daily school lives but hardly in evidence to the casual observer. The Nanking primary school where Tse Shu teaches is laid out in a fashion typical of the Chinese schools we saw—clusters of small buildings, each with half a dozen or so classrooms arranged around courtyards. Each room opens directly onto a courtyard with no space wasted on corridors. To move from one room to the next, one must go outside. The courtyards are used mostly as playgrounds. Walking around the school, which was really a small campus, we suddenly came upon a large area used for gardening: a small farm in the middle of a big city.

As we approached, the children put down their spades and watering cans and greeted us with applause. We passed a small brick building that exuded a powerful, foul smell. Five children were working collect-

---

8. Its full name is the Great Proletarian Cultural Revolution. It is considered *great* because of the breadth of people it encompassed and the depth of ideas and practices it challenged; considered *proletarian* because that is the class which led the struggle and in whose interests it was waged; considered *cultural* because culture in the broadest sense was the arena of the struggle; and considered a *revolution* because it was a thoroughgoing attack on the ideological and political power of anti-socialist beliefs and practices.

ing night soil there with buckets and carrying poles. We could see three fields, each of them with fifteen to twenty children weeding and watering. In one there was no teacher, yet the children seemed to be working diligently. As they got back to work, one of the teachers who had been helping them came to talk with us. She told us what they were growing—eggplants, tomatoes, cucumbers, sunflowers, sugar cane, string beans, onions, peanuts, spinach, cauliflower, maize, watermelon, and ginseng and other medicinal herbs.

There was at least one other crop, because the Little Red Soldier[9] who was my personal guide during our entire stay at the school picked a mint leaf in the garden and gave it to me, smelling it first so I'd know how to identify it. I took it, smelled it, and indicated that I knew what it was. We both smiled, pleased at our small triumph of communication. Later we went indoors for our discussion, and finding myself still holding the mint leaf, I dropped it into my cup of tea. This didn't escape my young guide's notice. She immediately went outside and returned a few minutes later carrying two handfuls of mint leaves which she passed out to everyone in the room.

The farm was only the beginning. The school is "smashing revisionism" through its many workshops, too. Located on the school grounds, from the outside they look like any other classroom, but inside there is another world. In the first one, three children were helping the teacher punch out oil filters for trucks at a large machine that spun and whirred in one corner. About a dozen others seated at a long workbench were stacking the filters. In the next room, children were bent over individual tables putting all their strength into filing and smoothing the aluminum castings that are attached to the steps of buses. A few doors down there was an electroplating workshop where some children were standing at sinks wearing large rubber aprons and others were sitting on benches, all of them vigorously cleaning and scrubbing the plates with wire brushes.

Sometimes we in North America have our children work with tools also. In those preschools and lower elementary grades that attempt this kind of activity, it is often done with pretend tools (plastic hammers, saws that don't cut, etc.) which the children use to pretend to construct something. In those classrooms where something is actually made, much of the work is commonly done by the teacher, and the product is

---

9. A member of a youth organization for primary school children. The organization is discussed in Chapter 6.

usually an "extra," a game or simple piece of equipment for the children's use. Then, in many school districts there is a long dry spell with little or no manual activity outside of art work until junior high when girls have cooking and sewing classes and boys carpentry and metal work. At this stage too, because of the setup and aims of these programs, students can make only a few things each year—perhaps a dress, blouse, and apron, or a stool, mailbox, and spice rack. The things they make are commonly for individual consumption, usually for themselves or gifts for their mothers. By high school, it often happens that those who are still taking "industrial arts" or "domestic science" classes are in such courses by default, having been judged insufficiently intelligent for the "academic" stream. In many schools, students by this stage are pretty well separated into those who "should" work with their hands and those who "should" work with their minds, it being unmistakably clear what their aspirations in life ought properly to be. This division generally follows class lines with middle-class kids going the academic route and kids from what is tellingly called the lower class going the manual work route. It need not be spelled out what the difference in pay and community status will be for them.

In China the work that goes on in school workshops is not a game. Starting in some places as early as the preschools, the children are not playing at work. The results of their efforts are actually used in production. They are making things not just for themselves and their parents but for all of society. The workshops at Chen Hsien Street Primary School are set up by factories in Nanking which provide the machinery, tools, materials, and teachers. After the students process whatever part they are working on, it goes back to the factory and is used. Whenever they see a truck, they can have the satisfaction of knowing something about how it was made, that they perhaps helped to build it. The same is true of the farm work. One teacher reported that the children say that the peanuts taste better when they grow them themselves than when they buy them at the market.

In China, work activities continue through school for all the students. They are not reserved for "the less academically inclined." They serve tᴏ break down class distinctions. Manual work is respected in China and the Chinese believe everyone should be involved in it. Nor is there sex segregation in these work activities. One would never see half the student population in a Chinese school busying themselves with pots and pans while the other half was engaged with chisels and screwdrivers. Schools are for the training of those skills that are not easily learned outside of school, skills that anyone might need. This is why all the students—regardless of their sex or family class background—learn industrial and agricultural principles and how to apply them.

The pots and pans skills are taught at home, because most homes contain at least one expert in this sphere of endeavor, and many contain several. By the same token, teachers of industrial and agricultural production are also very often experts. To avoid the frustration that goes with ineptitude, and to ensure that a usable product is turned out, the teachers of these classes are frequently workers and peasants. Except for the simplest jobs, the factories are likely to send workers to the schools to teach and supervise the shop work. The regular teachers often conduct the agricultural work at urban primary schools that have their own gardens, because this involves simply planting, attending, and harvesting a few crops. In addition, primary students also spend some time working on the communes with both their regular teachers and the peasants guiding them. In the middle school more sophisticated skills are taught, such as crop experimentation, farm machinery repair, and the raising of animals. The city students, along with their teachers, usually put in longer and more regular stints on the communes where the peasants are their teachers.

To make sure that the students do not envision themselves as isolated cogs in a complex and arcane process, they make frequent visits to the factories. The children at the Nanking primary school would go, for example, to the factory that produces trucks. There they can see and understand the connection between what they do in their school workshop and what is done in the factory. They already know something about the process because they have been doing it. They see the oil filters that they have prepared being assembled along with other parts to make a final product. They also have prior knowledge of more than just their own small part in the process because their teacher is from that factory and has discussed with them many of the principles, procedures, and problems involved in making trucks. Their trips to the factory serve to extend, verify, and deepen that knowledge.

The work in the fields and shops and the visits to factories and communes constitute the practical aspect of a course known as common or general knowledge. At the Nanking school I visited, it began in the fourth grade. A theoretical side was conducted in the classroom. The course started with basic information about nature and agriculture, then went on to the fundamentals of industrial principles, public health, geography, and history. This type of general knowledge course continues in the secondary curriculum with greater emphasis on the fundamentals of industry in the city schools and agriculture in the country schools. Such a course is often closely linked with the sciences and mathematics.

We visited a class on public health at a primary school in which the children were learning to identify herbs used in medical treatment. Using the herbs to demonstrate, the teacher described the characteristics—structure, color, size. They were passed around for the children to examine, with them commenting on the textures and smells. The teacher explained where and how they grew, telling the children, "The first thing to do is to look, use your eyes to identify an herb; the second thing is to feel the plant with your hands." The children also get practical experience by going out and searching for the herbs, in addition to growing a few varieties in their school garden.

This class reminded me of the herbal garden we had seen on a commune. It was part of a medical complex containing a hospital for in-patients and out-patients, a dentist's office, a pharmacy, and a pharmaceutical workshop. The garden was set up as an exhibit for the peasants. There were herbs everywhere and a large sign reading "Chinese traditional medicine and pharmacology are a great treasure house. Greater efforts should be made to explore this knowledge and raise it to a higher level." Each kind of herb was in a pot spaced apart from the others. The pots were labelled with the names of the herbs and their distinguishing characteristics. During their leisure time, the peasants could use the garden and learn to identify the herbs. Then when they came across them in the fields, they would know which ones were useful to collect. This educational venture was apparently quite successful, because the pharmaceutical workshop was able to produce 40 percent of all the medicines used on the commune (which had a population of over 66,-000) from the herbs collected by the peasants. Thus, it is not just the schoolchildren who are learning to combine theory and practice.

But what about young children doing farm and factory work? Doesn't that constitute child labor? That's certainly not how they see it at Chen Hsien Street Primary School. One of the teachers explained: "The purpose in having the children do industrial work and farming is so they will be able to apply what they learn in the classroom. We try to integrate theory with practice and mental work with manual work so the children will develop all-roundedly."

Middle school student in school's herbal garden.

The amount and type of work the children do is suited to their age and physical capabilities. In the lower grades at this primary school they help out with the simpler chores in the garden—getting rid of stones, weeding, and watering—the idea being to gradually familiarize themselves with farming, learn to identify crops, and become accustomed to physical work. Beginning in grade four, from the age of about eleven on, the work becomes more difficult and they spend more time at it, but we were assured, it is never overly taxing. Each child works afternoons for two weeks a term, half the time in the garden and half in the workshops. In the mornings they attend their regular classes; when it rains they don't work outside.

The teachers at the school pointed out that they are not training specialists at this early age. So that a child will more fully understand a particular process, he or she is assigned to one workshop for the entire week; the next time the child will go to a different one. This gives the children a good grasp of several different processes. It is basically the same principle that any teacher would apply to a math class. Children are not taught only to add and never to subtract. Nor are they given a choice which one they would like to learn. They need to know both. In the production activities at this Nanking primary school, the same thing holds—it is important that the children learn several processes well. The assignment of jobs, however, is always based on a consideration of the children's physical condition.

Though everyone benefits, no one profits from the children's work. The crop is divided among all the children at Chen Hsien. To bring home the things they have grown to share with their families produces real satisfaction. This arrangement corresponds closely with the communes where peasants work the land together and share the harvest. In the children's industrial production work, factories often pay the schools, which use the money to buy equipment and materials for the children, but this practice varies. In one middle school I visited, where the students were making wooden chairs for another school, everyone seemed a bit surprised when I asked about payment. The worker-teacher in charge explained that the other school had supplied the raw materials, but that there was no payment involved. "The purpose," he reminded me, "is for the students' education, not for money." Even in those instances where the schools were paid, the significance of the money was always played down and the educational value of the work emphasized. But, paid or not, such activities undoubtedly help to develop a collective spirit. The children learn early in life that collective efforts yield collective benefits.

Perhaps, however, the most telling evidence that the children are not being exploited is their appearance of well-being. The children of China are the healthiest and happiest I have ever seen. Any images of pallid, frail children tied to machines for a dozen or more hours a day, the images that come to mind when we think of child labor, could not be more out of place than when applied to China. My own impressions have been confirmed by other visitors. One, a Canadian, who before liberation had lived in China for twenty-two years, was incredulous when he returned for a visit many years later.

What did I look for?

I searched for scurvy-headed children. Lice-ridden children. Children with inflamed red eyes. Children with bleeding gums. Children with distended stomachs and spindling arms and legs. I searched the sidewalks day and night for children who had been purposely deformed by beggars. Beggars who would leech on to any well-dressed passer-by to blackmail sympathy and offerings, by pretending the hideous-looking child was their own.

I looked for children covered with horrible sores upon which flies feasted. I looked for children having a bowel movement, which, after much strain, would only eject tapeworms.

I looked for child slaves in alleyway factories. Children who worked twelve hours a day, literally chained to small press punches. Children who, if they lost a finger, or worse, often were cast into the streets to beg and forage in garbage cans for future subsistence.

I looked for children who had no hope of a future, education, love or a happy family life. I searched hard to find abandoned children . . . .

I found the Western world ignorant of the fact that Chinese children had become the most mentally, physically, and psychologically healthy children in the world.[10]

KINDERGARTEN TO UNIVERSITY

There is nothing unique about the industrial and agricultural work being done by the students at Chen Hsien Street Primary School. It is a regular feature of schools in China. Even at The East Is Red Kindergarten there is a sizable garden which the children help to cultivate. We were told that the garden was there before the Cultural Revolution but the teachers did all the work "so that the children wouldn't get dirty." But this attitude was criticized. Asked one teacher rhetorically, "If they don't plant beans, how will they know what beans look like?" Much of the work is still done by the teachers, but the children now assist at each step—planting seeds, watering, weeding, and helping with the harvesting. When we were there they had recently harvested and brought home the last crop—an occasion for great excitement—and planted a new one. The children were scrambling around on their hands and knees searching everywhere for any stray villain weed which might have

---

10. W. A. Scott, "China Revisited by an Old China Hand," *Eastern Horizon* 5, no. 6 (1966), pp. 34–35.

escaped their scrutiny. Because they actually work in the garden, they can now identify all the crops they grow, about ten of them plus a couple of types of medicinal herbs.

They also have a "workshop." In two spacious, airy adjoining rooms there were five children-sized green tables with six to eight little four- and five-year-olds sitting on small chairs intent upon their productive labor. A different job was being done at each table. At one, the children were putting strings on tags that would later be attached to sewing machines; at another, they were opening small plastic bags in which pieces of electronics equipment were to be placed; at the next, they were closing one end of small cardboard boxes in which locks were to be packed; at another, they were using scissors to cut apart and trim two attached plastic bottle caps; at the last table, they were separating the paper from the corks of used badminton shuttlecocks. All of the leftover materials—the plastic trimmings, paper, and corks—would be recycled (as is just about everything else that is reusable in China). The children carefully placed each tiny piece in the baskets in the center of the tables. They were learning not only manual skills, but the value of thrift as well.

While the work is simpler and the children spend much less time at it—two twenty-minute periods a week—the setup is similar in some respects to the Nanking primary school. The children visit the factories where the items they are working on are processed and the factories pay the school for the work done.

With this kind of background in kindergarten and primary school, students are able to take on quite advanced projects by the time they reach middle school. They often even set up their own factories. The senior middle school we visited on Da Li People's Commune operated two factories. At one radios were made and at the other alcohol was produced from the liquid waste of a nearby chemical plant. The daily output of alcohol was two-and-a-half gallons, enough to supply themselves and a neighboring school with sufficient quantities for all of their laboratory experiments. They also ran a small experimental farm of one-and-a-half acres which was used for cultivating improved strains of rice, wheat, and rape seed. It is common for schools in the rural areas either to have their own agricultural projects or to assign students to other agricultural activities on the commune.

The specific arrangements for the productive labor classes vary considerably, particularly at the middle school and university levels, but there are certain common features. The most basic is that all middle schools, universities, and institutes maintain such classes as a central part of their curricula.

In addition to working in their own factories and on farms, a great many middle school students devote a substantial portion of their productive labor time to working in established enterprises outside of the school. No longer do factories just send simple tasks to the school workshops for students to process and return. The students now go to the factories and work for several weeks at a time. We saw some middle school students at workbenches when we visited a machine-tools factory in Shanghai. Interspersed among them were older men and women, who had small flags on their tables indicating that they had earned the distinction of being model workers.[11] The students under their supervision could be secure in the knowledge that they were learning from experts.

Even at this stage, students do not usually become narrow specialists. Just as the youth in the countryside generally continue to improve their industrial skills rather than attend exclusively to agriculture, so the students from the cities also expand their knowledge of both. They go to the factories as well as working at school and they go to communes where they work closely with the peasants for several weeks at a time. Some recent visitors described one such type of arrangement:

> Physical labour in the countryside for students from urban middle schools centres on the 'branch school,' in most cases sited on an area of waste land on which teachers and students build their own living accommodation and classrooms. The size of the plots vary from 25 to 50 acres. To take one example, a Kwangchow [Canton] middle school with 26 acres grows rice, sugar cane, some vegetables and fruit, raises poultry, runs a small weather forecasting unit and a small hydroelectric station, as well as a workshop for making medicines from local herbs.
>
> The division of school time between work and study varies and depends on seasonal factors. Normally three days of the week are devoted to study and three to labour, although many sessions obviously combine the two. Teachers work alongside the students.

-----
11. Model workers are those who are seen to be most exemplary in their conscientious style of work, their cooperative attitudes toward workmates, and their overall socialist outlooks and conduct at their places of work. They are held up as models for other workers to emulate.

While living for the most part in their own quarters, contact with the local community is close. In the evenings the peasants and town students get together and exchange experiences. Lessons include writing the history of the village and biographies of the peasants. In the busy seasons the students work with peasants in the fields.[12]

This system is having the important effect of narrowing the wide gap that has traditionally existed between the city and the country. As in most parts of the world, the cities have been the centers of greater affluence, advanced education, and culture while the rural areas have been more backward in all respects. The split between the "city slickers" and the "country bumpkins" is still a major problem in China, but it is being consciously and vigorously grappled with by the large-scale flow of students from the cities going to live, work, and learn with the peasants.[13] In addition, the countryside is being industrialized. The Chinese want to develop the rural areas and to avoid the uncontrolled sprawl and other problems of congested urban areas that they see in the West, so industry is decentralized to a remarkable extent. I recently spoke to a man who had just visited his native county in China, a poor rural district, after an absence of twenty-eight years abroad. When he had lived there, not one factory was to be found; now there are 120.

For both the classroom work—the theory—and its application in factory and field the teachers are often workers and peasants—the experts in industry and agriculture. Some schools arrange an exchange between workers or peasants and regular teachers. A master worker might be invited to give classes in the theory of principles that the students require for factory work, spending several weeks or months working with the students, freeing their teacher to work in the factory for that period. At the same time the worker can supervise the application of these principles in actual production. Another method is that while students are working in factories outside, they might have one day or afternoon a week set aside for theory classes to discuss the operations they are doing; the classes might be given at the factories or back at the

---

12. Peter Mauger et al., *Education in China,* Modern China Series, no. 5 (London: Anglo-Chinese Educational Institute, 1974), p. 49.

13. This problem was certainly a concern in 1973. By 1975 when I returned to China, however, it had expanded into a movement to close the three big gaps: between workers and peasants; between town and country; and between mental and manual work.

Veteran worker-teacher demonstrates carpentry technique in primary school workshop where children are producing chairs.

schools, but in either case they are likely to be conducted by the people who best understand the operations both theoretically and practically. Or workers and peasants might simply become full-time teachers as was the recent case with 600 model workers and technicians in Wusih, a city of approximately 650,000 people. With the direct, broad participation of these new worker-teachers and peasant-teachers, the situation arises much less frequently where "machines are operated only on blackboards" and where students "can't distinguish between rice and grass."

At these levels of education, the time set aside for productive activities ranges from one to three months a year. In the middle schools, work time is usually divided between industry and agriculture; but at the higher levels, there is more specialization, students doing physical work that relates to their particular areas of study. For example, the students and teachers in the chemistry department at Peking University have their own factory that produces medicines.

Decisions about who should work where are guided by rational considerations of what the students are studying and how they can best gain experience in applying that knowledge, the result being that arrangements are strikingly sensible. The students at Sun Yat-sen Medical College spend one full year of a three-year course along with their professors, in factories and communes. There they continue their medical education and practice at the same time. This gives them an opportunity to learn about preventive medicine as they are where they can study firsthand such things as health and safety conditions and community hygiene and sanitation and offer practical suggestions. This is in addition to clinical work in the three general and two specialized hospitals connected to the College. One healthy looking, pigtailed student at the College commented on the new system: "Now the schools are run in an open-door way, and we have more contact with society. This helps us to combine what we learn in school with practice outside."

I ran into another very sensible arrangement in a friendship store[14] in Shanghai. While speaking to two clerks, I discovered that they were students from the Textile Workers' Institute who were studying English. The friendship store was their "factory." What better place to learn to apply the knowledge gained in class?

This is representative of the kind of setup used for students at advanced levels in disciplines outside of science and technology. The guiding principle is to "take all of society as a factory." A professor of philosophy at Peking University explained: "We can't run a novel factory or a history factory, so we use society as our factory. The students spend two or three months a year outside the campus making social investigations. For instance, while at the University the freshmen in the department of philosophy studied the Marxist-Leninist theory of class struggle, and then they went to a production brigade in the countryside. They held meetings with the peasants and discussed the concepts they had been studying at the University. Then they conducted studies on the characteristics of classes and the class struggle in that brigade and wrote more than thirty reports about it. They submitted the reports to the comrades at the brigade who thought that they were excellent and very helpful."

Another group of students, specializing in Chinese literature went to a different brigade where a number of peasants were trying their hand at

---

14. Friendship stores are department stores that cater to foreigners. They sell many standard items as well as things that foreigners are likely to be interested in—specialty foods, souvenirs, gifts, etc., all at standard prices. Foreigners are also free to shop in the people's department stores and small shops.

creative writing. Through seminars, they discussed writing styles, ana-
lyzed some classical and modern works, studied the Marxist view of
literature and collectively wrote several stories.

The field experiences and activities of students at the middle school
and university levels serve a dual purpose. While the students are serving themselves by deepening their own knowledge through combining
practice with theory, they are also at the same time performing valuable
services for others. (The workers and peasants are similarly of service to
the students who are learning from them.) Some peasants have improved their writing abilities; other peasants have learned about their
ideological strengths and weaknesses; medicine is being produced for
the people; middle school students on one commune make alcohol for
their experiments and the schools do not have to buy it; the country
might be able to produce better quality rice, wheat, or rape seed. These
things are happening in middle schools, universities, and institutes all
over the country. Even primary school children and preschoolers are
making social contributions—growing food and medicinal herbs,
adding their little bit to the manufacture of commodities, the older
children giving acupuncture treatments, etc.

Perhaps equally as important, young people are learning to take
initiative. They are being taught that they should serve others at every
opportunity, including ways not planned in the curriculum. There are
students in the cities who have organized themselves into groups to help
direct traffic, to do chores for old people, run errands for neighbors, etc.
Others in the countryside might give haircuts, repair shoes, sew clothes,
teach more advanced literacy skills to the older peasants—whatever
they can see that needs doing.

The benefit that is most stressed by the Chinese is the fuller integration of students into the workaday world of workers and peasants. This
integration goes beyond labor activities, encompassing numerous other
aspects of the educational process. There seem to be throngs of students
practically everywhere in China. Driving on back country roads, you
suddenly come upon hundreds of middle school students in long lines as
far as you can see. With their backpacks partially covered by straw hats
that hang loosely from strings around their necks, they may be hiking to
a commune or to a historical site. In the cities, one sees groups of thirty,
forty, or fifty children walking at a brisk pace, three or four abreast,
canteens hanging from their belts, khaki satchels on shoulder straps.
The air rings with their energetic voices singing "I Am a Little Red

Soldier,'' or "Learn from Uncle Lei Feng.''[15] They may be going to a factory, or park, a department store, a museum, a monument, a zoo, or a clinic. There are groups of tots, two and three years old, walking in lines baby elephant style, each one hanging onto the shirttail of the one in front. Apparently they have their field trips, too.

"Students used to study behind closed doors,'' many people can be heard to say. This is seen as a corrupting influence, because they learned to take for granted all the things that are produced by the hard work of others. "I have eaten rice all my life,'' remarked one aging university teacher, "but I never really appreciated a single grain. It never occurred to me how the peasants sweated to supply that rice for me because I myself never shed even one drop of sweat to grow rice. It is good that that is changing.''

"Yes,'' one of his students agreed. "The peasants have taught us young people to appreciate the rice we eat; we have worked by their side to grow it. Our sweat is mixed with theirs.'' This is what the Chinese mean when they say that now they run their schools in an "open-door way.''

THEORY AND PRACTICE

This emphasis that the Chinese give to the integration of theory and practice may sound somewhat strange. To the popular North American mind, theory is some sort of rather effete and sterile activity indulged in by relatively few people, mainly professors who cut themselves off from the world. These are often looked upon as people who spin out fanciful ideas that really do no one any harm—and seldom any good. Practice to most of us, on the other hand, means the repetition of an activity in order to improve a skill. Webster's Dictionary offers "exercise" and "drill" as synonyms for practice. Boys go to baseball practice; children practice the piano and the multiplication tables on the supposition that "practice makes perfect."

The Chinese would vigorously disagree with this maxim and with such ideas about what constitutes theory and practice. In the first place,

---

15. Lei Feng is a hero of the People's Liberation Army. See Chapter 6 for more about Lei Feng and other heroes.

they disapprove of the very idea of perfection. People are capable of development and growth, but at no point can it ever be said that someone has reached perfection in any endeavor. The concept of perfection would be regarded as counter-developmental and antihistorical because it implies that there is an ultimate, a fixed demarcation line beyond which humans can never go. It further implies that aspirations too should be limited by some boundary called perfection, a boundary which to them would necessarily be arbitrary. The Chinese as Marxists do not deal in absolutes. The only absolutes they recognize are struggle and change and the human capacity and energy to break through and transcend apparent limitations. What may seem a limitation at one point in time is conquered at another, presenting something else in turn that appears as a limitation, and so on endlessly. That is how they define human progress. For them to accept the idea of perfection would be to deny struggle, and hence progress.

Second, they would not accept that growth comes only through practice. Children, they argue, cannot truly develop their capabilities for multiplication if they don't understand the mathematical principles on which it is based. Children might be able to produce acceptable responses to specific questions from practice alone, but if they don't understand what multiplication is, its connection to other mathematical concepts and processes, its relevance and application, their competence in multiplication will not develop further.

To the Chinese, practice includes everything that people do. It embraces all activity and constitutes all experience. It is highly valued because people learn through experience. But unless guided by what the Chinese call "correct theory," meaning theory that is scientifically and morally grounded, practice can be very dangerous. For example, Chinese traditional medicine has evolved over centuries of practice. The history of successful application of acupuncture, moxibustion, herbal medicine, and other methods of treatment to a wide variety of diseases leaves a rich legacy to modern-day China (and to the rest of the world, which is just now beginning to appreciate its contributions). But without a sufficient knowledge of scientific analysis or sound enough theories about why treatments do or don't work, however, many harmful practices rooted in superstition also evolved. Han Suyin relates one of her experiences in the China of 1940, when as a midwife she was called to a peasant's house to try to save the life of a young woman who had given birth a week before. The afterbirth had not been expelled, and, according to local superstition, the umbilical cord could not be cut until it had. Lying between the woman's legs was a dead baby; the would-be mother had lockjaw and was close to death herself:

All over the bed, on the clothes of the rigid girl, sitting up like a pole, wadded blankets rolled as bolsters in her back, were strewn rice grains, scattered in handfuls as placatory offerings to the evil spirits that had locked the afterbirth inside the girl's belly; hanging outside the door and the room were streamers and untied knots of straw, signifying the untying of the "lock" within; on the woman's stomach had been painted some signs and also on her feet; there were feathers about, perhaps from sacrificed fowls.[16]

According to the Chinese, it is theory—people's interpretations of their experience—that shapes their practice. Everyone has theories about human behavior and acts accordingly. The theories might be based on prejudice, superstition, or scientific analysis; they might be selfishly or selflessly motivated, but they are theories nonetheless. The Chinese are not tolerant of any and all theories. They would disagree with the view that holds that everyone is entitled to his own opinion because it implies that all opinions are equally valid and invalid. What about opinions that do others harm, they would ask, opinions that are destructive of people's welfare, that enslave their bodies or their minds? What about the opinion that the afterbirth within the dying woman could be coaxed out by hanging untied knots of straw? Should those who know better "respect" that opinion by leaving it alone, or should they try to change it, to enlighten others? To earn the respect of the Chinese, a theory must be scientific. It must be based on observation and testing—on systematic practice—which must in turn lend itself to further testing—again, practice.

The Chinese see two basic philosophical orientations, two approaches to interpreting the world—materialism and idealism. Here again we have to disentangle the popular notions these terms often suggest to us from what they suggest to them. In our society, materialism is usually taken to mean the quest for wealth, that which is mundane and vulgar; a "moneygrubber" is materialistic. In contrast, idealism for some connotes the quest after selfless moral principles, that which is

---

16. Han Suyin, *Birdless Summer* (New York: Bantam Books, 1972), pp. 181-82.

high-minded (though often viewed as unrealistic). Someone who aspires to make a better world is frequently called idealistic.

The Chinese give these terms very different definitions. They hold materialism as that approach to life which takes all things as based on matter. The world is composed of people, animals, trees, air, molecules—things that are real and have a definite, concrete, material existence. All practice, all activity, derives from interaction among these concrete bits of matter in the real world. They constitute what the Chinese call "objective reality," which exists regardless of anyone's perception of it. Extending this reasoning, they maintain that these interactions are knowable; they lend themselves to scientific scrutiny and comprehension. As good materialists, the Chinese maintain that interpretations and understandings of life—in their words, "subjective orientations"—should correspond as closely as possible with objective reality.

Idealism, on the other hand, starts from the opposite perspective. Passing over material realities as the basis for comprehending the world, it begins with ideas. For idealists, ideas take precedence over material reality. Some idealists go so far as to claim total separation between the world of what they may call the mind, the spirit, or the soul from the world of matter.

Marxists, by their understanding of the word, identify different kinds of idealism. For example, each form of idealism could offer its own explanation for the existence of poverty: that's what God wants; it's fate; it's human nature (which implies that some people are lazy, stupid, and wasteful while others are hard-working, intelligent, and resourceful); poverty is psychological or the result of a "culture of poverty" (it's an attitude, a frame of mind, the way people come to see themselves more than anything else). Some idealists dismiss the relevance of poverty altogether saying people should be concerned with spiritual sustenance and disdain base physical appetites. Marxist materialists reject all of these as nonscientific falsifications. Poverty, they say, is the result of certain material, economic arrangements in society. They would ask: who owns and controls the material means through which the goods necessary for survival and abundance are produced? How are the material goods that are produced distributed—equitably or inequitably? And so on.

The Chinese claim that the superiority of materialism over idealism rests on the fact that as a scientific approach, materialism equips people to solve and overcome problems, to control nature and society, whereas idealism equips people to accept things as they are. As materialists they say that they analyze economic and social phenomena just as they analyze natural phenomena. They need not accept poverty; it can be understood and therefore controlled, wiped out—and they are proving it in practice.

It is for this reason that the Chinese and other Marxists are atheists. Religion is a form of idealism. It is predicated on an acceptance of God who is unknowable, whose mysterious ways are unpredictable, and whose final judgments must be accepted. A young Chinese university student explained why they have discarded religion: "In the old days, when the people lived a miserable, brutal existence, they prayed to God to give them happiness, to give them food, to improve their lives. They prayed very hard, but things did not change. While so many died of starvation, people still continued to pray. But the people finally came to know that there is no god who will save them; we must save ourselves. Food, houses, wealth, all these things are created only by the people, by the strength of the masses, not by any gods. So we must rely on our own energy, our own intelligence to create the things we need. We will not find happiness by asking some god to give it to us; we must make it through our own efforts. We no longer believe in such superstitions."

There is a folksong in China that says,

The cherry is good to eat;
But the tree is difficult to plant,
And happiness cannot fall down from the sky.

Planting the tree, as the Chinese see it, is a human endeavor, a difficult but rewarding one. That is the essence and spirit of materialism.[17]

Theory for the Chinese, then, must be scientific but it also must be rooted in a particular kind of moral motivation—the motive to serve the people. Nonscientific theories are rejected but that does not mean that all scientific ones are accepted. Just as they do not honor variety for its own sake, the Chinese also do not approve of pursuing any knowledge, any ideas simply because they are knowledge or ideas. A theory must be

---

17. For a lucid and thoroughgoing explanation of the Marxist view of materialism and idealism, the three short volumes by Maurice Cornforth entitled *Dialectical Materialism: An Introduction* are highly recommended. While all three volumes deal extensively with these two theoretical orientations, vol. 1, *Materialism and the Dialectical Method,* 4th ed. rev. (New York: International Publishers, 1971), contains a chapter that lays out their essential features in clear, concise form. See "Materialism and Idealism," pp. 17-28.

usable, applicable to real life problems in a way that will result in collective human betterment. It must, as the Chinese say, "Shoot the arrow at the target." The proliferation of non-biodegradable packaging that currently plagues some countries is the result of concentrated scientific research aimed, perhaps unknowingly, at benefiting the packagers at the expense of the people. That, for the Chinese, would be the wrong target.

Armed with this materialist conception of the world, the Chinese see the relationship between theory and practice as a crucial one. Stories abound about the poverty of the one without the other—the endless suffering of people who did, who practiced for so long without the benefit of scientific theories to empower them to control their lives; and the elitism, arrogance, and ineptitude of those who theorized in seclusion from the real world. Theory and practice for the Chinese must unite, interpenetrate; they must cross-fertilize and nourish each other.

Of the two, practice is regarded as the more basic, because, for the materialist, theory comes from experience gained by engagement with the objective world. Mao has stressed this point repeatedly over the years. Writing in 1935, he contended, "Reading is learning, but applying is also learning and the more important kind of learning at that. . . . It is often not a matter of first learning and then doing, but of doing and then learning, for doing is itself learning."[18] And later, "If we have a correct theory but merely prate about it, pigeonhole it and do not put it into practice, then that theory, however good, is of no significance."[19] Practice generates theories which are interpretations of that practice and which advance comprehension; the new theories are then tested in practice, enriching and refining them, over and over in an upward spiral.

This is what was being urged on the sign in the herbal garden—"Chinese traditional medicine and pharmacology are a great treasure house. Greater efforts should be made to explore this knowledge and raise it to a higher level." The practice of centuries should not be discarded simply because it is old. "Weed through the old to bring forth the new." Subject traditional medicine to scientific analysis, verify what is useful, comprehend its hidden principles, try them out again—this time more efficiently and effectively—then again study the results, say the Chinese.

18. Mao Tse-tung, "Problems of Strategy in China's Revolutionary War," *Selected Works,* vol. 1, pp. 189-90.
19. Mao Tse-tung, "On Practice," *Selected Works,* vol. 1, p. 304.

For improving traditional medicine, crop strains and yields, machinery—for just about everything, the same principle holds. For the Chinese, theory is not something that goes on in schools while practice happens outside, in life removed and apart from that theory. There must be a perpetual interchange between theory and practice both in and out of school. School must partake of life while life must penetrate the school.

PROBLEM-SOLVING

The integration of theory and practice has brought about a new kind of mass initiative and creativity. Before, when students were taught only to collect and store information without having much experience in applying it, they were stumped when they met real problems. With their learning locked away in that corner of the brain reserved for things memorized in school, they rarely realized that their accumulated knowledge could be of practical service to them.

Now, instead of experiencing bewilderment in the face of an unfamiliar problem or passing it on to an expert, today's Chinese youth are predisposed to tackle it themselves. Their behavior is consistent with what they learn, but now a part of that learning emphasizes the use of their knowledge in practical application to the real world.

During a discussion at a middle school in Shanghai, one of the teachers was criticizing the revisionist line of splitting practice from theory. To demonstrate how bad things had been he said, "In the past, even graduates of the College of Sciences sometimes couldn't install electrical facilities. Although they had a lot of theoretical knowledge about electricity, they didn't know what to do with it." We got a firsthand demonstration of how that situation is changing when we visited a small factory in the middle school where about fifty girls and boys were making transistor radios. Some were assembling, others testing, with much discussion about what they were doing, usually among themselves, sometimes with their teacher who was a factory worker. No one was working alone. There were diagrams on the blackboard and not an idle person in the room. Considering the small size of the room, the large number of students, and the kind of work they were doing, it was surprisingly orderly.

One of the people in our group was having some difficulty with his tape recorder. He explained his problem to some of the students and asked if they could repair it. They promised to try, and we left to visit other classes. His request struck some of us as a bit farfetched. How could a bunch of fifteen-year-olds who had never seen this kind of tape recorder before (it was not made in China) figure out how to repair it? Anyway, they were making radios, not tape recorders. To our amazement, a student showed up less than an hour later with the tape recorder back in working order. We had been wrong to suppose a static relationship between their theory and their practice. They were learning scientific principles, which, at that point, were being applied to the making of radios. But because they really understood those principles, they were able to marshal them in solving other problems as well.

This episode points up the inaccuracy of an expression I had heard many times—that China is turning out armies of "little blue ants," unthinking and mesmerized, spirit flattened so that they willingly accept the drudgery of turning nuts and bolts for the duration of their days, asking nothing more of life. But intellectual activity such as we saw is not typical of "little blue ants." Students so engaged must think; they have no choice in the matter. That is what being able to solve problems, to apply theory, means.

It is an active and even creative process. To teach students to combine theory with practice in the service of the people is to discourage passivity. Students are praised when they do more than wait for problems to be presented to them and then apply theory. They are most congratulated when they seek out problems, when they try to discover what the people need.

We were given a concrete example of student initiative at the same middle school by a student who was a member of the school's Revolutionary Committee. He was about sixteen, tall, with the bearing of a real leader in the making. He told us about his schoolmate, Wang Tse-fa, who had recently suffered from an ear disease that had affected his hearing: "Soon after his return to school, our class was studying theoretical and practical knowledge about electronics. We were learning about amplifying principles and we thought, 'Why not apply this knowledge to make a hearing aid for Comrade Wang? We should be bold and daring. This would help him, and it would also be a good way to combine our theoretical study with practice.'"

He talked about the problems the students ran into and the help they got from the medical equipment factory: "When the workers at the

Middle school students learn to apply theory to practice and to solve practical problems in their school workshops. Here they are working on a lathe, making parts for drill presses.

factory heard our story, they gave us every assistance, and with their help we succeeded in making the equipment. That was just a few weeks ago, and we are still trying to improve it. Comrade Wang was very moved by our deed. In the past he was usually quiet, but after we gave him the hearing aid he was so moved that he came to the platform to express his appreciation. Because of his poor hearing, his morale had become low, but now it has been raised and he tries to do some services for the other students to show his feelings. He has been coming to school very early in the morning to do some of the cleaning work before the rest of us arrive. He thinks that this is what he can do for the others.''

Though the hearing aid Wang would have received from the state may have been of greater technical quality, it is doubtful that it would have held quite the same meaning for him as this extraordinary gift from his classmates.

RESPECT FOR WORKERS AND PEASANTS

Around 300 B.C., Mencius, a disciple of Confucius, wrote:

> Some labor with their brains and some labor with their brawn. Those who labor with their brains govern others; those who labor with their brawn are governed by others. Those governed by others, feed them. Those who govern others, are fed by them. This is a universal principle in the world.[20]

> If there were no men of superior grade, there would be no one to rule the countrymen. If there were no countrymen, there would be no one to support the men of superior grade.[21]

The working people were mere beasts whose sole purpose was to supply a luxurious existence for that tiny layer of society's "men of superior grade." It was taken as a fact of life that they did not think, could not think. Mindless toil was their lot. It did not matter how much they suffered, how hungry, tired, poor, or wretched they might be. They were just insensitive, stupid, inferior brutes. It was the corpulent literati with long robes and long fingernails who held the monopoly on virtue and wisdom. Education was for the reproduction and perpetuation of that small ruling elite of superior men.

With historical suddenness, the Communists proclaimed: "The lowly are most intelligent; the elite are most ignorant." A thoroughly revolutionary assertion, turning the code of nearly two-and-a-half millenia completely upside down. But it is one thing to assert this—quite another to convince people, to inspire them with a real respect for those who labor and had been held in contempt for so long. How could it be that the workers and peasants (most of whom couldn't even read) were the most intelligent, and that those who had spent their lives studying knew nothing? Today the Chinese say that those who work create society's wealth; they experience life and therefore know it; they struggle and conquer, while those who just read books and do no work, the "parasites who live off others' labor," create only nonsensical theories like the one about their presumed superiority.

---

20. Quoted in Derk Bodde, *China's Cultural Tradition: What and Whither?* (New York: Holt, Rinehart and Winston, 1957), p. 49.
    21. Ibid.

It was only when the workers and peasants themselves began to benefit from their labor, to enjoy the wealth they created, when—beginning in 1949—the few were no longer allowed to extract it from them, that they began to feel their own power and to recognize more fully their own intelligence. And with that dawn of recognition, their intelligence was unharnessed. They were the creators of all of life's material goods; they could increase that wealth through hard work and knowledge—practice and theory. For the workers and peasants who had always practiced, had always worked hard, it has been much easier to integrate sound theories into their lives. A theory either improves practice or it doesn't; it should accordingly be embraced or thrown out.

It has been much more difficult for those who had only theorized but rarely tested their theories to accept the value of practice and to be willing to give up their privileges and actually work. How could they degrade themselves by digging in the fields with the peasants, by wearing clothes that made them indistinguishable from the workers? But this is what began to happen in the China of 1949. The landlord was given a plot of ground like everyone else, but now, if he wanted to eat, he had to take a hoe in his own hands just like the peasants. They had had enough of scratching at the earth to feed him while their own families went hungry; now they would feed themselves and their children, and he had to do likewise or suffer the consequences.

It is true that those who were formerly privileged were forced to work. Not in slave labor camps or chain gangs or by any other brutal techniques that may be imagined. They had to work, to create wealth, just as the peasants had been doing for all those centuries. The differences now were that everyone was expected to create the wealth and everyone would share in it.

It has been a strenuous battle for members of the former ruling classes to come to appreciate that their arrogance toward and dependence on those who work were loathsome. A great many, of course, have refused to face up to their new condition and have tried to resist or have left China. They felt demeaned and deprived. The old ideology was so deep that some even chose to die of hunger rather than "degrade" themselves by working. There are still many who are not entirely satisfied, who harbor secret thoughts about their superiority over the masses, who still disdain work and those who do it; some among them would go to great lengths to reverse the present situation. That is why the Chinese say that class struggle is far from over in China. But this attitude, which has been fought time and again, has been progressively diminishing. It becomes more difficult to sustain an inner sense of superiority when the outer trappings of it are rapidly being eradicated, and when the new heroes of the new society are people who don't mind getting their hands dirty.

Education had always been the avenue to exalted status. At the upper levels, many of the teachers themselves had been members of the privileged few. It was only to be expected that the schools would be one of the most intractable bastions for the old ideology. Only by having students work with those previously despised—go to factories and labor side by side with them at their machines, have them come into the schools and be the teachers, dig in their fields and live in their homes—only by these means could the new generations of students come to discover the workers' and peasants' intelligence, esteem their humanity, and learn genuinely to respect them.

It hasn't been easy. Even though this elitist outlook had been contested many times, the old ideology has a stubborn grip, and by the mid-1960s had again become quite problematic. This was in spite of the fact that, during the preceding years, several thousand half-work, half-study middle schools had been established. In addition, the sending of educated urban youth to rural areas to work had been going on for nearly a decade. Nevertheless, the desired lessons were not always being learned.

One of our guides, an engaging and ingenuous eighteen-year-old, told us about her experiences in a Peking primary school just before the Cultural Revolution. "You know, all youth should have gone to the countryside, but some of us were given privileged treatment. Even some of the older students didn't go or went only for a very short time. My class went to a commune only once, and we criticized everything there. The teacher warned us that everything was dirty on the communes, so we brought gloves with us and our own food—eggs, pork. We wouldn't eat the peasants' food and when we worked in the fields we wore gloves and we were so dainty, just picking around and making sure we stayed clean.

"When we got back to school, the teacher praised us and said we had worked very hard. We wrote a composition about it saying how good it was to do manual work with the peasants. But going to the countryside didn't really temper us because it was like camp or play. We had just gone through the motions of integrating with the peasants, but we really still looked down on them. The teacher taught us to study for our own prestige. She told us to serve the people, but actually taught us to be very selfish.''

The change that has come with the Cultural Revolution was evident wherever we went. In our discussion with the children and teachers at the primary school in Nanking we commented on the night-soil collecting that some of the children had been doing in the school garden and the potent smell that went with the job. "Many people in our country would consider that very unpleasant work. How is it decided who gets that job?'' we asked.

"Under the revisionist influence, the pupils used to compete to see whose hands would be whiter and softer, and whose clothes would be newer and more beautiful. But now that they integrate with the workers and peasants, the students compare themselves with each other to see who is capable of working the hardest. A new habit is taking shape in the minds of both pupils and teachers. Cherishing physical labor is regarded as glorious, and looking down on it as ugly. The teachers and pupils in the school feel the same. They vie among themselves to do the dirty work and sustain the hardships. It is true that we get our hands dirty, but we clean our minds.''

While appreciating the nobility of this sentiment, it would be naive of anyone to think that this problem has been solved once and for all in China, that every person everywhere in the country, given the choice, would, like the teachers and pupils of this school, elect to shovel human excrement. Such a utopian idea could result only from an underestimation of the depth of contempt in which manual work and manual workers were held in the Chinese mind of the past. This contempt has been too rooted and too pervasive for too long to be completely reversed within the short span of a quarter of a century. However, it has been seriously enough challenged so that "cherishing physical labor" holds a central place among the values being taught to young children in the schools.

This new attitude toward work undoubtedly accounts for the extremely low incidence of truancy at school and absenteeism at work. Work is not something to be avoided; it is coming to be seen more as a positive part of people's lives and less as a necessary evil. Surprisingly, the pace of work is leisurely and relaxed. It is conducted seriously and efficiently, yet without the tension and pressurized atmosphere that accompanies a too hectic speed. There does not seem to be any punchclock sense of time. Students, workers, and peasants work hard but they do not appear to be overworked. There is neither a hysterical obsession with their work, nor a frantic "get away" compulsion when it's over. Work appears to be enjoyed and easily taken in stride. People felt free, for example, to interrupt their work or study to discuss things with us, sometimes for quite extended periods, without ever sneaking looks at teachers or "foremen." They would also stay beyond normal work or school hours to continue our talks. When we asked how much time we had for our discussion at the primary school, one of our hosts answered, "As much as you like." We stayed until nearly six o'clock with about twenty children and almost as many teachers. No one looked like they felt imposed upon. Although the children had occasional little diversions (for instance, when one of the younger boys applauded at the wrong time, eliciting muffled giggles from the others), all were obviously interested and participated actively in the discussion; this was after a full day of work, study, and showing us around.

In schools and factories and on commune production teams, there are regular rest periods which are looked forward to as enjoyable high points in the day. Sometimes they are used for reading aloud and serious talk, sometimes for light relaxation. People catch up on their newspaper reading or discuss certain prominent articles. A lot of the time, of course, people just rest by themselves. Adults can often be seen catching catnaps; children play games. Or this time might be used to sit around in groups and chat or joke. Sometimes, they even put on short impromptu performances for each other, one or another group or individual getting up to sing or dance.[22]

One of the numbers in the performance we were given at the primary school, called "Dance in the Vegetable Garden," featured relaxation at the proper time. Children wearing straw hats, carrying hoes,

---

22. If someone is skilled at sleight of hand, that's a real treat because the Chinese apparently love magic. At the two acrobatic performances I attended, magicians were the main attractions. Except for the foreigners who were breathless at the spectacular acrobatic feats, everyone else in the audience seemed far more impressed with the magicians. They sat on the edges of their seats and watched closely, an incessant murmur rippling through the theater as people whispered to each other about what they thought the magician was up to; a brief silence before the climax of each trick; uproarious laughter when the magician succeeded in fooling us all; and loud, animated, appreciative discussion on all sides as everyone tried to find explanations—until the next trick, which again brought people to the edges of their seats in intense watching.

rakes, and watering cans sang and danced to the accompaniment of traditional musical instruments. They were planting a garden:

"Let's get the hoes."

"Let's get the rakes."

"You turn the soil; I'll bring the seed."

"You water; I'll bring the bucket," ran their lively musical interchange. And they raked, hoed, planted, watered, weeded, and sweated.

"Let's rest now. The most important thing is to have good health. When your body is not well, you can't get good results."

After a brief, pleasant rest, they got back to work with the same energy as before. If their results were an indication of their health, as they said, they must have been superkids. Up sprouted the most fantastic "crops" when they raised the props (which until now had been lying face down) presenting giant, bright orange pumpkins, huge stalks of golden corn, and brilliant red tomatoes almost as big as the children. A splendid crop indeed and well worth the effort!

There can be no question that the integration of productive work into the school curriculum is affecting students' outlooks at a very early age. The place of work in their lives is coming to be taken as a matter of course, not only as something that happens to them, but also as something they actively and voluntarily choose.

Before we left the captivating children at Chen Hsien Street Primary School, a boy came up to us with eight drawings done by children at the school. "We would like to give these to our friends here to present to the American children," he said. "The drawings are not very good in skill, but they will strengthen the friendship between the American children and the Chinese children." They were all lovely drawings, some in water color and others in crayon. As is always the case when children draw pictures of subjects of their own choosing, these drawings reflected those things that were important in their lives. Some were of children playing together; others showed children going to school, doing exercises, reading together. One of them, done by Yi Ling in grade two, was of a Little Red Soldier with rosy cheeks and a red ribbon in her hair. She was darning socks, and on the table were her sewing implements—a pincushion, scissors, and thread. The drawing was entitled "Work with Our Own Hands." Typically, the child in the drawing was smiling.

V: EVERY DAY IN EVERY WAY

So many deeds cry out to be done,
And always urgently;
The world rolls on,
Time presses.
Ten thousand years are too long,
Seize the day, seize the hour![1]

MAO TSE-TUNG

INTELLIGENCE

"In my class there are forty-eight students. Most of them do very well. Sometimes there are students who have difficulty, but by bringing forth their initiative, it can be changed. With much effort by them and with assistance from others, they can be educated to overcome their problems." The woman talking teaches English to fifteen and sixteen-year-old students at Pai Kwang Middle School in Shanghai. She appeared to be in her late fifties although her vigor and enthusiasm made judging her age not so much difficult as irrelevant. The school itself is a huge place with old buildings which used to be a police station before 1949. This school, which accommodates 2,800 students, is grayish and crowded— and exciting.

The teacher continued her narrative: "This student is an example," she said, indicating the boy sitting next to her. "He didn't like to study, so he was always misbehaving in class. He did very poorly in all his school work. Our marking system is based on 100, and 60 is a passing mark. In the past, he studied five courses, and the marks for all his courses put together totalled less than 60!"

I wondered if I knew for sure which boy she was talking about because the one she pointed out didn't appear to be the least embarrassed about being singled out in such an uncomplimentary fashion in front of his peers, teachers, and us.

"In class," she continued, "we discussed the past history of our revolutionary struggles, trying to show the relation of our studies to

---

1. Quoted in Joshua S. Horn, *Away with All Pests* (New York: Monthly Review Press, 1969), p. 5.

revolution so that the students would be encouraged to study well. We also take other steps to help those students who are temporarily lagging behind. So with this boy, for example, the other students and teachers would coach him after classes. Now he has caught up with the others. In the past he got zero in his English examination, and just recently he got 96! Perhaps Comrade Shi would like to tell you himself about his personal experiences.''

The smile that accompanied her introduction of Shi made it clear that calling him "comrade" was no mere ritual. Her obvious respect for her student made it clear why he had not been ill at ease. When the fifteen-year-old boy stood up, one thing was evident—Comrade Shi was short. As he started to speak, however, "standing tall" in every sense of the word, any concern about his height quickly disappeared from my mind.

"I didn't study well in primary school," he began in a clear voice, "so when I entered middle school, it was difficult, and the lessons seemed very deep to me. I could never understand what was going on, and so I thought, 'Let it be; it can't be helped. I just won't study any more.'

"But then I received a lot of revolutionary education from the teachers and students. We went to the countryside and factories, and when I saw with my own eyes how well things are developing in our country and how hard everyone works, I realized the importance of our studies, that we, the young generation, must share the responsibility of continuing the revolution. My study is not only for myself; it is for the revolution, for the people in the first place. I thought this question over and over, and gradually realized my mistake; I shouldn't 'let it be.'

"During this time, the students and teachers all helped me voluntarily. They would even come to my home to coach me after classes. My partner in the one-pair-red group[2] would come to my home after school to help me, even at night—sometimes up to eleven or twelve o'clock and once even up to two o'clock early in the morning!" (In China people generally go to bed around ten o'clock.) "His revolutionary spirit spurred me on. I thought, 'How can I ignore my studies when he is working so hard for my benefit?' So I became determined to work hard and overcome my difficulties."

When we tried to congratulate Shi, he quickly interrupted. "I still

---

2. The students in this school are organized into groups called "one-pair-red," two people who "work together to help each other become more revolutionary."

Everyone can achieve. A visitor talks with one pupil in a rural primary school while the others attend to the lesson.

am not doing as well as I should, so I have to try harder to make more progress, and,'' he added, his face, which until now had been very serious, softening into a broad smile, ''I will give you a report next time you visit China.''

This treatment of ''problem children'' not as incorrigibles but as full of potential to be developed is in line with our own highest educational ideals. The Chinese appear intent upon turning ideal into reality. Their concept of ''temporarily lagging behind'' leaves no room for labeling children as dull, slow, or stupid. They do not bifurcate the world into the smart and the dumb.

The Chinese sense of justice would be provoked at the idea that intelligence could be seen as a static entity that each person has so much of, no more, no less, like water in a glass; that anyone would be presumptuous enough to claim to be able to measure just how much each person has; and worst of all, that he would then feel free to shape another's future by suggesting that school and life aspirations not overshoot these false intellectual boundaries supposedly prescribed by nature.

The view that is considered most advanced in China today is that intelligence, like any other human attribute, lends itself to change. When I asked about intelligence, one teacher said, "Differences do exist in children's capabilities. But these capabilities are derived primarily from practice. We don't think that some children are born clever and others stupid. If a student does not do good work, we must first of all find out why. It is not because of stupidity. Maybe he isn't studying hard enough. If we know what the problem is, then we can help him more efficiently."

Depending on circumstances, then, a person can learn to think and act intelligently—or stupidly. Precisely because the middle school student Shi was seen as "temporarily lagging behind" rather than incapable of learning, he was treated as someone with passing problems who, with appropriate treatment, could overcome them. And he became more intelligent. He need no longer think of himself as a victim of a world he could never quite understand.

To look for the limitations in people's intelligence is, in a way, to create them. Growth can be squelched and potential can be stymied by taking such a negative perspective on human potential. A look at China's own past shows that, under wretched material conditions and with an ideology that branded most people as inferior, people were taught to lack confidence, to mystify the world, to plod along without purpose or understanding. Depending on their circumstances, people can learn to become stupid by being stupefied or they can learn the opposite. In China today, people are expected to think and behave intelligently, and, as is usual with expectations that are set forth consistently, they are learning to do so.

Ideas about human potential in any society are rooted in a conception of human nature. For example, in many countries, it is common to see all people as, by nature, competitive and greedy; to see women as inherently weak-willed, emotional, and fickle; to see blacks as intellectually inferior; and to see some people as naturally less capable than others. An extensive vocabulary of clichés reveals this viewpoint that sees human capacities as fixed.[3] The implication is that there are certain

---

3. Here are a few: "A tiger can't change its stripes"; "Water reaches its own level"; "Like father, like son"; "You can't teach an old dog new tricks"; "The apple doesn't fall far from the tree"; "You can't change a sow's ear into a silk purse"; "Blood will tell"; "Cream always rises to the top"; "Once a ———, always a ———."

things that can and cannot be done and people should learn to restrict their aspirations and activities to the possible. In its most extreme form, this outlook takes on the coloration of cynicism. It disparages ideas of human betterment. A cynical outlook is one that sees as naive any efforts to undo or transcend the "rules" of human nature.

The Chinese would say that people who think this way are mistaking capitalist ideology for human nature. Capitalist society, as they see it, is by definition composed of a hierarchy of winners and losers; many losers are required in order for there to be relatively few winners. But since that sounds too painfully unjust for societies that claim to be democratic, an ideology is needed that will obscure and justify this unequal state of affairs. What better than one that attributes disagreeable characteristics to nature? If we are born selfish and competitive, no more can be done about it than about the fact that we are born with noses and knees. People are destined to be stupid or intelligent just as they will be short or tall.

A not too dissimilar view of human nature used to be perpetuated in China: some people were thought to be superior—they were the wise and the virtuous; others were inferior—the stupid and immoral. The important thing was for the inferior people to be unmistakably convinced of their inferiority and to never strive beyond it. China's many peasant rebellions, especially when they failed as they usually did, have been interpreted by former ruling classes as foolhardy attempts to upset a natural order. Those few that did succeed were likewise attributed to human nature as the victor legitimated his claim to the throne by citing his "Mandate from Heaven." What then mattered most, as the Chinese now see it, was for the class forces in society to remain static.

> Dirty frogs want to feed on crane,
> Poor scum hope for great happenings in vain.
> Look at yourself in some ditch water, do!
> What great deeds can be done by the likes of you?
> Can snow fall in mid-July?
> Can the sun rise in the western sky?[4]

The present-day Chinese say that all such notions about what human nature is and is not and about what human beings are and are not

---

4. Landlord Ts'ui, from the opera, "Wang Kuei and Li Hsiang-hsiang." Quoted in William Hinton, *Fanshen: A Documentary of Revolution in a Chinese Village* (New York: Monthly Review Press, 1966), p. 26.

capable of achieving are just so many fictions designed to prop up obsolete social systems. "Is there such a thing as human nature?" asks Mao.

Of course there is. But there is only human nature in the concrete, no human nature in the abstract. In class society there is only human nature of a class character; there is no human nature above classes. We uphold the human nature of the proletariat and of the masses of the people, while the landlord and bourgeois classes uphold the human nature of their own classes, only they do not say so but make it out to be the only human nature in existence.[5]

Thus each class creates its own idea of human nature.

According to the Chinese, it is the new proletarian view of what constitutes human nature that now prevails in their country. Certainly there remain strong vestiges of the old ideology but people are expected to struggle against them. That is what the anti-Confucian campaign was all about. And with each successive struggle the Chinese people are drastically altering their perceptions of human capabilities. Their conviction is that, with diligence and determination, the working people can conquer and transcend those things which appeared impossible in the past. They need no longer be bound by the old fabrications about their unchangeable nature. To the Chinese this is not some fancy theory that has been conjured up for them. They point out how they have been living it and proving it over and over again for the last quarter-century. Ex-prostitutes now hold responsible jobs; previously illiterate peasants have high government posts; women are productive and self-respecting members of society; former landlords till the soil without loss of dignity. By "studying hard" students like Shi can "make progress every day" and need not lag behind. There are nearly as many examples as there are political, economic, and social situations to prove them. People in China no longer doubt that they are capable of change; they can improve, grow, develop. In a word, all people are educable.

The Chinese are striving to create a situation of real equality through the educational system. The stress is on equality of condition as opposed to equality of opportunity. Some people—for example, children from minority or poor peasant backgrounds—have histories and even present circumstances of much lesser affluence than children of the

---

5. Mao Tse-tung, "Talks at the Yenan Forum on Literature and Art," *Selected Works of Mao Tse-tung,* 4 vols. (Peking: Foreign Languages Press, 1961–65), vol. 3, p. 90.

formerly privileged classes. They need more opportunities, more assistance, if they are to succeed. To simply provide equality of opportunity would, by the Chinese reckoning, only continue and increase already existing inequalities. Had Shi not been given more opportunities than the others, he could not have hoped to become equal. Strange as it may sound, the Chinese are attempting to move toward equality through what might look to us like inequality of opportunity.

Since their revolutionary efforts are all geared toward the eventual elimination of classes, the Chinese disparage any hierarchical arrangement of society. No one, they say, deserves to be considered superior to anyone else, regardless of abilities. It is for this reason that the very idea of "giftedness," of a special intelligence unattainable by most people, is also thoroughly renounced by the Chinese. Part of their criticism of Lin Piao is connected to what they consider his unscientific conception of intelligence, a throwback to the Confucian ethic:

> While completely denying that knowledge is the reflection in the mind of the external world and that it comes from social practice, Lin Piao advertised wherever and whenever he could that a person was born with "natural ability" and "special endowments" or was born "a genius" and alleged that knowledge and talent were "innate in the womb."[6]

This viewpoint is regarded by the Chinese as dangerous because it furnishes the ideological justification for perpetuating inequality. It paves the way for condoning privilege for those who regard themselves as intellectually superior.

This does not mean that the Chinese do not recognize excellence. On the contrary, they reward it with praise and esteem, provided that it is put in the service of the people. That is what is meant by socialist emulation. However, people with unusual skills or abilities who expect special privileges or who use their excellence to pursue only personal goals are not considered good socialists. Those who excel are expected rather to take on additional responsibilities. So, for instance, good students should not only develop their own abilities but also help those who "lag behind." It is those who apply their excellence to furthering the general welfare that are most looked up to.

It is how excellence is used rather than the excellence itself that is

---

6. Hsin Feng, " 'Upside Down' Philosophy and Capitalist Restoration—Criticizing Lin Piao's Bourgeois Idealism," *Peking Review* (January 25, 1974), p. 5.

important. Therefore, lesser degrees of competence that are well motivated and directed would be viewed as more worthy than greater competence which is less purely motivated and directed. Mao, in his essay
on Norman Bethune,[7] has clearly stated that the amount of social contribution a person is able to make is not as significant as the fact of the
contribution.

> We must all learn the spirit of absolute selflessness from him. With this
> spirit everyone can be very useful to the people. A man's ability may be
> great or small, but if he has this spirit, he is already noble-minded and
> pure, a man of moral integrity and above vulgar interests, a man who is
> of value to the people.[8]

CREATIVITY

Like their idea of intelligence, the Chinese also have a conception of
creativity that is unfamiliar to many outsiders. In our society, for example, creativity is seen primarily in artistic terms. The creative people are
the painters, musicians, writers, actors. These are the talented, the
gifted; they possess creativity while the rest of us have little or none.
The inborn human nature theory is applied to creativity even more
stringently than it is to intelligence. Creativity is totally mystifying in its
origins and development: some few people simply "have" it; most do
not. If it is there, it will inevitably bloom regardless of the nourishment
it receives or is denied. By the same token, for those who supposedly
lack creativity, nothing will help. If there is no seed in the soil, no
amount of sunshine and rain will produce a flower. It is seldom imagined that people can learn to be creative as they can learn other things,
that it lends itself to development like everything else.

---

7. Norman Bethune was a Canadian doctor who went to China in 1938 during the
Anti-Japanese War. He conscientiously attended the wounded in the guerrilla regions.
Less than two years later, weakened from self-imposed overwork, he died of septicemia
(blood poisoning) contracted when he cut himself during an operation. He is revered in
China as a model of internationalism. Mao's short essay, "In Memory of Norman Beth-
une," written to commemorate his death, is one of the three most widely read works in
China. For more about China's Canadian hero, see Ted Allan and Sydney Gordon, *The
Scalpel, the Sword: The Story of Doctor Norman Bethune,* rev. ed. (Toronto: McClelland
and Stewart, 1971).
8. Mao Tse-tung, "In Memory of Norman Bethune," *Selected Works,* vol. 2, p. 338.

The Chinese differ markedly from us in both their definition of creativity and their explanation of where it originates. To them, creativity can be expressed in a myriad of forms. An artist might certainly be creative, but that is just one kind of creativity. The peasants who figure out how to increase their crop yield, the workers who innovate new machinery, the neighborhood residents who come up with new insights on how to tackle community problems, students who take initiative in their studies—all these people are no less creative than the artists. Great emphasis is put on having all this creativity equally recognized and valued.

In China, it is often said that down through the ages real creativity has invariably come from the masses, the working people—"the creators of all of life's wealth." The celebrated and priceless Ming vases were, after all, not the "product" of an emperor (any more than the pyramids were the "product" of a pharaoh). They were the glorious result of endless hours of experimentation and toil by working men and artisans who conferred upon that dynasty an aura of beauty it hardly deserved. By contrast, the ruling classes, those who luxuriated in the wealth created by others, were more inclined to self-indulgences.

The Chinese do not any longer perceive the world as a small luminous island of special, sensitive people surrounded by a sea of thick-skinned pedestrian philistines. Everyone, they believe, can be creative, because creativity, like other accomplishments, is a result of experience. It is a learned, not innate quality; rational, not mysterious. All that is necessary is for conditions to be favorable to its development. One of these conditions, a fundamental one, is cooperation. Here, too, there is a major difference in our two perspectives on creativity. Creativity to the Chinese is not a purely individual affair, a tempestuous force that inhabits the artist and with which he (rarely she) struggles alone and in isolation from others until his creative spirit finds expression and bursts forth into the world. They do not see creativity as private. Creativity to them comes from the combined intelligence and efforts of many people. Not only is everyone capable of creativity, but they should all work hard to develop it, to learn to become more creative, because that is how they will collectively and individually progress—through the initiative and creativity of the people. The need to contribute to the solution of shared problems is the basis for the development of creativity, a creativity which the Chinese see as without limit.

Perhaps the difference in outlooks is most clearly revealed in the following statements. The first was made by a noted American political scientist, former Cornell University professor, and author, a man who is considered liberal in his views. He puts in unadorned terms a cultural viewpoint which others tend to phrase more delicately, but which, regardless of how it is expressed, is one that prevails.

> Most people are ordinary. And ordinary people are ordinary, regardless of the time or society or setting in which they live. Moreover, ordinary people are relatively unintelligent, incapable of abstraction or imagination, lacking any special qualities of talent or creativity. They are for the most part without drive or perseverance; easily discouraged, they prefer the paths of security. Whether slave or serf or sweated worker, most people in the past have displayed these traits. And most who inhabit the present, whether scientist or suburbanite or sophisticate, continue to manifest these tendencies.
>
> This is the human condition. . . . In any society all save an exceptional few will lack the capacity for attainments that transcend the mediocre.[9]

Here are some of the things that Mao, the ideological leader of China, says on the same subject:

> The people, and the people alone, are the motive force of world history.[10]

> One [a leader] certainly cannot make an investigation, or do it well . . . without shedding the ugly mantle of pretentiousness and becoming a willing pupil. It has to be understood that the masses are the real heroes, while we ourselves are often childish and ignorant, and without this understanding it is impossible to acquire even the most rudimentary knowledge.[11]

> Every comrade must be helped to understand that as long as we rely on the people, believe firmly in the inexhaustible creative power of the masses, and hence trust and identify ourselves with them . . . we can . . . overcome every difficulty.[12]

9. Andrew Hacker, *The End of the American Era,* (New York: Atheneum, 1970), pp. 161–62.

10. Mao Tse-tung, "On Coalition Government," *Selected Works,* vol. 3, p. 257.

11. Mao Tse-tung, "Preface and Postscript to *Rural Surveys,*" *Selected Works,* vol. 3, p. 12.

12. Mao Tse-tung, "On Coalition Government," *Selected Works,* vol. 3, p. 316.

CURRICULUM

A mere listing of the courses studied in the schools does not, by itself, give adequate representation to the great innovations occurring in the schools of China. A number of the course titles sound similar to those of relatively developed school systems all over the world.[13] A better indicator of the unusual character of the Chinese educational experiment is to be found in the underlying principle that guides the construction of curriculum and the content of educational programs both for the schools and for society as a whole. This principle, called "all-rounded development," sees education as more than intellectual training. Citing their own past history and the dangers of revisionism, Chinese educators frequently point out the shortcomings of "one-sidedness" in education. In its elongated form, the principle states that education must enable each person "to develop morally, intellectually,

---

13. The work in the primary schools centers on Chinese language, mathematics, music, art, and physical culture. These are constants throughout the primary grades. (The kindergartens, which large numbers of the primary school children have attended, especially in the cities, supply some advance preparation by teaching the children several characters and a bit of simple arithmetic.) Other subjects are politics (starting in grade one in the schools where I inquired) and general knowledge, which incorporates productive work in agriculture and industry, history, geography, and science. Sometimes a foreign language—very often English—is given. Military training is frequently included as part of the physical culture program. At this stage, combat skills are not usually taught, the emphasis being on learning from the PLA and developing discipline and organization. There is some variation in the grade levels at which these subjects are introduced.

With some differences from one school to the next, the secondary curriculum generally consists of: Chinese language and literature; mathematics, physics, and chemistry which are often offered as part of the fundamentals of industrial knowledge course; biology which is usually linked to agricultural fundamental knowledge; hygiene or physiology; a foreign language; politics; history; geography; physical culture and military training; revolutionary art and music.

At a comprehensive higher institution like Peking University, most courses taken by a student are within her or his area of specialization, but certain ones are common to all—Marxist-Leninist philosophy and economics and the history of the Communist Party. In addition to the regular courses, Peking University holds weekly general meetings in the social sciences and natural sciences which everyone may attend to broaden their knowledge beyond their fields of specialization.

There are a few schools that specialize in music, art, and dance for students who show keen interest and skill in these areas. An emphasis in these specializations supplements the basic curriculum. Admission to such schools, some of which take students from primary through middle school, is by recommendation from schools, communes, or factories. (There are other special schools for children who require special teaching and care. The Chinese are known, for example, for their work in the deaf-mute schools where acupuncture, among other techniques, is widely in use.)

and physically and become a worker with both socialist consciousness and culture."[14]

The industrial and agricultural fundamental knowledge course seems to incorporate all three kinds of development very well. Other subjects achieve varying degrees of integration of moral, intellectual, and physical development but generally tend to emphasize one or another of the three. It is in the total school program, however, that the balance is to be achieved and the objective of producing working people with "socialist consciousness and culture" realized.

Moral development very largely involves learning to comprehend and embrace socialist principles.[15] It is an integral part of virtually all courses and teaching materials all the way through school. Intellectual development, seen as the learning that results from the interplay between theory and practice, is of course also stressed throughout. An intellectual emphasis of a bookish nature had always been the center of educational endeavors in China's past, the change now being in a greater connection to practice and in more balanced importance relative to the other two forms of development.

The third in this trio, physical development, has an unusually prominent place in the curriculum compared with other school systems in most parts of the world. Several hours a week are devoted to physical education classes and regular exercise periods. This is in addition to the extracurricular athletics in the ongoing school and neighborhood programs, and to the physical activities connected with the practical work of the common knowledge course. Physical development is not limited to a select group. Both girls and boys at all levels of education participate, although there tends to be sexual segregation for these activities among the older students.

Like moral and intellectual development, it is now considered of utmost importance that people of all ages, but especially youths, main-

---

14. Mao Tse-tung, "On the Correct Handling of Contradications Among the People," *Selected Readings from the Works of Mao Tse-tung* (Peking: Foreign Languages Press, 1971), p. 459. It has been pointed out to me that although this is the statement that appears in the Chinese translations, it is misleading. The original Chinese, *lao dong zhe,* meaning a person who works or a laboring person, has imprecisely been translated as "a worker," which could give a false impression if taken in the Marxist sense of industrial worker. The statement instead refers to any working person.

15. Moral development is an essential feature of political education, the purpose, content, and handling of which are discussed in Chapter 6.

Children do morning exercises under the leadership of a fellow pupil.

tain physical fitness.[16] This is a fairly new emphasis in the curriculum. Mao stressed its importance in 1953 when he said:

> New China must care for her youth and show concern for the growth of the younger generation. Young people have to study and work, but they are at the age of physical growth. Therefore, full attention must be paid both to their work and study and to their recreation, sport, and rest.[17]

Apparently, however, his words were very often forgotten before

---

16. For many foreign visitors, the most exciting time in China's cities is around five-thirty or six o'clock in the morning. Groups of workers can be seen jogging down the streets; in the squares, schoolchildren practice the martial arts and old people do the intricate and highly controlled movements of *tai ji* and other traditional exercises; young people play badminton on makeshift courts put together by stringing nets between the trees on the sidewalks. Exercising, in one form or another, seems to be the first order of business for many Chinese every day.

17. Mao Tse-tung, "Talk at the Reception for the Presidium of the Second National Congress of the Youth League" Quoted in *Quotations from Chairman Mao Tse-tung* (Peking: Foreign Languages Press, 1966), p. 293.

the Cultural Revolution when students were greatly overworked. At a talk in 1964, Mao scolded his audience:

> At present, there is too much studying going on, and this is exceedingly harmful. There are too many subjects at present, and the burden is too heavy, it puts middle-school and university students in a constant state of tension. . . .
> The syllabus should be chopped in half. The students should have time for recreation, swimming, playing ball, and reading freely outside their course work. . . . It won't do for students just to read books all day, and not to go in for cultural pursuits, physical education, and swimming, not be able to run around. . . .[18]

We frequently heard stories about that period when students were expected to do nothing but study. By the time they reached university they would be spending twenty-five or more hours a week in classes, frantically copying every word of the lectures, with little or no discussion. They exhausted themselves outside of class trying to memorize the lectures—with not much time, energy, or inclination to think or talk about the ideas.

The heavy work load and the meaninglessness of so much of that study were attributed to the revisionist influence that encouraged students to study for personal advancement. Therefore, these problems were among the prominent aspects of the educational system that were attacked during the Cultural Revolution. From what I could gather, conscientious efforts are now made to give students plenty of time to think, discuss, and enjoy themselves. While the amount of work has diminished considerably, commitment to that work seems to have greatly deepened.

Physical activities and rest are interspersed throughout the school day. At Pai Kwang Middle School, we stopped in on a class where students were doing eye protection exercises by massaging the acupuncture points near their eyes. Later, in conversation with a young man in his mid-twenties who had studied English in university, I mentioned this and commented on how few young people I had seen wearing glasses. "Yes," he said, looking at me through his rimless spectacles as I gazed back at him through mine, "the students' health is now well looked after, and they take care to guard against eyestrain. Those of us who

---

18. Mao Tse-tung, "Remarks at the Spring Festival," February 13, 1964. Quoted in Stuart Schram, ed., John Chinnery and Tieyun, trans., *Mao Tse-tung Unrehearsed, Talks and Letters: 1956–1971* (Harmondsworth, Middlesex: Penguin Books, 1974), pp. 203–4.

were students before the Cultural Revolution," he continued, indicating himself and his similarly bespectacled friend seated nearby, "worked too hard, and now our eyesight is not very good. We agree with your proverb," he added with a twinkle, "that 'all work and no play makes Jack a dull boy.'"

While the concept of all-rounded development is the general guideline for the schools of China, the specifics of what this means in practice vary considerably. At all levels and in most areas of study, there is wide diversity in the curriculum. Contrary to a popular impression outside of China that "under communism" all children in the same grade are reading the same page in the same textbook on the same day throughout the country, there are very few statements about the curriculum that hold uniformly. This is true even of those practices that many other countries have centralized, such as externally composed standardized exams and national diplomas. People in China are trying to consolidate and implement the lessons of the Cultural Revolution and thus experimentation and initiative are widely encouraged. The curriculum also provides for the study of subjects that cater to the needs of specific localities and conditions. Therefore, not all the same subjects are taught in all schools, nor are they given the same emphasis.

Teaching materials are generally prepared by research groups at provincial, county, or municipal levels. Regular classroom teachers are members of such groups, and they take to their meetings the ideas of the teachers and students in their schools. In addition, the department responsible for the preparation of educational materials actively solicits teacher and student opinion. Workers and peasants also often have representation in such groups. By university, and occasionally even middle school, students might be working in teams with professors and workers or peasants, not only in drafting teaching materials but sometimes in designing the total curriculum for a particular area of specialization. [19]

With such an experimental approach, mistakes are made, but gener-

---

19. There is apparently much local initiative in generating new materials at all educational levels. For example, when I was in Shanghai in 1975, students and teachers in all the primary and middle schools were using their own materials—songs, poems, paintings—to learn about the heroism of a young Shanghai girl who had sacrificed her own life to save another child. Although the actual event had occurred only two-and-a-half weeks before, by the time I arrived in the city her deed had already become central to the curriculum, with abundant school-produced materials in use to teach this very important lesson.

ally results are not fully accepted until they have been well tested. Given the revolutionary view of progress as stemming from the endless flow of practice to theory and back to practice, it seems unlikely that the Chinese will settle upon inflexible school procedures. And given their belief that people learn by doing, that they should be bold and take initative in exploring new possibilites, one could venture to predict that some degree of experimentation will remain as a permanent feature of their educational system. Needs change, people understand things more deeply over time, everything can be improved; curriculum and methods must evolve accordingly.

While decentralization and experimentation make for a great deal of local variation, there is considerable cooperation at the same time. For instance, in industry ordinary workers might concentrate on problems at their own factory—perhaps giving a part of their time to developing new machinery, working out better production techniques, or discussing improved methods of self-management—but they would also communicate the knowledge or information they gained to other factories as well. There is no such thing, for example, as a patent in China. If advanced machinery is innovated in a particular factory, no individual or small group owns the idea. The design is channelled through more centralized agencies and disseminated to factories doing similar work in other localities. The objective is for everyone to learn from the best efforts of others and to progress together. So too in education. Good ideas are shared, not hoarded. A notable example can be found in the Kirin program. Taking its name from a province in North East China, a county revolutionary committee in that province designed a fully elaborated program in 1969 which was considered so excellent that it was widely publicized and discussed, with people in each locality weighing and evaluating its applicability to their own circumstances and needs. Many of the current educational practices commonly found in China originated with the Kirin recommendations.

One of the more significant curriculum changes with the Cultural Revolution is the shortening of the number of years of schooling at all levels above preschool. It was felt by many students and teachers that much of the material being taught was irrelevant, out of date, unduly repetitive, overly intellectualized, and pedantic. A professor at Peking University complained that before the Cultural Revolution, students were overburdened with courses in an attempt "to train them to know everything just like encyclopedias rather than just giving them a basic

education so that they could analyze and solve problems themselves.''
Another professor at Sun Yat-sen Medical College said that their old
textbooks ''devoted several hundred thousand words to the history of
famous physicians, when they had graduated from university, where
they had gotten their degrees, and other such useless information.''

The Chinese want the schools to be more closely geared to the
general line for socialist construction:[20] ''Go all out, aim high, and
achieve greater, faster, better and more economical results in building
socialism.'' They ask: why waste six years on complicated, unnecessary material when urgently needed doctors can be just as well trained—
perhaps better—in three years? Mao's educational principle of ''fewer
and better'' has been taken seriously. After the Cultural Revolution
people all over the country began discussing what the schools should be
teaching in order to better fulfill the goal of an all-rounded socialist
education. Teams of teachers, cadres, workers, peasants, and students
got together to analyze existing curricula and to eliminate those parts
they considered unnecessary. Primary schools have been cut from a six-
year to a five-year program. Middle school education, which also used
to be six years, has been reduced to four in some places, five in others.
University, formerly five or six years in length, now is usually three.[21]

Not all of the changes are aimed at simply cutting down the amount
of work covered. ''Fewer'' is only half of Mao's directive. The other,
''better,'' requires critical and painstaking analysis of the what and how
of everything that is taught. This has brought qualitative changes in
many subjects, changes which could not always mean ''fewer.'' In the
medical colleges, for example, more material has been included on
traditional Chinese medicine, which, before the Cultural Revolution
was taught little, having been discredited, the Chinese claim, by the
revisionists.

The principle of ''fewer and better'' has not meant simply scrapping
everything old or foreign on the grounds that all such things are by

---

20. The term socialist construction refers to socialist economic development.

21. In actuality, there is usually even less formal class time than is apparent from
figures showing the amount of time students spend in school. For instance, a typical
school day in the primary and middle schools generally lasts five to six hours. However,
part of each day is used for exercises and rest breaks and, in a great many schools, for
activities after class. School is in session for six days a week, but in some schools students
have special programs one or two afternoons while teachers prepare lessons, have meetings, etc. And while the school year lasts ten months, this includes the time spent in
productive labor.

definition "decadent" or "reactionary." Though this position was advocated among some groups during the height of the Cultural Revolution, it has since been condemned as "ultra-leftist." The opposite is said to have been a more common problem, what the Chinese refer to as the "worshipping" of all things old or foreign—the revisionist line. The revolutionary response to these two positions, both seen as extreme and incorrect, is: "Make the past serve the present and foreign things serve China." This is to be done by "discarding the dross and selecting the essential, eliminating the false and retaining the true."

METHODS

Much can be learned even from "the dross" and "the false." In the large library at Peking University, there are many volumes on communism that would today unquestionably be considered revisionist and many works in the social sciences that the Chinese say are bourgeois and reactionary; there are Buddhist scriptures, writings by idealist philosophers, etc., the same books that many "China-watchers" claimed were destroyed by the Red Guards in the late 1960s.

"From our point of view," said a philosophy professor at Peking University, "truth and nonsense coexist. For example, idealist philosophers have exerted a powerful influence, so we must let the students know some theory of idealism. Only in that way can they be clear on the struggle between idealism and materialism.

"Before the Cultural Revolution, the students also studied both, but too often passively and uncritically. The teachers introduced Marxist-Leninist works divorced from practice, so that it became dull, purely academic knowledge. It lost its power. You know that Marxism holds that we must not only understand society and be able to explain the objective world; it is more important to use knowledge, to apply it in order to actively change society. But because of the way Marxism-Leninism used to be taught, there was no revolutionary spirit, no dynamism, and so the students missed its real significance. At the same time, the idealist works were taught, but uncritically. The teachers thought they were being objective, but to be uncritical is not real objectivity. They were actually propagandizing feudal and capitalist idealism in their classes; they were turning on a green light to capitalist philosophies."

Interestingly enough, his very appearance seemed to add weight to the arguments he was presenting. This professor, like all the others I met at Peking University, was something of a surprise. Throughout our time in China, whenever we asked our guides questions of a philosophical nature, they would always end their explanations with a comment such as, "But maybe that doesn't answer your question very well. We will be visiting Peking University soon and you can ask some people there; they will be able to tell you more." As a result, I was prepared to meet some rather awesome figures. Although the weather was hot the day we went to the University, it did not quite seem to warrant the beads of sweat that gathered on our interpreter's brow as he strained to be precise. All of our guides were more intent than usual; Peking University was a place where they could expect to learn a lot and where teachers were held in the highest esteem. Only our most skillful interpreters translated that day—the ideas might be complex and they wanted to get them just right. The youngest and most inexperienced one was not working, yet she never relaxed her attention, listening first to one language and then to its translation, dictionary always at the ready. But, instead of intimidating academics, we were most pleasantly faced with simple, unassuming people like this philosophy professor who, from his manner and outgoingness, looked more suited to field or factory than to the lecturer's podium.

He continued. "Now we do things differently. We put emphasis on analyzing and criticizing these idealist works so that the students will understand them more deeply and develop a proletarian theory. The students read certain pertinent works, and we assign them questions that will help them expose contradictions in the readings. Then they hold discussions among themselves relating their readings to practice. The discussions help them to identify the contradictions more fully. Following that, the teacher meets with the students and discusses whatever questions and problems they have encountered. Together we analyze concrete situations and examples, and eventually solve the contradictions. Then we have a summary through mass debate. This way of doing things stimulates the students and they become more active; their thinking is alive, vivid, and dynamic. Their study is no longer passive or boring and unrelated to the real problems in society. They feel anxious to solve problems. Their motivation to study also increases."

The Chinese strongly disclaim that teachers and textbooks can be neutral and nonpartisan. They agree with Mao that "every kind of thinking, without exception, is stamped with the brand of a class.''[22] To teach about idealism without condemning it is, to the Chinese, to condone it. The ideology of one class or another is reflected in everything taught in the schools. The question is: which class? It is the difference between reading four-year-olds fairy tales about princesses or true stories about heroes who distinguished themselves by serving the people; between math problems that ask students to calculate bank interest or crop yield; between having advanced microbiology students do "pure" research in labs at universities isolated from the community or having them get together with iron refinery workers to study the use of sulfur-metabolizing bacteria for removing sulfur from low-grade iron ore.

While the method of self-study and the expectation of intellectual independence on the part of students, especially the older ones, have been encouraged by revolutionary educators for some time, they have received renewed emphasis with the Cultural Revolution. The same professor talked about how the more enlightened methods evolved: "You know that imperial education has had a very long history in China. For many, many centuries students just crammed and memorized. It didn't matter whether they understood anything or not. Anyway, it was thought that the teacher was master and knew everything while the students knew nothing. So they had to recite abstract theories by heart. We were also influenced by capitalist education which began with the Industrial Revolution in England, and, more recently, by Russian revisionist education. Such ways of teaching and learning don't die easily, and it was impossible for the proletarian revolution in education to be successful in a few years. So despite some gains, many of us continued to use some of the same old methods. The teacher would just lecture from the platform and the students would copy everything down mechanically.''

His eye caught the tape recorder we were using to record the discussion, and he added, pointing to it, ''Just like that tape recorder. We call that the old injection method. We thought we could inject knowledge into students like serum into a patient.''

The students I spoke to were understandably happy about moving away from the old injection method and were openly enthusiastic about the advantages of the self-study approach. A first year university student

---

22. Mao Tse-tung, ''On Practice,'' *Selected Works,* vol. 1, p. 296.

said, "Some books are very difficult to understand, but we must overcome our difficulties and read them again and again and have discussions to learn from each other. Sometimes we have to refer to other materials for help. These books express important things and are very helpful to us. But I think the more important thing is for us to learn not to always rely on the materials or the teachers but to think by ourselves, to use our own brains. Otherwise we will not be able to understand the real meaning of theories and their connection to practice, and we will not be able to solve the problems we encounter."

Self-study is most commonly used in the universities, but not exclusively. It is also in evidence in the middle schools. A middle school teacher of literature told me how she used this method in her class.

"The students were going to study a poem written by Chairman Mao about snail fever.[23] It describes how the people who suffered from the disease in the past were very poor and how the situation has changed since liberation.

"The students started by reading the poem. Then they went to the countryside to make a direct investigation among the people who had suffered from snail fever in the past. They split into different groups and went out among the peasants; they stayed with the peasants, asked them questions, and listened to their stories. They found out about the life cycle of the parasite, how it affected people, and the great suffering it brought; they learned how the peasants have struggled to fight this terrible disease. When they returned to the classroom, each group selected a representative to describe what they had learned. Their experiences made their discussion vivid. Then they discussed the poem and

---

23. Snail fever, or schistosomiasis, is a disease caused by parasites that lodge in the intestines and the liver. It can cause hardening of the liver, distension and severe hemorrhage of the stomach, stunted growth, impotency, and death. According to Dr. Joshua Horn, an English surgeon who practiced medicine in China from 1954 to 1969, there are a quarter of a billion sufferers of schistosomiasis in Third World countries. Its popular name derives from the fact that the snail is the parasite's host during part of its life cycle. It is also sometimes known as the unconquerable disease because it is so difficult to combat. In the areas affected in China, there has been a massive campaign to eliminate the disease, especially at the snail stage of the parasite's cycle. This has involved intensive education, dogged determination, and the sheer hard work of searching out the tiny snail shells, less than one-quarter inch long. Through these means the Chinese have nearly conquered the once-dreaded "unconquerable disease." Joshua Horn's fascinating and readable book, *Away With All Pests* (New York: Monthly Review Press, 1969), tells the whole story. Written for the layperson, it is highly recommended reading for anyone interested in China's remarkable achievements in medical care and public health.

Learning takes place outside the classroom. A Shanghai teacher with students at the dockyards for an art lesson.

because of their practical, direct experience, they could understand it more profoundly. Using this method, students can develop creative viewpoints. They learn to analyze and solve problems, to think independently."

I remarked that in this situation the students were actually the teachers and I asked, "When students take leadership like that in teaching, is it usually initiated by the students themselves or assigned by the teacher?"

"Well, I think the teachers should take responsibility for planning, so we design the projects. But very often we will invite students to help us, and we are all very happy to work together. So it really is a combination—the teachers take the overall responsibility for planning the lessons and the students help us."

Hers appears to be a representative viewpoint. The Chinese would not accept the position of encouraging kids to "do their own thing," to pursue whatever interests them in school. They would see this as both "bourgeois" and "idealist." Bourgeois, because it puts self-interest ahead of community interest. To do "your own thing" suggests that it is different from and more important than anyone else's, what the Chinese call selfishness. To serve the people well, personal interests must to the greatest possible extent be in harmony with those things that are good for the group. When they are not, a revolutionary will forfeit the former.

Idealist, because by implication this attitude attributes mysterious origins to self-interests. Where does someone's "own thing" come. from, the Chinese would ask. Is it inherent or learned? The ideology of "doing your own thing" hints that everyone's "thing" is different from everyone else's regardless of people's class, experience, or conditions, that people just happen to have certain "things" or others. Inexplicable, so, by implication, they seem to be inborn. If they are not common or shared, but are instead unique concerns, it logically follows that only the person with a particular "thing" can express or develop it, and that the only help anyone else who does not also happen to have "it" can offer is to leave that person alone—also, by the Chinese definition, bourgeois.

As materialists, the Chinese would unhesitatingly place this outlook on the nonsense tray of their truth and nonsense scale. People's thoughts, actions, and interests, they say, are learned. Some of these are good, meaning beneficial to others and oneself, while others are not. Those which are good should be developed and expressed; those which are bad should be discouraged. However, people cannot develop the good things and replace the bad easily or well if they operate in isolation from each other. Everyone benefits by outside assistance, and teachers, because of their experience, are among those who can provide the needed leadership and direction for young people. To deny that leadership would be considered irresponsible. Therefore, according to the Chinese, the work of the schools must be rational; it must be the result of planning, and teachers have the primary responsibility as planners. The role of students as planning assistants and as critics (in both the positive and negative sense) can help to guard against teacher authoritarianism.

As one teacher put it, "We can't teach students everything, and we shouldn't. Our job is to help supply them with a framework so that they will be equipped to analyze any material and solve any problems them-selves.'' This kind of approach was discussed at every school we vis-ited, from primary through university, and was visible in most of the classes we observed. However, it seemed to me that in the primary schools more traditional methods were in evidence. I mentioned this to a fourth grade teacher: "Yes, it's true. When the children learn to read and write Chinese they must first learn some things by rote. There are many characters and in the first few grades they must learn several hundred every year. Some words are very difficult and must be memo-rized and repeated often. Otherwise the children will not be able to read the characters and form them correctly. They must read some things aloud because this is the easiest way to correct pronunciation.

"But memorizing and reciting are not suitable for other studies. In arithmetic lessons or in the basic knowledge of industrial and agri-cultural production class, the children spend more time in solving prob-lems. In their lessons on politics, they learn to analyze theories. Recitation is of no use. You may be able to recall a paragraph but if you are unable to apply it, to use it for understanding a problem and solving it, it's useless. No amount of recitation will help you." In her school, at least, the old inflexible methods appeared most often in the Chinese language classes, but this is not necessarily true of all schools. The stiff methods inherited from the preliberation tradition, whereby students memorized the Confucian classics by reciting them in unison over and over again, have not yet been fully eradicated. There is a great deal of unevenness from one school to the next.[24] But from my vantage point as

---

24. William Hinton, in a talk in 1972, confirmed this unevenness in methods prac-ticed at different schools from the experience of his own three children who had attended both an urban and a rural primary school during their stay in China a year earlier. In the Peking school, the teachers set a rigid atmosphere, relied heavily on rote learning, and established strict expectations: "There are in various parts of China unreconstructed schools. How come all the reforms haven't broken them loose? Well, I think in Peking these teachers come from the old society. Though they like the socialist revolution, they haven't revolutionized their thought enough to revolutionize their teaching, in spite of plenty of efforts to bring it about.

"Now in the countryside they didn't have much in the way of schools before, and when they create a school they don't have that whole tradition of having taught under the Manchus, and they have a much more creative program. I don't mean that there aren't primary schools in Peking that are creative. My kids didn't happen to go to one. When they got down in the countryside they went to a school that was much more flexible, where they had work and the work was very meaningful and their study was linked to the village and to the problems and the kids. They didn't want to leave. In fact my kids still want to go back to that school. They like it much better than the supposedly very advanced school they go to at home." (William Hinton, "Reflections on China," *Monthly Review* 25, no. 2 [June 1973], pp. 39–40.)

a visitor, it seemed obvious to me that the balance weighs in favor of an adoption of progressive methods—investigation, elicitation, self and mutual help—over the old ways.

That is why I was dismayed when, after returning from China, I read an article in *Reader's Digest* written by its vice president of public affairs, C. R. Devine, who began his account of the impressions he brought back from China thus:

> I traveled through Nazi Germany in 1938, and saw the vigor with which the Third Reich regimented its citizenry. Yet that didn't hold a candle to the systematic sublimation of the individual that has taken place in China during the last 24 years. . . . From earliest childhood, this "new China" generation has learned by rote the vague and frequently confusing "teachings" of the Great Leader, Mao Tse-tung. . . . One can't help but wonder how succeeding generations will turn out, with schools fully regimented from kindergarten on.[25]

Another of the largest circulation magazines told of "ranks of chanting, ten-year-old martinets . . . memorizing verses that told them of their ineradicable debt to Chairman Mao."[26]

Could it be that the new "China-watchers," who at last can watch from within China rather than from Hong Kong have mistaken diligence for regimentation? School work is a serious affair in China. Students do interrupt their classes to hospitably greet and bid good-bye to visitors, but in between they attend to their studies. Remarkably, their involvement and interest are rarely distracted, even by a dozen or so foreigners flitting around their classrooms with flashbulbs popping, movie cameras humming, tape recorders listening.

Could these journalists have mistaken a superficially somber appearance for oppressive relationships? The schools are far from posh and modern-looking. China is not an affluent country, and the schools are often old, sometimes not in the best of shape (although clean), and they are almost always crowded. The desks, which are arranged in rows, are riveted to the floor in a style familiar here not long ago which still remains in some of our older schools. But these facts by themselves tell us nothing about the quality of the relationships that exist among the people in the schools.

Though stilted methods can still be found in use in some class-

---

25. "Behind the Lines," *Reader's Digest* 103, no. 620 (December 1973), pp. 19–20.
26. "Confucius is Alive in Canton," *Time* (November 26, 1973), p. 37.

rooms, as generalizations about Chinese schools, these statements from two mass circulation periodicals negate the remarkable progress that has been made. They are simply inaccurate. Whether these observers were unable or perhaps unwilling to see the larger truths about trends in current Chinese educational methods, they have managed to misrepresent the facts to a dangerous degree.[27]

Observation of the direction of development and the strength of the forces leading that development is crucial in order to judge the strengths and weaknesses of any social system. Sound judgments can never be made on the basis of a few casual observations if individual items are viewed in isolation from each other and as static.

Referring to their own experience, the Chinese are quick to point out that they must consciously control the direction of their development, that progress cannot be taken for granted, that it is easy to slide into

---

27. Fortunately, this is not the only kind of reporting on China. Many returning visitors make more balanced statements about what they have seen and heard. These, however, less often find their way into the large circulation journals and consequently far fewer people are exposed to "the other side." Here is a brief sampling:

"Imagine schools where teachers and students exhibit great respect for each other, and where both groups talk about their eagerness to keep learning and their willingness to teach others." (Albert H. Yee [Educational Psychologist and Dean of Graduate Studies and Research, California State University, Long Beach], "Education in the Land of Mao: View I," *Learning* 2, no. 3 [November 1973], p. 22).

"I have to stress that the children certainly were not unhappy or parrotlike in anything they did. Their enthusiasm was strong and unforced." (Doreen Croft [Associate Professor of Early Childhood Development, DeAnza College, Cupertino, California, and Director of Greenmeadow Nursery School in Palo Alto, California], "Education in the Land of Mao: View II," *Learning* 2, no. 3 [November 1973], p. 27).

"The pre-Cultural Revolution notion of the teacher and the textbook as the center of the classroom was severely criticized and teaching methods have now changed to an emphasis on individual or independent study and group discussion." (Stewart E. Fraser [Professor of International and Comparative Education, Peabody College, Nashville, Director of the Peabody International Center, Chairman of Phi Delta Kappa Commission on International Relations in Education, author and editor of three books and numerous articles on Chinese education] and John N. Hawkins [NDEA Fellow in International Education, Peabody College, co-author of a book on Chinese education], "Chinese Education: Revolution and Development," *Phi Delta Kappan* 52, no. 8 [April 1972], p. 497).

"Medical students . . . are educated and trained to 'serve the people', to be oriented towards problem-solving and . . . to do manual labour alongside—and to learn from—the masses." (G. Gingras [C. C., M.D., A.B.P.M.R., F.A.C.S., F.A.A.P.M.R., F.R.C.P. (C), President, Canadian Medical Association, and Director, Institute of Rehabilitation, Montreal] and D. A. Geekie [B.P.H.E., C.P.H., Director of Communications, The Canadian Medical Association, Ottawa] on behalf of the Canadian medical delegation to China, "China Report," *Canadian Medical Association Journal* 109, no. 2 [July 21, 1973], p. 150).

complacency, that rigidity and passivity can occur and recur in any school at any time if teachers and students become lax in the demands they make upon themselves and each other. There are educators in China who are acutely aware of these dangers, such as the teacher at a technical institute who asked, "Has socialist education been achieved throughout China? Can we now sail ahead with ease? The very nature of socialism," she asserted emphatically in answer to her own questions, "makes this impossible. Wherever things are stagnant, revisionism must be strong. There have been many battles and many victories— over whether to study for marks or to learn how to analyze and solve problems, over how to integrate theory and practice, over developing new and more meaningful methods and materials, and many, many other problems. But each of these battles must be fought today, tomorrow, and the next day in each school. Of course with every victory that is won, it is easier to win new victories provided that we don't deceive ourselves into thinking that the victory was a once-and-for-all achievement. We must always be alert to problems; we must always guard against becoming uncritical of our work."

STUDENT EVALUATION

The means of gauging student progress are undergoing as great a change as the teaching methods. The teachers and students at Pai Kwang Middle School recounted the injustices of exams in the pre-Cultural Revolution days: "Under the influence of the revisionist line, the method of surprise attack in examinations was often used; the greater the surprise, the better. Teachers would try to trick the students when they were off guard by asking catch questions and out-of-the-way questions. This was the way the teachers tried to show that they had superior knowledge."

The teacher who spoke was middle-aged and had been teaching for a number of years. I wondered if he were one of those who used to lay in ambush to spring "surprise attacks" on his students. Another teacher, a young woman with bobbed hair and clear shining eyes, continued. Judging from her age, she looked as though she were quite possibly speaking from direct experience.

"In the past, the students studied only for good marks. They would have to spend too much time preparing for the examinations, and sometimes their health would suffer. They would be very afraid and tense when examination time approached." Just the week before, a professor at the medical college in Canton had told us that the real, though not always consciously intended, purpose of this way of conducting exams was to degrade some students and find grounds to expel them. This was the easiest way for the teachers to do their weeding and get rid of anyone who was having difficulty.

"More often than not," he said, "those expelled were the children of the laboring people, and by these means the examinations kept the old elitist system going."[28]

Their remarks brought to mind an account I had read before coming to China of the imperial examination system, the long-term ancestor of the revisionist approach to exams; it was recorded by a Jesuit missionary to China in the sixteenth century.

There is an immense palace built especially for this examination in every metropolitan city, closed in by a great wall. In it there are a number of suites, secluded from all distraction, which are assigned to the examiners ... while they are discussing the submitted manuscripts. In the centre of this palace there are more than four thousand small cells, just large enough to contain a small table and a seat for one person. The cells are so constructed that the occupant cannot converse with the one in the next compartment, or even see him.

During the time the manuscripts are being examined both day and night, a guard of magistrates and of military sentinels is in continual circulation to prevent all contact by word or by writing between those who are engaged in the palace and those outside. The same three days are set aside for this examination throughout the kingdom. Those taking part in the examinations are permitted to write from dawn to sunset, behind locked doors, and they are served with light meals, prepared the day before at public expense. When the candidate bachelors are admitted to the palace, they are carefully searched to see that they have no book or written matter in their possession. Entering the examination, they are allowed to have several brushes for writing, the writers' palette, and also ink and paper. Their clothes and even brushes and palette are carefully

---

28. In his book, *Hundred Day War: The Cultural Revolution at Tsinghua University* (New York: Monthly Review Press, 1972), William Hinton relates incidents of differential treatment of students depending upon their backgrounds. When several students rebelled, they were "prematurely graduated," removing them and their rebellion. See pp. 38–40 for examples.

examined lest they should contain anything deceitful, and if fraud of any kind is discovered, they are not only excluded from the examination but are severely punished as well.

When the bachelor candidates are admitted to the palace and the doors closed and sealed on the outside with a public seal, each of the two presiding officers appointed by the king, explains in public three passages. . . . He then presents these passages as the general subject matter, and a separate paper must be written on the selection made by each examiner. Then four passages are selected from any one of the Five Books of Doctrines and assigned for additional matter for examination . . . these seven written papers must show evidence not only of proper use of words but also of a proper appreciation of the ideas contained in the doctrines and a strict observance of the rules of Chinese rhetoric. No dissertation should exceed five hundred characters.

On the second day of examination, after two days of rest, and behind closed doors as formerly, topics are offered for examination relative to things that have happened in the past, to the annals of the ancients, and to events which may be expected to happen in the near future. These papers are written in triplex, in the form of an advisory document addressed to the king, as to what would be the best course to follow for the good of the empire in such eventualities.

On the third day three difficulties or arguments are offered for examination. . . . Each one must also recopy his manuscript into a copy book prepared for that purpose. At the end in addition to his own name he signs the names of his parents, grandparents and his great grandparents.

Then the book is so sealed that it can be opened only by the deputies.

Each one does this with as many copy books as he may have used, and he presents them personally to the deputy. These books are again recopied by the librarians appointed for that purpose. To prevent any partiality, the books are marked with a particular character in red, before they are presented to the examiners, and the autographs are omitted. These are the ones that are presented to the examiners for rating. The autographed copies are numbered to correspond with the markings on the manuscript presented. This method is followed to prevent recognition of manuscript and to conceal the author's identity and his handwriting.

The first set of examiners is chosen from the local magistrates who go through the papers and reject the poorer ones . . . the number of papers coming up to the regal examiners will not be more than double the number of candidates for the degree. If 150 degrees are to be granted, three hundred manuscripts are chosen.

When the examinations are over and the ceremonies at an end, the royal examiners publish a book distributed throughout the whole empire, containing the results, the names of the new licentiates, the outstanding manuscripts on the various subjects. The book is published as a deluxe edition.[29]

Before I left China I visited the Forbidden City built in Peking in the early 1400s to house the Ming emperors. One of the most extraordinary buildings in this fabulous palace-city, called the Hall of Preserving Harmony, was for a period the place where examinations to select the country's highest officials were administered. Three thousand scholars at a time would gather to write the three-day examinations; a few would actually die of exhaustion, and among those who failed some could see no alternative but suicide.

The mentality that kept this examination system going for centuries on end—a system which in its brutal search for "the men of superior grade" often brought tragedy to the failures—does not disappear without struggle. Persistent re-education has been the modern weapon used to attack this ancient dragon, and Mao has been its chief designer.

"Chairman Mao teaches us," said the young woman teacher at Pai Kwang who spoke earlier, "that we should cultivate in the students the ability to analyze and solve problems. We must do this in our examinations as well as our daily lessons."

By this time, our hosts at Pai Kwang Middle School had become quite animated. One after another they began to tell us about their unusual new ideas on examinations. A politics teacher said, "Last semester, the Revolutionary Committee discussed this very question. We must take the students as the masters of the school and no longer deal with them as an enemy. So we asked the students to discuss this problem: how should we conduct examinations? The students were very enthusiastic; they all joined the discussions earnestly and conscientiously. A great many opinions and suggestions were raised. This comrade," he said, pointing to the English teacher who had told us about the problem of the "temporarily lagging behind" student, "collected all the opinions and summarized them. Now we are trying out some of the suggestions forwarded by the students and teachers, those that we all agree are the best."

One of these new ideas was described by a teacher of fourteen-

---

29. Matteo Ricci, quoted in Hilda Hookham, *A Short History of China* (London: Longmans, Green and Co., 1969), pp. 150–51.

year-old students. "We try to put the students in an active position, to let them have some control over the teaching affairs of the class. Before, the students were always made passive in examinations. The teachers would make up the questions and the students would answer them, and at the end the teachers would give the marks. That was the normal way. But now we are trying to transform this situation, because we think the old way was not educational. The students didn't learn anything; they were just frightened.

"So before the last examinations, the students were asked to raise questions; what kind of questions did they think were suitable to be asked? All the suggestions were written on big-character posters[30] and hung on the walls of the school. They aroused a lot of interest among the students. They had hot discussions among themselves. 'Oh, this question is not so good.' 'This question should be put another way.' 'What is the best way to answer this question?' Such discussions went on among the students for several days and finally they decided which questions should be asked in the examination and how they should be phrased. This is just one example, and you can see the students learned a lot in preparing for the examination. They had to think and bring their creativity into play rather than just cram as in the past."

Another, not too dissimilar method was described, in which students formed into small groups with one or two teachers in each. The students by turn took on the role of the teacher, devising and asking oral questions which they all discussed until they reached what they considered to be the best answers.

Reminding us of the university science graduates earlier mentioned who could not install electrical facilities, the same teacher spoke again: "The teachers in our industrial fundamental knowledge classes criticized this revisionist separation of theory from practice and said we should change this situation. The students all agreed. Before, the students were given only written examinations, but now they combine some practical experiments in their examinations. They work together and discuss a problem, and then they conduct the necessary experiments and record the results on paper. They might also be examined on the spot; for instance, perhaps they would go to a factory where they would

---

30. A big-character poster is a sign or essay that anyone can write and hang up in public places, usually on walls in the streets. It provides a channel for the expression of opinion and was widely used during the Cultural Revolution.

be asked to explain and demonstrate certain practical operations, or they may be given blueprints and examined on how they make calculations. Of course, these new methods have reduced the tension, and the students can do better work."

A chemistry teacher in another urban middle school told me how the same goals were achieved in his examinations. After collecting different kinds of soil from several fields, he had the students together analyze the chemical elements of each and decide which plants would be most suitable for cultivation in which kinds of soil.

A similar approach is sometimes tried in subjects that might appear far less suited to it. A Chinese literature teacher at Pai Kwang reported, "We also have students go outside of the school and conduct investigations in factories or communes to gather information and ideas firsthand from the workers and peasants. Some of us invited veteran workers to come to the school to tell about their personal experiences. After listening and asking questions, the students studied and discussed these things among themselves. When their investigations were completed, they wrote stories and articles about what they had learned. So this is another kind of examination that integrates theory and practice."

One of the most unusual forms that the new exams take is to allow each student to determine the topic he or she would like to write on. It can be on any aspect of the work studied or a general summation of what has been learned. One student, a former radar operator who recently began to study at the Talien Mercantile Marine Institute where he majors in navigation, wrote such an excellent first-year chemistry exam using this method of summing up his studies, that it received wide publicity—being printed in its entirety in several journals. His professor commented, "As a teacher for more than a dozen years before the Great Proletarian Cultural Revolution, I'd never seen such a good examination paper which is difficult to evaluate in terms of a mark."[31]

On the face of it, allowing students to select the topics for their own examinations might bear resemblance to the "do-your-own-thing" syndrome. This isn't the case, however, since such choices in China occur within a context of coherent and agreed upon principles and goals. Student preference is not based on "transcendental inspiration" or personal whimsy but on the expectation that the choice will derive

---

31. "No Mark Can Do Justice to This Examination Paper," *Peking Review* (June 21, 1974), p. 14.

from its objective social relevance and that its treatment will be focused and disciplined.

Another method that seems to be gaining acceptance in some schools is the open book exam. The description I heard differs from what we usually mean by open book in that students are permitted not only to use written reference materials during the examination, but also to discuss the questions among themselves. The old standard exam in which students do not have access to books or each other is also still in use. Called a paper examination, it is being used more sparingly than in the past—mainly, it was emphasized, to test students on information that is deemed essential to be memorized. But this too has lost much of its impact as a "surprise attack" in many schools, because the questions are often pretty well known in advance. Teachers sometimes prepare what they call questionnaires for the open book and paper examinations which are given to the students in advance to enable them to review the necessary material.

"For reviewing lessons, the students are organized into many small groups so that they can help each other and teach each other. Most of our students learn a lot from this method, and pass the examinations very well," one of the teachers remarked.

These are local experiments. While examples of some of the more enlightened new forms, they are undoubtedly not highly developed in all schools in China. Like every other battle, this one too "must be fought today, tomorrow, and the next day in each school." These forms do, however, highlight the attitude of questioning traditional ways which has been renewed with the Cultural Revolution. By such methods as these, examinations are themselves coming to be learning experiences. They are one part of a continuing process. The old idea that students should try to learn as much as possible and stop all learning activities during examinations is being challenged as unjust and educationally unsound.

The definition of what learning should be extends further. To those most engaged in educational change learning means not only being able to recall something or understand it intellectually; it should entail a depth of comprehension that affects people's actual behavior and outlook. If what students are taught has no bearing on how they act, Chinese educators would consider that it has not been learned, that their teaching has been a failure.

A lively professor who teaches courses in Marxism-Leninism at

Peking University provided us with an example of just that kind of failure. "When I was a student eighteen years ago," he recalled "I had a classmate who could memorize *everything*. He could recite works of Marx and Lenin by heart. He could repeat all the sentences in the textbooks about materialism and on all of his examinations he always got 100, the very best grade! But, when he went home. ..." Here he interrupted himself as he started to chuckle. "When he went home during vacations, the first thing he would do is pray to God!"

An absurd situation from the emerging Chinese perspective of what education is all about. To the Chinese one is either a materialist or an idealist and if the student had spent less time memorizing and more time trying to *understand* Marxist-Leninist materialism, he could not possibly have behaved like an idealist. Because he was completely unaffected by his study, it had been, in the eyes of his former fellow student, nothing but a fruitless, mechanical, and stupefying exercise.

The influence of teachers who prefer such old cut-and-dried robot-like teaching and examination styles still exists, in a number of schools, with some strength. At the same time, as new forms are tried and prove themselves, as more teachers become convinced of their worth, and as students become more critical and unafraid, it becomes increasingly difficult for conservative teachers to perpetrate outdated methods.

From the students' position, there is no question of the superiority of the new system. Examinations are being stripped of the awe they once held. A university student told me, "It's hard to get over the fear of examinations and to change the habit of cramming. Sometimes that still happens, but that's bad because we will forget the things we cram. They are unconsolidated and temporary, and that is not progress. But that doesn't happen as often any more, because now we really have nothing to fear."

Others said they liked the new kinds of examinations because they were not boring and pointless like the old ones. The students felt challenged and appreciated their new active role. The cooperative aspect seemed particularly important to them. A ruddy-complected girl in middle school commented:

"In the examinations we solve problems just as we would at any other time. Most of the problems we will face in life we will analyze together with our comrades; that is what we need to know—how to solve problems by thinking and working together in a collective spirit."

The collective spirit is one of the most impressive aspects of the new

examinations. It is an ingredient common to a great many of them. Even the paper examinations which students write individually involve cooperation in those schools where there is group study and review beforehand. Chinese students now have far less cause to shudder than in the past when they faced—each one alone and frightened—the terror of a punitive examination system that separated them into life's successes and failures.

But failures must exist in China, too. If there are examinations, there will be grades and failures. Some of us were uncomfortable with the idea of any students failing and wondered why examinations were thought to be necessary at all. We asked an older teacher at Pai Kwang Middle School: "At first when we began to criticize the revisionist line in education, some people said, 'Eliminate all examinations; they are all revisionist,' but we thought about it and decided that was wrong—from one extreme to its opposite, what we call ultraleft. The new examinations are useful for summing up our work and discovering the strengths and weaknesses of both the teachers and the students. On the basis of the examinations, we can work out new teaching plans to overcome the weaknesses and develop the strengths."

"What happens in this school to those who fail?"

"It does not very often happen that students fail. You see, before the examinations are given the students are organized to help each other and to study together to review their lessons. I will give you an example. Last semester each class selected several students who studied very well and asked them to help those students who were temporarily lagging behind. The teachers also gave them extra coaching. So the number of students who have difficulty with the examinations has greatly decreased. Of course there are still some who do not pass. When this happens, the teachers and students give further help.

"Before, we didn't care if the students passed or not, if they understood the work or not. Under the revisionist influence, many teachers would just talk all the time in class without stopping, and after class they thought they had finished their work. If some students didn't understand, the teachers wouldn't help them. Sometimes the students didn't show the right cooperative spirit either, because they were competing for high marks. But now we teachers do not take the students as our enemies. The relationship between teachers and students has improved, and the purpose of the examinations has also changed. Now we are all comrades, so we want all the students to do well and to under-

Students giving mutual aid in a crafts project.

stand their lessons. The examinations test their ability to think, not just to remember. And they test *our* success in teaching.

"We think that the phenomenon of students not passing can be overcome. There are two main reasons why students sometimes lag behind. One is that they might be poorly motivated, and so their enthusiasm is not fully mobilized. The other reason is that students might have a poor foundation, a weak basis for further education before they enter the school. To solve these problems, we try to string ties between the school, the family, and the community. Education, you know, is a three-in-one combination responsibility, so we are all involved when a student is lagging behind."

It was also mentioned that the family of such students would be contacted to see if there were any problems at home. Not only at this school but in others where the question of failure was discussed, the emphasis was always on providing extra help, and everyone seemed to get into the picture. Students work together to give "mutual aid"; the teachers do whatever their time permits. Parents, retired workers, and cadres in the neighborhoods are relied on as coaches after classes.

The failure rate is not at the zero point, but it is close in many schools. If a student fails a course, he or she can usually take a make-up exam after receiving extra coaching. There are some variations in different schools and at different levels, but it seems to be the case in some schools that if a student fails on the second try in two major courses, the grade must be repeated. However, this regulation is applied with flexibility. When, for example, failures are the result of illness or some other unavoidable cause, students will not usually be held back but will receive even more concentrated help from the others. In some schools, students organize tutoring groups among themselves to visit those who are ill so that they will not get behind in their studies. Therefore, repeating a grade is not very common, even among students who have missed a lot of school. In one primary school in Peking, out of 1,040 children, only seven had to repeat a grade. At Sun Yat-sen Medical College, where students can take a make-up exam in one subject only— with two failures they must repeat the year—out of the approximately 1,700 students enrolled or graduated by 1973, this rule had not been invoked once since 1969! (That was the year that the College adopted the new student selection policy of admitting people recommended by workers and peasants.)

It appears, however, that even if a student is not promoted, his disappointment need not necessarily be accompanied by disgrace nor signal the beginning of reduced opportunities in life. Nor is failure considered a sign of stupidity. As in the case of Shi who went from a 0 to a 96 in English, it might well be an indication to everyone around that perhaps *they* had neglected their responsibilities to *him*. They should all know long in advance of examinations just who is having problems and why, and then try to do something about it in good time.

Perhaps the teachers succeed so well with their students, even though there may be as many as fifty and sometimes even more in a class, because they receive so much help. The students themselves are in effect their assistants. They are being transformed from receptacles into partners. In a number of schools they participate in every stage, from helping to plan lessons, prepare materials, and teach each other, to criticizing the teachers, designing their own examinations, and even evaluating the results of their work.

In such schools, teachers no longer have ultimate and potentially punitive authority over students through the weapon of marks. Children in the primary schools can have some say in evaluation through their freedom to criticize teachers and express opinions. By middle school, their power often becomes more institutionalized through discussions with their teachers that are aimed more specifically at determining the criteria to be used for evaluation and in some schools even assigning grades to themselves and each other. Like other parts of the educational process, this procedure is neither secretive nor private. The students, under the direction of their teachers, openly review each other's performance and "devotion to work," a concept which bears some similarity to what we call effort. The difference is that "devotion to work" is also not seen as a private matter having to do with the student's efforts only in relation to his or her own work. Instead, it includes such qualities as respect for workers and peasants, modesty, cooperation with others, and concern for the collective.

In the schools where mutual assessment is practiced, it is assumed that the students are capable of offering reliable evaluations because they have worked together regularly in school, after school, before, and sometimes even during, exams. Therefore, such assessments are taken seriously and are included along with each student's own self-evaluation in the reports issued at the end of the term. Together with criticism and self-criticism meetings between teachers and students, this kind of joint evaluation is also useful to teachers in planning the work ahead.

Among the more innovative schools, the assignment of grades is not a mechanical process; it is not simply a particular number of "right" answers that are sought. When exams are intended to develop and test problem-solving skills, there can be many acceptable ways of handling questions. Creativity and initiative are valued, and students receive higher marks when there is evidence of real thought than when they approach problems in a bookish way. This method of evaluation was urged by Mao in a talk delivered in 1964:

> If one sets twenty questions on the *Dream of the Red Chamber* [a famous Chinese novel], and some students answer half of them and answer them well, and some of the answers are very good and contain creative ideas, then one can give them 100 per cent. If some other students answer all twenty questions and answer them correctly, but answer them simply by reciting from their textbooks and lectures, without any creative ideas, they should be given 50 or 60 per cent. . . . We must do things in a lively fashion, not in a lifeless fashion.[32]

---

32. Quoted in Schram, ed., *Mao Tse-tung Unrehearsed*, pp. 204–5.

DISCIPLINE AND SELF-DISCIPLINE

Since the Cultural Revolution, abuse of students in any form has become a matter that warrants the most serious attention. From the time the schools first began to reopen in 1967 questions of discipline and treatment of students by teachers have become foremost concerns, especially among the students. Reporting on some schools she visited in late 1970, one Western writer reproduced a big-character poster she saw in a middle school. It was written by the students:

> During class, when discipline leaves something to be desired, some of our teachers suddenly assume a threatening air; they take out the rod, striking it against the desk like deaf men, or use their hands instead. This we will no longer permit. This does not mean that teachers should refrain from severely criticizing infractions of discipline: on the contrary, such disturbances should be criticized. But how can they threaten us by waving rods and banging on desks? How can they treat us like this? Such things should not happen in our socialist schools. We think that teachers should patiently and scrupulously perform their ideological duties with their students. Teachers should reflect and say to themselves: Can the rod and hand replace ideological work? No, they can never replace it.[33]

When this same visitor discussed the message of the big-character poster with some students, one, a thirteen-year-old member of the school's revolutionary committee, said, "Anyone can scream and bang on a desk. Chairman Mao teaches the opposite: to convince others, you must persuade them, not force them. The only result of force is that you've coerced rather than convinced."

Our observations of Chinese classrooms and our discussions on the subject confirmed that they have made great strides in changing their conception and handling of indiscipline. It is significant that, just as academic difficulties are seen as a temporary lagging behind rather than a permanent incapacity, students who present discipline problems are described as mischievous or naughty rather than as "bad." Significant, because adjectives like "mischievous" and "naughty" most often refer to unacceptable behavior, connoting pliancy, the possibility of change, whereas the word "bad" usually refers to deeper, more perva-

---

33. Maria Antonietta Macciocchi, *Daily Life in Revolutionary China* (New York: Monthly Review Press, 1972), p. 453.

sive and unacceptable character failings, implying inability to change. One of the teachers at Pai Kwang Middle School made this quite explicit when she said, "Only a few students are somewhat mischievous, but I think they are still good children. With help they will improve, but in order to help them we must first find out the cause. Sometimes a child might think it's heroic to misbehave. Or he might not understand the importance of revolutionary discipline. We must investigate, not punish."

"I can give you an example of how we help naughty children," offered another teacher. "In my class there was a naughty boy; he was always disturbing the others with pranks. One day he brought a cricket to class and concealed it under his shirt. He often did things like that. I criticized him for his misbehavior, but he didn't accept it. He drew a caricature of me showing an angry face. I thought about what to do and realized that we should approach everything with a one-divides-into-two viewpoint."

Here, one of our guides—an outspoken man with a booming voice, who appeared gruff but was often unexpectedly gentle—interrupted to explain. This was a rare occurrence since the guides were always careful to allow conversations to flow unhindered and directly between us and those we were interviewing without adding their own views or interpretations. "There are contradictions in everything," he said. "Everything has two opposite sides. Whenever we analyze a problem, we look at both sides. In philosophical terms this is called the dialectical viewpoint, the unity of two opposites. In everyday language, we call it one-divides-into-two."

The teacher resumed his story, explaining that he had failed to apply the one-divides-into-two viewpoint in his dealings with his student: "I had been annoyed at him; his behavior had made me angry." A good part of the reason for the problem, he decided, had to do with his own approach to the boy. Perhaps he had seen only the mischief and not the strengths. Perhaps he had too readily given vent to his own irritation and had not tried hard enough to be of help.

"I thought, 'I should try to understand him; I should try to get closer to him. Then we could have a better relationship.' When I got to know him better, I discovered that his family had been very poor in the past, and so I invited his father to come to school to give the class an account of his past misery. He came and told the students that before liberation they had no money and that none of them could go to school. He said that his son, the boy in my class, was the first one in his family ever to attend a middle school, and this story made the boy lower his head.''

I waited for him to continue. The teacher had said that his purpose was to help the boy, that his plan had evolved from his own new positive attitude. Yet he had made the student feel ashamed. I wondered if this was his idea of a constructive approach. As he went on it became clear to me that his purpose had not been to belittle, but rather to teach. There was a forceful lesson to be learned, and the teacher had chosen to present it dramatically. And, it had worked. ''After receiving this kind of re-education, his behavior and schoolwork improved. But the process of his transformation was not a smooth one. There were also some reversals. Although he behaved well in many classes, he still acted the same old way in English class. So I had a private talk with him and asked him why. He said, 'I don't want to be an interpreter when I grow up, so why should I bother with English?' '' The five English interpreters in the room found this remark very funny, and we all joined in their laughter.

The teacher continued. ''When he said he shouldn't study English, I related the story about Dr. Norman Bethune, the Canadian doctor who came to China from afar during the Anti-Japanese War period and how he had sacrificed his life for the Chinese people. This is the spirit of internationalism. I told him about many of our workers who go to friendly countries to help build railways and our doctors who go to offer medical assistance to the working people there. I wanted him to understand that the Chinese people should support all the revolutionary people in the world, that we learn not only for ourselves. These stories enlightened him and he began to see that all our work is for the revolution, and that we, the Chinese people, should also learn from the experiences of other peoples; we should learn from each other and support each other. He was also given an assignment to study the heroic deeds of the Paris Commune[34] fighters and then was asked to give an account of his personal experiences, what it had meant to him to study this historic event. So through such means, he gradually came to understand the importance of learning a foreign language.

''His behavior and interest improved steadily from then on. He has

---

34. The Paris Commune refers to the working class revolution that occurred in Paris in 1871. Lasting only three months, the Commune was the first example of a working class taking political power. Even though it failed, it is celebrated in socialist countries for ushering in the modern era of socialism.

since graduated and is now a member of the Communist Youth League[35] and the People's Liberation Army. From this kind of experience we are convinced that in dealing with these so-called naughty children we should not punish them. We should try to give guidance on the merits of each case. We should apply the one-divides-into-two viewpoint in dealing with them and in this way bring their initiative into play so they can surmount their shortcomings."

In a very real sense, Chinese educators like this man are not talking about discipline as it is usually conceived, discipline that is imposed from outside; rather it must be discipline that is internalized. Punishment, which they scorn as suppression, can bring temporary compliance, but that is just the appearance of discipline and will, over time, only aggravate, not solve the problem. Real change must be rooted in understanding. The boy had to be shown his family's past deprivation in order to appreciate his present good fortune. He had to be educated about the heroic deeds and sacrifices of others before him, acts that have resulted in his own present circumstances. It was necessary to "raise his political consciousness." Only then could he comprehend his responsibility to others, and only then would he be convinced of the need to put in the effort required for real change: "A student must first have the idea of serving the people. Then he will work hard to develop the ability to serve the people."

Because of this growing basic optimism about everyone's potentialities—this conception of humans as transformable rather than rigidly fixed—and the consequent humane and developmental approach to difficulties, very few children present behavioral problems in the schools, and among those who do it is generally short lived. As with academic failings, they are very likely to receive encouragement and assistance to help them improve from a number of others around them. They are given both reasons and support for pulling themselves together, and these, along with the countless exemplary models that surround them, are powerful persuaders.

Even in the army, discipline does not mean unquestioned obedience to commands if they are arbitrarily issued from above. In fact, the very origins of this outlook on discipline—the inner commitment to deci-

---

35. The Communist Youth League is an organization for exemplary youth. Membership, like membership in the PLA, is considered an honor because only those dedicated to the principles and practices of socialism are selected, and they are looked up to as models for others to emulate. See Chapter 6 for further elaboration on the League.

sions and rules that are comprehended and agreed upon—can be found in the Red Army of the 1920s, and it continues as standard operating procedure in the PLA today. Imagine an army in which new recruits have the right to criticize seasoned high-ranking officers. Problems should be thoroughly discussed with the rank and file; all viewpoints and objections should be aired—persuasion, education, discussion—with the aim of reaching consensus. But once a decision is agreed upon, that decision must become a commitment, and it is a matter of self-discipline for each soldier to honor it to the fullest. This generally works out well, because soldiers, like increasing numbers of students in the schools, are essentially carrying out their own rationally agreed upon decisions rather than someone else's orders whose rationale may be unknown to them. They can therefore be counted on, to a large extent, to monitor and discipline themselves and each other, with there being less need for their "superiors" to patrol their behavior and enforce discipline from outside.

This sense of self-discipline is the opposite, yet united, aspect of freedom in the Chinese dialectical, or one-divides-into-two mode of thought. Freedom and discipline appear as opposites, and in one sense they are for the Chinese. But they also say that at the same time, freedom and discipline are united because the one is meaningless and retrogressive without the other. Like hot and cold or any other set of opposites, freedom cannot be meaningfully known without discipline and vice versa. A university student told me, "We are working to create a situation in which we have both freedom and discipline. Only by developing both can all people enjoy real freedom."

Freedom itself is also seen dialectically. Freedom *from* sets the precondition for freedom *to*. The Chinese consider their new freedom from want, hunger, disease, and ignorance as a real liberation, a profound and essential aspect of any genuine freedom. This, they say, allows them, for the first time in their history, to all be free to live, experiment, cooperate, and progress. Discipline to most Chinese does not limit this freedom. On the contrary, it assures that their new freedom may flourish.

VI: SO GROWS THE TREE

We can learn what we did not know. We are not only good at destroying the old world, we are also good at building the new.[1]

MAO TSE-TUNG

POLITICS/MORALITY/POLITICS

"Schools must put the ideological transformation of the students in first place," they say. "Put proletarian politics in command!" they say. Learn to be "red and expert." "Study hard for the revolution." "Keep our hearts red," they say. Little children sing about "the red sun shining in our hearts." People of all ages study "in order to make Chairman Mao's thoughts part of our daily lives." Huge billboards on the streets depict smiling workers and peasants hard at work while in the background the top half of an enormous blazing, fiery red sun emerging on the horizon illuminates everything with a startling brilliance and intensity. No matter where you look or who you talk to in China, these are the things you see and hear.

To a Westerner the idea of such billboards and songs may seem ridiculously melodramatic; the constant references to Chairman Mao might suggest the exhortations of fundamentalist religion. Words like politics, revolution, masses, proletariat, and red coming up over and over again would seem to have a mesmerizing impact.

Even a visitor from the West sympathetic to the immensity of the Chinese experiment might imagine, before entering China, that the Chinese people must be overwhelmed, constricted, or at least bored by constantly reiterated messages. Yet it takes little more than fleeting

---

1. Mao Tse-tung, "Report to the Second Plenary Session of the Seventh Central Committee of the Communist Party of China," *Selected Works of Mao Tse-tung*, 4 vols. (Peking: Foreign Languages Press, 1961–65), vol. 4, p. 374.

experience with the Chinese in the flesh to realize that what sounds like vacuous sloganizing to us is simply everyday normal language to them. More extensive contact leads to the recognition that this everyday language appears, for the most part, to have real meaning for both speakers and listeners.

At this point of realization, we are forced to question some very basic assumptions about our own interpretations of life. As with any experience that shakes a well-established prejudice, we begin to look for the reasons for such taken-for-granted blinders. In my own case, the discovery of a people who seem to all say similar things, which are deeply meaningful to them but which would be mere slogans to most people in my own society, turned my attention to our use of certain key words and our feelings about them. Indeed, we may learn much about ourselves by actually encountering people like the Chinese, who behave in ways so dissimilar from what we have been taught to expect of them. For example, consider some of our connotations for words that we are likely to balk at when a Chinese is using them:

—"Revolution" is used in our context largely as a Madison Avenue superlative; so much of our experience with "revolution" stems from TV and magazine ads about "a revolutionary new deodorant" or "a revolutionary breakthrough in automotive design." Despite the fact that we once had a revolution of our own, the meaning of the word has been diluted to the extent that the Chinese often sound to us like fanatics when they use the word, infusing it as they do with its real and full meaning.

—We don't talk about "the proletariat." The closest thing to it are concerns expressed, rarely in glowing terms, about "labor unrest" and "labor problems," implying troublesomeness on the part of workers. The Chinese, by contrast, see all the trouble as coming from the capitalists who hold down the working people. To them, any "restlessness," demands, or rebellion by workers is necessary and just.

—"Politics" in our society is often seen as the dirty business of the few who manipulate the many, certainly not something you want to teach your kids.

—"Red" brings to mind agitation and the "extremists" who want to change everything. It is, in the popular image, their purpose to breed dissatisfaction even if it's not warranted. They know only the method of violence.

—"The masses"—well, when this term is used at all to refer to people, it's not complimentary. We tend to think of a mob, an indistinguishable blob of impressionable and manipulable people, unworthy of anyone's respect. The contempt brought to this concept is tellingly summed up in the term *"rabble*-rousing."

The meanings intended by the Chinese could not be more different. For instance, the educational objective of all-rounded development—to educate students "morally, intellectually, and physically"—could in some ways be understood as *"politically*, intellectually, and physically." Politics, to the Chinese, is not shenanigans and deals; it seems, on many occasions, to be interchangeable with morality. But the Chinese are not talking about morality just in a personalized ethical sense. Personal integrity and honor, if isolated from their actual social consequences, are what Chinese revolutionaries would consider hollow remnants of earlier class societies.

To educate youth morally in China is to "put proletarian politics in command." Proletarian politics refers to the standards, both in outlook and in practice, of those who are the most conscious and committed. To put these high standards in command is to provide "the masses"—the working people who comprise by the Chinese calculation 95 percent of the population—with a model of progressive thought and action toward which to strive. And so when the schools put proletarian politics or the new morality of the proletariat in the forefront, they are teaching students to "be red," to transform their ideology by ridding themselves of "the me-first mentality that seeks to put oneself in the limelight and strives for personal fame, position, power, and profits." In short, the new morality is aimed at teaching youth to respect, identify with, and serve the working people. The slogans are simply expressions of the most advanced political thinking and indicators of the direction of further change. People are expected to actually apply them in their daily lives.

The difficulty for many outsiders comes in trying to grasp how this happens. How do they live every day by the revolutionary principles of proletarian politics, of "serving the people"? Even though the Chinese use the term "struggle" often, they do not appear to take it lightly. It's hard, *very* hard, but, in the Chinese experience, repeated strenuous exertion has time and again borne positive results—concrete, tangible, visible. They are surrounded by what they call "the fruits of struggle," everything from the food in their bellies and the clothes on their backs to their plump healthy children, their opportunities to all learn and grow, and their unprecedented security about their futures. Thus, when the Chinese tell their children to "study hard; make progress every day," it does not seem to be an empty piety, but a noble call to action.

POLITICAL EDUCATION

Political education, in its most comprehensive sense of ideological formation and transformation, is perhaps the most important single ingredient in the educational program all the way through school. It is generally undertaken as a formal course beginning in grade one, but politics seems to permeate all other courses as well, to be contained in all features of all educational undertakings, to be fundamental to just about all school practice. It is therefore difficult and misleading to attempt to draw too sharp a distinction between the course on politics and everything else in school. For instance, the productive labor programs, while not specifically subsumed under any politics courses, have undeniable and extremely important political objectives and content. The same can be said for all other parts of the school curriculum, including those that might appear to be far less related to politics. Even school athletic events might have explicitly political content, like the kindergarten sports meet that featured such races as building-a-house relay and planting-trees relay. In the delivering-the-grain-to-the-state race, a number of three-year-olds pulled toy dump trucks attached to strings, stopping at a designated point to load the "grain" into the truck. The object was to get to the finish line quickly but without spilling any of the precious contents.[2]

Without attempting, then, to be exhaustive, we can identify a few other highlights of political education in China.

Revolutionary models are heavily relied upon to imbue students with an understanding and acceptance of socialist values from very early on in their education. The military is one of the most abundant sources of heroes. Soldiers are pointed to as models for building socialism every bit as much as for defending it. Lei Feng is one such model, perhaps the best known among China's youth. There are wall posters of him in schoolrooms, but they do not depict a soldier with fist clenched

2. See "Kindergarten Sports Meet," *China Reconstructs* 23, no. 10 (October 1974), pp. 16–17.

in a dramatic gesture of military triumph as might be expected. Instead, we see a smiling, surprisingly gentle-looking man holding a book and talking with some children. The caption reads "Learn from the Good Example Set by Uncle Lei Feng." There are songs and stories about him, but none of them tell about prowess on the battlefield. He died in 1962 at the age of 22—not in combat, but in an accident. In fact, the only point that ever seems to be made about him as a fighter is as a potential fighter—his readiness and willingness to fight and die to protect his country.

Lei Feng is an army hero of a new type. He is a model of selfless and tireless service to the people. The stories about him tell of his miserable childhood as an orphan. Most of his family had been tortured and killed by the Japanese and Kuomintang; his one surviving brother died at the age of ten, the victim of tuberculosis caused by working long hours in a factory under intolerable conditions. Lei Feng himself was severely abused at the hands of a landlord. When he was nine years old, his village was liberated by the PLA, and for the first time in his life, he had enough food and clothing, was cared for, and even went to school.

The contrast between the old and new society indelibly imprinted upon him, Lei Feng later joined the army and vowed undying commitment to building socialism. "Human life is limited, but serving the people is not. I will put my limited life into unlimited service of the people." The main point of the Lei Feng stories is how he did just that in the span of his very limited life. In the face of growing revisionist tendencies in the China of the late 1950s and early 1960s, he unfailingly chose socialism and selfless dedication, becoming a model of the revolutionary line in the two-line struggle. His deeds were not particularly spectacular. Whenever he saw people working, he would instantly pitch in, insisting upon doing the most difficult jobs. He never sought praise or money. He used every spare moment to help out wherever he saw the opportunity, for example, working as a volunteer after-school counselor in a primary school which has since been renamed after him, sewing on buttons for his comrades, taking care of them when they were sick, sending his pay to flood victims in another part of China, etc. While to some of us, Lei Feng may sound like a Boy Scout "do-gooder," in China his deeds are taken seriously and are esteemed.

Compared with most of the heroes presented to our children—the Bobby Orrs who accomplish extraordinary feats that lie outside of the opportunities and competence of most people and the fictional Captain

Kindergarten children absorbed in a story about a revolutionary hero.

Marvels who do things unrealizable by *anyone*—the Lei Feng-type hero is quite another matter. He was real; he did simple things in the real arena of everyone's daily life. Anyone can do the same, child or adult. What is required is selflessness, modesty, eagerness to take initiative, and dedication to the well-being of others. Since so many of our heroes are beyond reach, they are often a source of frustration to us, especially to our children; Lei Feng, by contrast, is a source of inspiration to the Chinese. To them, the most important thing they can say about him is not that he was unique but that "there are hundreds of thousands of Lei Fengs in China."

The PLA is one place where many of them can be found. Soldiers are expected to lead exemplary lives, to all strive to be Lei Fengs. This is quite out of keeping with the usual activities of an army. In most times and places, armies have been set apart from the rest of society and have pursued their own affairs which, on a day-to-day basis, have had little connection to the rest of the population.

The Chinese army, however, is a type unique to twentieth century revolutions. It has been designed to be a people's army. It is not a parasitic organization that drains the resources of the country while sitting around and waiting for wars. Army people in China are productive members of society. You see PLA men and women everywhere, singly and in small groups and almost always unarmed. You see them not just on the streets, but in factories, communes, and schools, working and learning along with others, distinguishable only by their uniforms which are the same for "privates" and "generals" alike.[3] They are integrated into the ongoing life of the community and what they contribute to its well-being in production and services at least equals what they consume.

Soon after the Red Army was first organized in the late 1920s, rules of discipline were formulated insisting on total respect for the peasants in the guerrilla zones and unswerving honesty in all dealings with them down to the last detail of literally never taking a needle or piece of thread from the people without paying. This was in stark contrast to the armies of the Kuomintang, which were notorious for corruption, pillage, and suppression of the people. The practices of the Red Army remain the norms of conduct for the PLA today. The PLA's first duty is "to serve the people wholeheartedly." Units of army men and women play a vital role in supplying relief in emergency situations such as floods and epidemics; they take the lead in initiating numerous large-scale projects such as afforestation and pollution control programs and the building of power stations, dams, roads, railroads, bridges, and housing projects.

One result of all this is that the PLA is loved by the people. So when children say they want to become PLA members, as so many of them do, it doesn't necessarily mean that they are full of dreams of combat. This is not to suggest that the PLA is not a military organization. Like

---

3. On the army bases, officers and rank and file share the same living quarters, mess halls, and recreational facilities.

any other army, it is prepared to fight.[4] Moreover, even students in the schools receive military training. The crucial issue has to do with what makes up the content of that training. The stress is always on one or both of two objectives: military defense and public service.

Contrary, then, to a view sometimes expressed outside of China, the children are not learning to be bloodthirsty[5] or militaristic. All that they are taught appears to be consistent with the national policy of preparedness and defense. Younger students are taught about the exemplary working style of the PLA—their self-discipline and heroic deeds. The older ones learn self-defense and have target practice. Students of all ages sing songs about "defending the socialist motherland"; in the after-school model airplane construction class that we visited at the Children's Palace, there was a sign on the wall which read, "Establish a powerful contingent of people's air force to safeguard the motherland and be prepared to defeat any aggressors." During our stay at Chen Hsien Street Primary School in Nanking, we asked several children what they wanted to be when they grew up. One ten-year-old boy answered, "I would like to be a PLA man to defend our motherland." Another, age nine, hoped "to support the Chinese revolution and the world revolution" which he saw best filled by becoming a peasant "to produce more grain." These are certainly not the words of children who

---

4. The Chinese have never claimed to be pacifists; what they do claim, indeed insist upon, is that they are not and never will be aggressors. The policy is, "We will not attack unless we are attacked; if we are attacked, we will certainly counter-attack." As proof that their defensive posture is real, the Chinese often point to the fact that although China has the largest population on earth, not a single Chinese soldier is posted on foreign soil. Nor, unlike the superpowers, are the Chinese known for espionage. Consistent with their policy of maintaining a defensive position, their nuclear capacity was developed, they say, to make them less vulnerable to attack from others, but they have vowed never to stockpile like the superpowers or to use such weapons first. They have urged repeatedly, and so far in vain, for a worldwide conference on nuclear disarmament. They refuse to negotiate privately only with other nuclear powers on this question on the grounds that the whole world would be involved if there were a nuclear war, and to exclude others is to engage in "big power chauvinism, bullying and blackmail."

5. It is worth bearing in mind the fact that by the time the average North American student has graduated high school, he has watched 14,000 hours of television (roughly 3,000 hours more than he has spent in school) encompassing 18,000 murders and an uncountable number of other violent acts of a physical and psychological nature. This says nothing about the impact of violent films, "comics" and other cruelties he has directly or indirectly encountered. Furthermore, most of this violence is presented for sensational reasons. It more often is portrayed as an end in itself than as a necessary means to important and just ends.

are learning that their country should "take over the world." These children aspire to help defend and feed others, not to subjugate them.

There are also innumerable nonmilitary models as well, like the ones depicted in the very popular true story of the two sisters of Mongolian nationality who lived on the grasslands in the Inner Mongolia Autonomous Region. The story tells about how Lungmei, eleven, and her nine-year-old sister Yujung took over the sheep tending for their father when he was called away to help a neighbor. A storm blew up, frightening the sheep; they ran in the direction of the wind which was away from the girls' home. Rather than abandon the sheep, the children followed, for the animals were the property of the commune—they belonged to the people. Lungmei and Yujung bore a heavy responsibility and they were determined to do their very best. All night long the blizzard raged; the temperature dropped below zero; Yujung lost a boot in the snow and so Lungmei carried her; but they stayed with the sheep. Tired, hungry, and nearly frozen the girls were finally rescued the next morning by some railway workers. They had wandered several miles from home and had not lost a single sheep.

Heroines and heroes of minority and majority nationalities, children and adults, workers, peasants, soldiers—all doing realizable yet noble deeds—this is some of the stuff of political education in China's schools.

What might be called revolutionary patriotism holds a prominent place in the political education of China's young people. They study revolutionary movements past and present, primarily in China, but also in other countries. Besides developing a theoretical comprehension of revolutionary social change, the purpose, as expressed by a twelve-year-old primary school student, is "to learn the spirit of patriotism and internationalism."

Explaining, she said, "We study current affairs in China and other countries. We also learn about the importance of unity."

A younger boy sitting next to her added, "In the course on politics the teachers quite often tell us about the progressive struggles of the American working people."

"Yes," the first child continued, "and they teach us the importance of the friendship between the American people and Chinese people."

This emphasis on looking outward serves a dual purpose. On the one hand, it instills the socialist value of proletarian internationalism.

At the same time, it helps to further erode lingering remnants of suspicion toward foreigners that date both from traditional Middle-Kingdom chauvinism and from the intense maltreatment suffered by the Chinese people at the hands of foreign powers in the nineteenth and twentieth centuries.

The Chinese make a clear distinction between governments, or ruling classes, and the people. The American government is characterized as imperialist and therefore dangerous, although in certain respects not as dangerous as the Soviet Union which they see as a growing imperialist power hiding behind a mask of socialism. And the children are taught this lesson, but they are also taught not to confuse the common people of every nation—who are their friends—with certain governments that are enemies. It was not the least bit uncomfortable to be Americans in China; not once were we made to feel responsible for the actions and policies of the American government. As the Chinese see it, those actions and policies that they so vehemently condemn are engineered by the ruling class, not by ordinary people like ourselves. Beginning with the preschoolers at The East Is Red Kindergarten and going all the way up, the students demonstrated that whatever they had learned about us and any other *people* was positive. Good-byes were always moving moments with repeated and spontaneous expressions of friendship from the children: "Send our greetings to the American children." "Tell the American people about our friendly feelings for them and we will tell our schoolmates about the friendly feelings you have shown to us."

When we walked in on an English class at Pai Kwang Middle School in Shanghai there was a discussion in progress about the location of countries. The teacher asked questions and the students answered, using a pointer to illustrate their answers on the world map at the front of the classroom. The teacher asked in lovely, fluid English, "Where is China? Who can answer this question?"

"It is in Asia," answered a student, overpronouncing and separating each word and syllable as if they were all complete sentences.

"Yes. Here is Vietnam; it is also in Asia. Where is Vietnam?"

The students by turn answered her questions, each one in stiff but confidently and carefully articulated English. "It is in Asia, too."

"Where is the United States?"

"It is in North America."

"Please translate this sentence into Chinese: The American people

are our true friends." It is translated. Then, "We have friends all over
the world. Can you translate this sentence into Chinese?" It too is
translated, and so on.

The first thing a visitor sees on entering China from Hong Kong is
the sign on the bridge that marks the border: "Long Live the Great
Unity of the People of the World!" At the airport in Shanghai: "Serve
the People of China and the World!" These are all expressions of
international friendship and solidarity, the way the Chinese show their
hospitality to visitors. But such sentiments are shown not only when
schoolchildren say good-bye to foreigners or when Americans sit in on
their English classes; the signs appear not only at borders and airports.
They are for the consumption of the Chinese people as well and are part
of their political education. In a soccer stadium in Canton are huge
billboards, advertising not razor blades and soda pop but proletarian
internationalism: "Workers of the World Unite!" and "The People, and
the People Alone, are the Motive Force in the Making of World History!" On street corners and at school entrances, the familiar sign: "We
Have Friends All Over the World!"

The study of the Paris Commune undertaken by the middle school
boy who had been a behavioral problem, the stories he was told about
Norman Bethune and about the contributions of Chinese workers in
other countries—these are representative of the ways in which the
schools put flesh on the slogans of international solidarity. Students
learn about other countries' revolutionary movements of the past and
present with special emphasis on current liberation struggles of Third
World countries, a subject which, at best, is paid scant attention in most
schools in the West.

Internationalism in China is not inconsistent with patriotism. The
Chinese feel that they can be both patriots and internationalists at the
same time because their patriotism is not of a narrow nationalist type.
Rather their internationalism is an extension of their nationalism. The
slogan at home, "Unite to Win Still Greater Victories," is the more
immediate and national expression of the broader slogan, "Workers of
the World Unite." "Serve the People of China and the World" is an
extension to the whole world of the national guideline, "Serve the
People."

The frequent references in China to "our state" and "our country"
should not be mistaken for jingoism. The words people, state, government, country are often strung together, and even seem to be used

Even very young children learn about class struggle. The cartoons satirically depict Confucian ideas.

interchangeably at times. They generally come up in a context that refers to some collective past accomplishment or collective future task, indicating not so much chauvinism as unity of purpose and effort.

Judging from the comments made by a grade one teacher, quite explicit values are contained in the Chinese concept of patriotism. "Besides teaching the children to love their country," she said, explaining the objectives of the politics program in the lower primary grades, "we also teach them to love the people, to love labor, and to love public property." I did not get the feeling in China that the kids are learning, "My country right or wrong." It seemed to be more of a matter of, "I must do my part to make sure that my country is right!''—meaning, of course, revolutionary.

"We study about class struggle to develop a proletarian ideology," a junior middle school student said. The whole point of political education in China seemed to be summed up on the blackboard in one rural primary classroom where the problem was posed, " 'I worked harder than the others. Therefore I have more of a right to take a rest.' What kind of ideology is this?''

The class struggle is central; the only satisfactory and final conclusion to this struggle is the full triumph of the proletariat—materially and ideologically. It can be said that this is the overriding concern of the Chinese and that all other aspects of political education can be included within it. From the Chinese point of view, everything can be studied in one of two ways—from a revolutionary perspective which puts the class struggle of the proletariat in the center, or from a counterrevolutionary one which either sees the class struggle from the vantage point of privileged classes, or ignores or denies its significance altogether. Therefore, the specific contours of the two-line or class struggle as manifested at any particular time or place receive special attention. It is deemed crucial for students to be able to analyze class forces—the strengths and weaknesses of the bourgeoisie and the proletariat, their ideologies, their strategies and tactics, their subtleties and nuances. To equip themselves theoretically students study Marxism-Leninism, applying it to particular social problems and specific historical contexts.

By middle school, students in a number of places are analyzing difficult questions like the issues involved in the two-line struggle as it has developed since the inception of the socialist revolutionary movement in China. In the early days of the Communist Party, for instance, the right wing of the Party opted for closer ties with the Kuomintang to the point of merging with it and potentially losing any independent identity. The ultraleft wanted no alliance whatsoever with the Kuomintang but they also saw no future in trying to make revolution among a backward peasantry, placing their emphasis exclusively on the urban working class. Mao and others said that they should ally with the Kuomintang because, while it was not socialist, it had at the time some progressive patriotic aims consistent with those of the Communist Party. On the question of the peasantry, Mao held that they could and would be reliable allies of the proletariat.

Students might examine the implications of the rightist position, the ultraleft position, and Mao's position. What were the objective conditions of the peasantry at the time? How were they being exploited? By whom? What was the Kuomintang doing about it? What were the class positions and the national aspirations of the Kuomintang then? How did they later change? What was the subjective orientation of the peasantry, their consciousness of their exploitation? What were the revolutionary activities of the urban workers? Of students? How could they link up with the peasantry? Subtle and complex questions all, and questions whose answers are often equally complex, but they are the kind of questions that it is felt students must be able to handle if they are to gain any real understanding of the class struggle.

This sort of educational activity is obviously not just an academic exercise, a study of "dead history." Students are learning to appreciate the dynamics of the social changes which have been and are continuing to affect their world and to think critically about complicated and important issues. One might say that they are in training to analyze and deal with social problems equally as complex and important that will inevitably arise in their own futures.

But what's to prevent them from doing what the Peking University professor's classmate of eighteen years ago did, the young man who apparently learned everything about materialism but showed by his persistence in praying that he had actually learned nothing? How does the classroom and textbook study of class struggle cultivate "red hearts"? By itself it doesn't; and by itself it won't.

Certainly, students must be able to analyze the class struggle, to develop revolutionary theoretical positions. But without a deep and genuine commitment to socialist revolution their theories are at best useless and at worst harmful to that cause. They must develop sentiments to match their theories—no less than an ardent dedication to wage the class struggle on behalf of the proletariat. Certain commonly repeated phrases make it clear that this is the number one educational priority: "All the work in the schools is for the transformation of the ideas of the students" and "Schools must put the change of ideology of students in first place." The new generations must:

> take up the revolutionary cause and preserve the fruits of socialism, . . . [and] have the revolutionary thinking and spirit to take China forward into communism.
>
> It is unimaginable to think that after our working people made such sacrifices to win power we should fritter it away just by neglecting to educate the succeeding generations in what it took to obtain that victory.

To think only of their present happiness, of exposing them only to the "peaceful sunshine" and "clear blue skies" would be wrong and doing an injustice to their future well-being. It would be laying down a carpet for the restoration of all the ills of the old society.[6]

But having been raised with so much "sunshine," how can they be alert to the danger lurking in storm clouds they may never have seen? None of the hundreds of millions born since 1949 have direct experience with the brutal exploitation suffered by their predecessors. No one under thirty has the vivid and torturous mental images of a past reality that so inflamed their parents' and grandparents' sense of outrage as to arouse in them the pledge to make sacrifices of unfathomable proportions to rid China of misery and wretchedness. How can young people live up to the expectation that they "carry the revolution through to the end?" They have never known agonizing hunger; they have not been beaten, sold, or raped. When they are sick, someone takes care of them. They go to schools and recreation centers. They are accustomed to the cheerful sounds and sights of people whose lives are secure and productive.

The distance separating China's youth from the actual experience of unhappiness and despair was pointedly driven home to me by a rather humorous incident. While leisurely strolling along the Yangtse River Bridge in Nanking with our lovable teenage guide, I paused and the two of us stood quietly absorbed in the expanse of water and sky. Gazing down at the yellow-silted river rushing far below, my thoughts "naturally" turned to the phenomenon of suicide. I looked up at her suddenly and asked, "Do people ever jump off the bridge?" For a brief second she looked stunned; then she tossed her head back and let go with ripples of uninhibited laughter that trailed off into a soft giggle. She didn't answer my question; she didn't even seem to *get* it. I persisted. "Jumping off bridges is a common form of suicide in North America. Does that ever happen here?"

Her face showed that she was finally beginning to realize that I had actually asked the question seriously. Her smile disappeared, her laughter stopped, and her eyes widened. Dumbfounded, she asked, "Why would anyone ever want to do that?" Now it was my turn to be taken aback. I, too, recovered and then we talked for a while about suicide and its occurrence in North America. The discussion jogged her mem-

---

6. Soong Ching Ling, "For Succeeding Generations of Staunch Revolutionaries," *Peking Review* (May 28, 1965), p. 7.

ory and she said that she did remember hearing three or four years ago about a very old woman who was sick and had taken her own life.

It is quite true that this young woman was rather naive. It is also true that suicide still does occur sometimes in China and it is not limited to sick, old people. What struck me about her reaction was her own shock and total inexperience with the kind of suicide that is generated by alienation and despair. I could not imagine having such a conversation with an eighteen-year-old, no matter how naive, back home. Yet suicide is sufficiently rare that this young woman of new China cannot imagine that which was commonplace when her mother was her age.

A full understanding of and feeling for China's terrible past can perhaps never be grasped in all its profundity by a generation that has never had to live it. Models like Lei Feng represent an ongoing revolutionary spirit consistent with the revolutionary heroism of the past—that helps. Students work in factories and fields alongside workers and peasants, bringing the significance of socialist construction closer to home—that also helps. But these alone are not enough. Young people must know as deeply as possible what kind of past they come out of before they can be intensely committed to the kind of future they must work toward. A veteran worker, when recounting his own biography before liberation, remarked, "Lenin was right when he said that to forget the past is to betray the present." The older generations of China know that "the bitter past" must somehow be sharply represented to the youth if they are to dedicate themselves to continuing the revolution. Bringing this past to life is one of the main methods of inculcating strong proletarian feelings.

Plays, operas, literature, and films re-enact the horrors of the past, always laying stress on their conquest through revolutionary action. These undoubtedly make an impact because the past can be seen and felt and the enormous change to the present better understood and appreciated. All memorabilia of the past are also extremely important. The "news" that we in the West got during the late 1960s about Chinese revolutionary leaders urging youth to destroy museums because they wanted to obliterate their past is absurd, since museums contain some of the most vivid representations of the past.

Artifacts are treasured for their power to instruct politically as well as for their beauty. A visitor to the Forbidden City, for example, can only marvel at the breathtaking splendor and incredible beauty of the gardens, pavilions, fountains, pagodas, jewels, jade carvings, incense burners, golden cauldrons, the fabulous Halls of various kinds of Harmony (Supreme Harmony, Complete Harmony, Preserving Harmony), the bronze and gold dragons, lions, cranes, and much, much more. At the same time, visitors also find out that the labor of 100,000 artisans and one million workers was required to construct the Forbidden City with its more than 9,000 rooms—all for one man and his family, servants, and concubines; that he would not allow a single building in Peking to be constructed over two stories high so as not to obstruct his view; that a moat, wall, and armed guards surrounded the City and that the stones in the huge courtyards are fifteen layers deep—all precautionary measures to keep the common people out. These are pointed lessons, especially when it is realized that now an average of nearly 100,000 people visit the "Forbidden" City every week.

Those who go to the Summer Palace, which like all such places is now a public park, know that less than a century ago the empress collected millions of dollars on the pretext of building a navy but used the money instead for the reconstruction of a palace which had earlier been destroyed by foreign troops. The day I was there many working people were sunning themselves and relaxing on the famous and phenomenal marble boat, the "boat" that couldn't go anywhere but which they knew had been fashioned to enable the empress to enjoy the reflection of the water on the mirrors inside. They also knew that the empress insisted that her table be decorated with 128 courses at each meal and that any one of her meals (which cost on average about six pounds of gold) would have fed 5,000 peasants who were meanwhile starving.

Or when they visit the tombs of the Ming emperors they discover that forty concubines and twelve serving women of the palace were buried alive with the emperor to attend to his every whim and desire in the next world. One of the tombs outside of Peking is fully excavated and visitors can see the marble and bronze walls of the burial chamber and the trunks and trunks that were full of silks and jewels. They can also see two unobtrusive charts on the wall. One shows the amount of labor required for the construction of the tomb—30,000 workers working for six years, amounting to well over 65 million work days or the equivalent of an average of 6.5 days of labor from every family in the country. The other chart calculates the cost of the tomb—double the total income of the entire country for a year, or, more graphically, when converted into rice, a quantity sufficient to feed one million people for six-and-a-half years. An exhibition hall constructed above ground shows the crude weapons used by the peasants in their uprisings against such outrageous injustices, side by side with the emperor's carved jade ornaments; the rags worn by the peasants next to the fantastically opulent gowns of tiny gold discs connected by golden threads worn by the emperor; paintings of peasant uprisings, and one of a young virgin being dragged away from her family to be thrown into the kiln to improve the quality of the emperor's porcelain. There are always schoolchildren at these places imbibing the sights and the stories that go with them, learning the lessons of class struggle.

These are some of the more spectacular lessons. Obviously not every student in China can get to places like the Forbidden City, Summer Palace, or Ming Tombs. But there are many museums all over the country that preserve the artifacts of China's earlier class inequities. There is even a museum on the Pai Kwang Middle School grounds in Shanghai. Despite the overcrowded conditions of the school, which used to be a police station, the jail has been left intact.

The students and teachers of the school have chosen not to convert it into classrooms, thus sacrificing the luxury of badly needed elbow room for what they consider to be the more important priority, the political education to be gained by its presence.

Shau Chih-ming, Chairman of the school's Revolutionary Committee, explained: "These buildings were formerly used for the suppression of the revolutionary people. During the imperialist occupation, this was a police station, but it has since been returned to the hands of the people and transformed into a school. The jail is as it was before; it has been preserved to teach the young people of this school what life was like before liberation."

There are two tiny cells for solitary confinement called black rooms because they are so dark inside. Next to them is a larger cell, about fifteen feet square, with concrete walls and floors, bars in front, completely bare save for a "toilet" which is nothing more than an open hole in the floor. As many as seventy to eighty prisoners would be herded into the cell at a time; even if there had been sufficient space, they were not allowed to sit but had to stand jammed together. The toilet was a relatively late addition to the cell, having been "the fruit of struggle." A sign next to it explains, "This was obtained only after a struggle waged by the imprisoned revolutionaries and innocent working people. In the beginning no such toilet existed in the cell and the waste was allowed to just spread all over the floor. It reeked; there were many flies and mosquitoes; epidemic diseases threatened the imprisoned people. Then they united to wage a struggle against the enemy demanding that the sanitary conditions be improved. But nothing was done and so the imprisoned people continued to struggle. They waged a hunger strike and finally obtained victory. Although the enemy was compelled to make this hole for a toilet, there was still no lid on it. You can see the cruel oppression the Chinese people have suffered in the past."

Perhaps the most effective way for young people to see this "cruel oppression" of the past is through the very impressive and moving experience known as "speaking bitterness." Middle-aged and old people get together with youth in schools and communities to tell about their lives in the old society. There are endless stories; the storytellers often sit for hours with their listeners, recounting their own separate nightmares, each one unique, yet all of them the same—hunger, premature death, exploitation, unimaginable abuse. Tears flow unashamedly on all sides, from men and women, children and adults. Sometimes people of a whole village meet in a central square and sit huddled together in the cold on small blocks of wood, eating coarse dry grain as in the past and telling each other about a mother raped, a baby sister drowned, a father beaten to death by an enraged landlord—all this done to restore to life the old society in the minds and hearts, not only of the youth, but of each other, and to reinvigorate their commitment to building a new future.[7] The stories always end with the profound transformation of people's lives that began with liberation. The contrast is explicit and always sharp; the stories, though excruciating, are always uplifting and inspiring to speakers and listeners alike.

We heard many such personal accounts in our travels, the same kind of stories that students hear at every opportunity. At Ho Lai People's Commune in Kiangsu Province northwest of Shanghai, for example, we visited the home of a fifty-five-year-old peasant woman. Her physical appearance somehow matched the appearance of her house and the commune village itself. Old, with the signs of past ill use, there was a solidity that seemed to reinforce the feeling of strength and purpose and that made each smile, each gesture of warmth and friendliness the more genuine.

---

7. It is of interest to note that the practice of comparing the old with the new has at times been used for conservative rather than revolutionary purposes. During the Cultural Revolution, for example, revisionists sometimes conjured up the horrors of the past to highlight the happiness of the present, the message being that people should be satisfied with their conditions and cease any agitation for further change.

She welcomed us and invited us to sit down in her living room-bedroom. It had been raining all day and the unpaved paths of the village had left our shoes caked with mud; over her strenuous objections we removed them so as not to soil her spotlessly clean floors. Two younger neighbors were also on hand to greet us and were quietly pouring hot water into glasses from large flower-decorated vacuum jugs. (Many Chinese believe that hot water is healthy, and it is always served to guests, usually as tea but sometimes by itself.)

She was obviously delighted with her foreign visitors and we kept the translators busy as we chatted about some of the things we had seen in her village. Then someone asked her about her life before liberation. Her answers came just as openly as before but a subtle change took place in her eyes and her voice as she spoke. For the Chinese, "speaking bitterness" is not a ritual; it is a reliving of the past.

"Before liberation, we were very poor. When my younger sister was born, my parents had no food and could not maintain her life. They had to give her to another family, and so we never lived together." She had watched her mother's belly swell and had probably even witnessed the agonies of birth. And the memory of having to "give away" this squalling bundle of new life had obviously still not left her.

"Our poverty got worse and worse and finally my father could not get any work at all from the landlord. He had to go to the city to work in a factory and he worked very hard. All the time he worked very hard, but he was paid so little that he could barely support just himself, and there was never money to send to us. My mother went to the rich landlord's house to be a domestic servant and my brother and I also worked for the landlord when we were very young. We used to cut firewood and herd oxen for his wife, but she was never satisfied, and would scold us and beat us. We had no tools to cut the firewood, and we had to break it with our hands. Even now my fingers are still scarred from it." Tears welled in her eyes as she extended her hands to show us the scars. "My brother and I suffered very much from the pain. We had only three months supply of grain for a year so my mother and us children had to dig for wild vegetables. Usually we had only porridge and the wild vegetables to eat. All of the poor peasants were treated this way by the landlords before liberation. We were all extremely poor and suffered very much. In my village," she continued, her eyes cast downward, "many children and adults died of hunger." When she looked up, her eyes were flashing, "But the landlords only laughed! When the landlords ate, they lorded it over us, over the poor peasants, saying, 'We have enough food, and you don't have any.' They would even give their scraps to the pigs rather than to us, and so we were very hungry— and very bitter.''

She reached for a handkerchief to wipe the tears from her cheeks. She took a deep breath and went on. ''When I was seventeen years old, I got married. My husband was also a poor peasant and so our lives never improved in those miserable days. My husband worked for the landlord as a hired hand but the landlord only let him work for seven months because he only wanted him during the busy season. There was no work during the slack season at all. We had six children; two of them died because we couldn't afford a doctor to take care of them when they got sick. We didn't have enough food for the others, two girls and two boys. Many times we couldn't even give them porridge to eat.'' The voice of our translator began to show the signs of the same emotion we were all feeling.

''Before liberation, we didn't have a house to live in. We stayed crowded together in a straw hut beside a fish pool. We tried to feed ourselves by catching fish. In the winter we all slept huddled together to try to keep warm. But after liberation, the government gave us this house. We were given three rooms.''

A smile appeared on her face; her eyes glistened through the tears. The heaviness dropped from her voice. ''Since then,'' she said with pride, ''we have added on another room; so now we even have a guest room. Before we had only a small straw hut and now we have a sturdy house with a *guest room*! Who would have ever dreamed in those days when we suffered so much that the poor would some day be so rich?''

While her home was still very modest and far from ''rich'' in our eyes, contrasting it to her past unimaginable deprivation—which is the only reasonable kind of comparison—she was indeed rich. From the straw hut without porridge to feed her children to a five-room house (she hadn't counted the small kitchen) with electricity, a stove for heat, and plenty of food. In the room where we were sitting were a bed and quilt, two wooden tables (one spread with an embroidered cloth), several bamboo chairs, a sewing machine, and a breakfront with dishes and fresh eggs. Her bedroom had a double bed with pillows and quilts on it, a small table and chair, and a bureau with a mirror, a clock, and four frames full of small family snapshots. The other bedroom and the guest room were similarly furnished, but the guest room also obviously doubled as a storage place. What's more, the family enjoyed a surplus, something unheard of for a poor peasant before. There were baskets of nuts, some cookies, tomato saplings, and a huge round container of sorghum. There was a speaker in the room that connected to the commune radio station, but the family also owned a transistor radio. The hallway too was used for storage and had a long ladder, a few tools hanging neatly in rows, and several more large baskets stacked inside one another, hanging from a hook near the ceiling, waiting to be filled with more surplus. The baskets themselves were sign enough of their new prosperity. In the past, only the rich ever had any need of baskets for storage. What would poor peasants ever put in them if, by chance, they owned such baskets?

The good smells of supper cooking filled the house. That night they would have soybean and tomato soup, pork fried with eggplant, rice and bread. They ate fish or meat twice a week, and this was one of those days. "I raise chickens, so we get four eggs every day. We also grow vegetables in our garden. We have one-tenth of a mou[8] for self-gardening. Many times we have more than we can eat, so we store food in the baskets." The sprinkling of flowers in the small garden also testified to her new wealth. If her family had been so fortunate as to have had any land of their own in the past, they could never have afforded the luxury of growing anything just for beauty.

The walls of the house were almost completely plastered with revolutionary posters, especially pictures of revolutionary ballets. We commented on the posters, and asked if she liked ballet. "Oh, yes, very much. I have seen 'The Red Detachment of Women' three times and I never get tired of it!" On the wall in her bedroom was a picture of the composer of "The Internationale," the song of proletarian international solidarity and struggle. Beneath it were the words:

> Arise, ye prisoners of starvation;
> Arise, ye wretched of the earth,
> For justice thunders condemnation,
> A better world's in birth.

> No more tradition's chains shall bind us.
> Arise, ye slaves, no more in thrall.
> The earth shall rise on new foundations.
> We have been naught; we shall be all!

---

8. One mou equals one-sixth of an acre.

Her husband had died before liberation. All of her children were married and she had three grandchildren, two in kindergartens and one in the brigade primary school. Two of her children and their families lived with her. The others lived and worked in Shanghai but came to visit during Spring Festival. Because she was not very strong she did light work at the nearby fish ponds. "I weed and cut grass to feed the fish, simple jobs like that. Although I'm getting old, I can still do something more for the revolution according to my abilities."

In the old days no one in her family had ever gone to school. "All of us began to get cultural knowledge only after liberation. I attended night school and learned to read and write some characters. I also belong to a study group, and we meet every Thursday night to study the works of Chairman Mao and discuss production affairs. We discuss ways to raise the fish yields in the ponds and other such problems. Before the Cultural Revolution the yield was 500 kilos of fish per mou of water surface. We have since increased it to over 600 kilos. Now we have all this," she said with a sweep of her scarred hand indicating the new wealth surrounding her, "*and* the bitterness is gone from our lives."

She leaned forward intently. "Chairman Mao and the Communist Party have led us out of our poverty and misery. We owe all that we have to their wise leadership. Now everyone works hard, but we all work together and everyone's life improves all the time. We cooperate and share the fruits of our work; so you can see why we are dedicated to socialist construction."

A more convincing argument would have been hard to imagine, but, like the children in China's schools, we were to hear many more. At the dockyard in Shanghai we were introduced to Sung Chi-chuan, a veteran dockworker, now a member of the Revolutionary Committee of Shanghai Harbor's Fifth Working District. Sung belongs to the Committee's section in charge of "the welfare and daily lives of the workers." He is a striking man, large, square, and powerful-looking, whose very presence seemed to command attention and respect. At fifty-eight he is a model veteran worker, highly regarded by his workmates for his wealth of experience and unflagging revolutionary spirit.

We admired the efficiency and cleanliness of the docks. One of the most noticeable things about the whole area was the absence of litter or dirt. The dockyard was alive with the movement and sounds of cranes, trucks, and forklifts (many of them operated by women) yet there was none of the offensive filth or the grimy smell I had always associated with large freight ports. Instead, the docks were spacious and pleasant; there were trees with big blossoms and small patches of flowers less than 100 yards from the water. Sung smiled appreciatively at our comments, transforming his deeply-lined square face into one large, warm crinkle. "It hasn't always been this way, far from it! This is just *one* of the changes here since liberation. I have worked on the docks for thirty-seven years, more than ten years before liberation, and more than twenty years since, and I have seen a lot. Before liberation, this Fifth Working District consisted of four wharves all owned by capitalists—foreign and Chinese.

"The workers were miserably exploited. The capitalists never employed any fixed workforce so the men would have to come early every morning and hope they would be chosen to work for the day. That's how they tried to divide the workers and make us passive. There were only three machines on the docks and all the work of loading and unloading was done by hand. No matter what distance we had to carry the loads, and no matter how heavy they were, we had to carry everything on our backs or shoulders." He half rose from his chair, his back stooped to illustrate the weight of the burdens the men had to carry.

"Of course the efficiency was very low. For instance, to unload 10,000 tons of rice would take ten days and ten nights; raw steel took even longer. Some pieces of steel weighed several tons, but everything, every bit of it, was handled by human labor!" He stopped to look at us as if to make sure that we understood what he had just said—an indication that even he, who had actually experienced it, found this fact extraordinary.

"We were called 'dirty coolies,' and we were driven as if we ourselves were machines. To squeeze more work out of us, the capitalists hired foremen. Every day these mercenaries would flog the workers to make us speed up. They carried whips and batons in their hands to beat the workers.

"Meanwhile we were suffering from hunger and cold. In the winter, we had only odd pieces of jute bag to cover our bodies and straw sandals for our feet. Some of the dockers had no place to live and would have to find shelter at night under the eaves of houses. But the old workers suffered the most. By afternoon they were very weak from carrying heavy loads all morning without a break. Often they carried 100-kilo bags on their backs from the berths to the warehouses. 100 kilos,'' he repeated. ''That was a distance of six to seven-hundred feet, and they would have to climb the steps and go up as many as six stories in the warehouses, always watched by the foremen who would whip them when they stumbled or slowed down. You could sometimes see their whole bodies trembling from the weight. Many of the old men just collapsed, and when they did they were thrown out and reduced to begging for a living.''

All this time, Sung sat on the edge of his seat, his huge gnarled hands making profuse gestures to accentuate his words. ''The wharves owned by the foreign imperialists were the worst. Before liberation, most of the wharves in Shanghai were owned by the Japanese, British, and American imperialists. They tortured us by every means. The British company which used to own this wharf set up a jail right in this building to imprison dockers when they thought we were not working hard enough. A British jail! Right here! The workers had no protection at all; the bosses could do whatever they liked to us. Do you see those two trees in front of this building?'' His excitement growing, he stood up to point out the window at the two trees side by side near the entrance, eyes wide and blazing with indignation. ''We called them the trees of the emperor of the palace of hell. When a worker would fall beneath the weight of the load on his back, they would hang him from those trees, a rope around each wrist, and whip and beat him so that we would 'all see the power they had over us. In truth, when the dockers went to work, it was just like entering a living hell on earth.''

He sank back into his chair and paused, the long lines of his face taut as he lingered for a brief moment with these stark memories. But when he started speaking again his face slowly softened into the same wonderful smile it wore when we met him. ''But exploitation and oppression are now things of the past. Since liberation, these wharves have been returned to the hands of the people, and the workers have been liberated. We dockers have become the masters of the wharves instead of being slaves!

''The working people of China have been politically liberated, and we are the masters of the motherland. And we have been liberated economically as well; we are no longer exploited by capitalists and imperialists. Our living standards are improving all the time with the development of production. We now enjoy what we call 'labor insurance regulations.' These regulations guarantee our livelihood and they also provide guarantees for our old age, sickness, and burial. We don't have to worry about these things any more.

"Before liberation, we were afraid of becoming old. I can remember when I was only twenty-one and started working on the docks— these very docks. Although I was strong enough to carry the heavy loads, I was already afraid of becoming old because I saw with my own eyes many old people who couldn't bear the weight and how they would be kicked off the docks by the bosses. And even I, who used to work fifteen or sixteen hours every day, couldn't get married because I wasn't paid enough to support a family. I stayed a bachelor. I got married and had children only *after* liberation.

"We don't have these worries any more. According to the labor insurance regulations, workers doing heavy manual work can retire at the age of fifty-five. The women workers can retire when they reach fifty.[9] After retirement, they will still receive seventy percent of their last pay. They also get complete free medical care and other benefits, so they have no worries at all. All the dockworkers get working clothes free from the state, including heavy padded coats for winter, gloves, shoes, and protective helmets.

"Also in the past there was no limit to the working hours, but now we have stipulated an eight-hour working day which includes mealtime and work breaks. During those hours nobody is made to work too hard. The three machines on these wharves before liberation have now grown to nearly two hundred, and more than 75 percent of the work is mechanized. Before, if there were two ships anchored here, there might be as many as 2,000 workers to unload and load them because it was all done by hand. But now, even if there are five ships at a time, you won't see many people on the wharf because those jobs have been mechanized. The workers do only the jobs in the warehouses and the holds of the ships; all the heaviest work is done by machines. We used to hear only the groaning voices of the workers straining under their burdens, but now you can hear only the humming voices of the machines."

He went on to tell us about the wage scale and how individual wages

---

9. Women generally retire before men (except on communes where peasants do not actually retire as long as they are able to work). The reason for this earlier retirement, we were told, is because women suffered very much in the past and consequently, older women are often in delicate health. But retirement, both for women and men, is not forced. Anyone who is able and so chooses may continue to work and many old people maintain some connection to their workplaces. At fifty-eight, Sung is a good example of a fully active worker who is not yet ready to retire.

were determined. They range from forty-six yuan a month for apprentices to ninety yuan for veteran workers.[10] When Sung retires, he will get sixty-three yuan a month for the rest of his life; he will also get full medical care free and the guarantee of a "decent burial," a level of security he dared not even dream of when he first came to the dockyards as a young man. The workers determine their own pay (within, of course, an accepted scale). They get together and assign themselves and each other to particular wage categories by measuring each person against three criteria—length of experience, level of skill, and political attitude toward work and workmates. "Before the Cultural Revolution, we put a lot of stress on skill, but that is a bourgeois way of doing things. Now we mainly pay attention to political attitude and experience. The workers decide," said another dock worker.

The workers also decide who their leaders will be. Bosses and foremen have disappeared. Sung, along with others, was selected by his workmates to the Revolutionary Committee, whose members regularly put in a stint of manual work like everyone else. If they abuse their position and begin to act in an authoritarian way or try to counter the interests of the workers, their authority can be challenged by the workers who are empowered to remove them from the Revolutionary Committee just as they put them there in the first place. The possibility of the reappearance of authoritarianism and elitism has undoubtedly not yet been completely eliminated from the Shanghai docks, or from the workplaces of China in general. But a commonly expressed belief is that institutions like the Revolutionary Committee, as well as the growing sense of self-confidence and self-reliance among the rank and file which were further enhanced by the Cultural Revolution, are encouraging signposts in the "10,000 li long march" toward communism.

Sung also told us about the canteen, the athletic facilities, and the recreational center with its ping pong tables, music rooms, and library

---

10. In June of 1973, one yuan equalled fifty-three cents but the exchange rate changes as the result of inflation external to China. The rate of exchange, however, tells nothing by itself. Several facts are of significance. Three generations often live together, bringing in two or more incomes per family. Prices are uniform and stable throughout the country. Rent runs in the vicinity of four to five percent of family income; food is cheap; prices of other necessities like clothing are reasonable; all medical care is either free or close to it. Most families are able to afford a few luxuries and have bank accounts. If, for some reason, a family is in need of necessities, the state will grant subsidies.

that have been set up for the workers' use at the Fifth Working District of Shanghai Harbor. There is a nursery on the docks for the workers' babies, a clinic for minor ailments and injuries, a spare-time school for the dockers after working hours, and amateur writing and theatrical groups. One of the favorite performances is the opera well known in China, "On The Docks," which depicts the dockers' working lives as revolutionary and heroic. A famous aria proclaims: "We dockers move grain in millions of jin[11] with our left hands, while our right shift steel by the ton. Neither mountains nor seas can block our revolutionary fervor. We send our sincere friendship to all parts of the globe."

This is just one part of Sung's story, and only a minute episode in the epic of the Chinese people's past wretchedness and degradation and their new happiness and pride. There was also the man who had gone to work in the silk factory when he was nine years old, who remembered the fatigue of working twelve hours straight in a hot room enveloped in steam and the excruciating pain of having boiling water poured over his head the time the foreman caught him napping. He still works there and recalled the poem composed all those years ago by his adult workmates, a poem which, he announced happily, is now long out of date.

> The lives of silk factory workers
> Are as bitter as ginseng.
> We come to work when the cock crows
> And go home in the middle of the night.
> Every inch of silk contains the sweat of the workers.
> We can't see the sun, only the mist.

And then there was Wang Pei-chang, the sixty-five-year-old woman who measured her new wealth by quilts. As a child she had shared one ragged quilt with the seven other members of her family in their feeble and pathetic attempt to stave off the biting cold of North China's fierce winters. But today there is one quilt for every two members of her family; the quilts are new and puffy, decorated with flowers and colorful designs. And she has a stove for heat. "How could I ever think of having such a good life? How could the working people of China be so much respected? In the old days we were treated like a piece of grass,

---

11. One jin equals approximately 1.1 pounds, or one-half kilo.

but in the new society, we, the working people, are seen as precious. We have been liberated, and today we are our own masters!''

There is a poster that hangs in many classrooms showing an old man with his arm around a young child, his hand resting on the boy's shoulder. They are both looking off into the distance at the faint outlines of chains, squalor, and scantily clad people huddled together, the snow whipping their almost naked bodies. These are all in the background, the past. The boy and the old man, neatly dressed and well fed, are of the present. Their faces look solemn as the old man tells the child about life before liberation. The characters along the edge of the poster remind students, ''Keep the memory of the past alive in our hearts.''

''Our lives were agonizing,'' said one old man, summing it all up. ''It's very painful for us to speak of our past miseries. But we must always recall the bitterness of the past to taste the sweetness of the present.''

The youth of China can ''recall'' this bitterness only through others, but from these stories they will learn enough, their elders hope, to ''treasure the new sweetness.'' ''It is up to them to make the future even sweeter.'' Their education would be useless if they didn't learn this, their first and most important lesson.

THE TWO LINES

''By having workers select who goes to university and by emphasizing politics so much in the schools, aren't you losing out? I mean, what about a student who does well in school but maybe isn't all that interested in politics? It seems to me that by your philosophy of education your country is losing some very clever and talented people who could perhaps make an important contribution to some field of knowledge.''

I overheard this criticism-question addressed to my Chinese friends studying in Canada by a woman who seemed quite upset by the Chinese educational system. It is the kind of question often asked of the Chinese. I have heard several different replies, all very similar, given by both students and teachers in China and abroad:

''How could someone who is not fired with the spirit of serving the people but is concerned only with himself make a contribution to others?''

"How much knowledge a person has is not the most important thing; what matters is how he applies that knowledge; is it to serve the people, or to serve only himself?"

"We don't believe that there is such a thing as individual genius, or that progress comes from the work of a few people. So, in China, all the people are mobilized to further socialist construction. All our advances come from the collective efforts of the masses who work together scientifically and cooperatively."

"Someone may have a huge amount of knowledge, he may know many things, but if his orientation is wrong his knowledge is worth nothing. That is for the bourgeoisie."

The answers have a ring of finality about them; yet the question is far from settled. This question has been at the center of educational debate since the founding of the People's Republic and it remains there today. It forms the crux of the two-line struggle in education.

What the Chinese call the revisionist line has been based on the contention that because China is a poor country just beginning to industrialize the need for scientists and technicians looms large; priority should go to the training of specialists, regardless of their political outlook. A chemist can do good chemistry whether his thinking is bourgeois or revolutionary; that's beside the point. The real point is that China needs highly skilled chemists, and soon. Anyway, goes this argument, the Communist Party is now in power so there is no need to worry about the class struggle any more. Of course universal education is important but it will have to stay in the background until there is a well-trained core of experts who can lead in developing the country and building an industrial base. Otherwise China cannot hope to catch up to the industrialized countries. That's how all other countries have developed, so why shouldn't China do the same?

The ramifications of this position are enormous. In industry, for example, it has meant the difference between who runs the factories— "experts" or the workers. If it's to be experts—people who have learned about the operations in principle but may be confounded when they see machines, people who decide "for" the workers how much they can produce, how fast the machines should run, what the workers should be paid, etc.—then what's the difference between a socialist and a capitalist enterprise?

Many capitalistic practices were in evidence in the factories of

China, especially during those years before the Cultural Revolution when the revisionist line so often held sway. Workers were given bonuses for higher productivity, leading to competition and invidious gradations among them; they became more acquisitive; interest in improving the productive process by innovating machinery and furthering cooperation lagged; bureaucracies developed; authoritarianism spread. Factory leaders were ignoring the workers' suggestions when they didn't suit their purposes; they became more concerned with turning out products that would yield the highest returns rather than those most needed by the country. Large numbers of individuals were striving more and more for their own narrow self-interests—higher paychecks and higher status—while ordinary working people were looked down upon, and the exhortation to serve the people took on a hollow sound. "We were becoming the slaves of money," one worker remarked. Similar things were happening on the communes. Every kind of work was affected. It seemed that every job site wanted "experts." But where were they to come from?

Obviously, the schools. It was in the schools that the ideological center of this many tentacled octopus, revisionism, resided. To train "top notch" professionals, the schools concentrated on those with a head start, the children of the former privileged classes—the landlords and the bourgeoisie—and the children of the newly developing privileged class of cadres. Many teachers were authoritarian and prohibited dissent; they were punitive toward the children of workers and peasants, favoring their own "class brothers" who were more "cultured" and less "crude." They set examinations that got rid of the "less intelligent," they "put marks in command," and the university authorities followed suit by accepting the "most capable." The curriculum trained intellectuals and scholars by methods devoted only to "book knowledge" and "divorced from politics, production, and the masses." A new elite was in the making, an elite which saw itself apart from and above those "mere" working people with dirty hands and "inferior" minds.

Class distinctions were sharpening and the class struggle had to be intensified if socialism was not to be lost. Hence the Cultural Revolution. In the course of the Cultural Revolution an opposite line developed in response to revisionism. Also considered to be wrongheaded, the ultraleftists swung in the other direction. In their most extreme expression, they claimed that everything from the past contained only reactionary politics and should be scrapped. Card playing reflects bourgeois decadence; it must be prohibited. How can red mean stop in a socialist country? Traffic signals must be changed. Everyone must carry the quotations of Chairman Mao at all times and constantly study them. Every manufactured product, every park, street, and bus must carry revolutionary slogans. One group of ultraleftists proclaimed: "Scoundrels of the bourgeoisie are not allowed to wander around or visit parks at will. . . . They cannot indulge in wild fancies."[12] In the schools, the ultraleftists debunked all technical and professional training; only ideological education was important; "book learning" was of little use and should be replaced by practice, by integration with the masses. Of course, ultraleftism also took more subtle forms—for example some people advocated that all examinations should be eliminated.

All redness and no expertise, the ultraleft line at that time was not seen as a threat on the same scale as the more common form of revisionism in China, despite the extreme headlines it generated in the Western press. Our media portrayed the Cultural Revolution as if it were purely and simply a mad scramble to denounce everything and everyone for not being revolutionary enough, as if it were a deification of Mao as the god of revolution. When many of us think of China, we see angry crowds shouting wild slogans and waving red books of Mao's quotations.

It is true that all this did happen during the Cultural Revolution, but it was a less significant aspect of a huge multifaceted movement and did not gain large throngs of adherents in most sections of the population. While many of the leaders of the ultraleft were experienced, which made them all the more dangerous, most of their followers during the height of the Cultural Revolution were overexuberant youths. This is not to say that there could not be conditions in which ultraleftism could well become a major problem in China. In fact, it did become a real enough threat at a later point in the Cultural Revolution when many of the factions which had developed in the heat of the struggle refused to unify. The "holier-than-thou" and "we-are-the-only-revolutionaries" attitudes of ultraleftists then became a smokescreen for an attempted

---

12. Maoism School of Peking, "The One Hundred Items for Destroying the Old and Establishing the New," *Chinese Sociology and Anthropology* 2, no. 3–4 (Spring–Summer 1970), p. 221.

traditional grab for power by Lin Piao and his followers. The more important point here, however, is that during most of the Cultural Revolution ultraleftists were seen more as an immature and passing nuisance, easier to contain than revisionism was to uproot.[13]

This is why the two-line struggle of the Cultural Revolution refers fundamentally to the struggle between the revisionist ideology that overemphasized expertise on the one hand, versus Mao's revolutionary position of insisting upon both redness and expertise on the other. Education, according to Mao, should stress both political commitment and technical competence. The implications of this line are just as far-reaching as they are for the revisionist line. This outlook sees everyone as capable of expertise; it credits the masses of people with intelligence and creativity.

The whole society has been shaken by the triumph of the red and expert line. To again take the factories as an example, the more invidious material incentives like the bonus system have been largely replaced by moral incentives. Workers of course are still paid and that payment derives basically from the socialist principle of "to each according to his work," but the competition for more money or easier jobs or the favor of cadres has diminished. There is more emphasis on being "red"—on increasing production, taking more initiative, improving cooperation, making a greater contribution to socialist construction and, in general, on serving the people more meaningfully. Workers select

---

13. Revisionism, because it is entrenched in that centuries-old tradition of selfishness, privilege-seeking, and slavish obedience to professionalism and authority, tends to be silent, diffuse, recalcitrant, and therefore difficult to identify and counter. Ultraleftism except in its more blatant and excessive manifestations can also be difficult to identify and counter in a revolutionary society because it appears to be moving in a revolutionary direction. Ultraleftists often clamor for rapid and thoroughgoing changes which are inappropriate to the circumstances and therefore cannot bring about meaningful revolutionary results. To Chinese revolutionaries, both "ordinary" revisionism and ultraleftism are seen as having a common class basis, as being isolated from the needs and demands of the masses, and therefore counterrevolutionary in consequence. For this reason, they see standard revisionism and ultraleftism as essentially two sides of the same coin. Their assessment appears to have been confirmed by the Lin Piao affair in which ultraleftism was indeed one of the chosen instruments utilized by Lin in the essentially rightist conspiracy against Mao, thus corroborating Mao's characterization of ultraleftists as those who "wave the red flag to oppose the red flag." (The Lin Piao affair and its implications require further study. For more on the Chinese explanation the reader is referred to the numerous articles that have appeared in *Peking Review* following the discovery of the plot to assassinate Mao and Lin's subsequent fall and death. Also see the short pamphlet by Yao Wen-yuan, *On the Social Basis of the Lin Piao Anti-Party Clique* [Peking: Foreign Languages Press, 1975].)

their own leaders and participate more fully in making their own decisions. While they are developing their ideological commitment to building socialism, more and more workers are, at the same time, learning to become more expert in translating that commitment into practice.

If it comes to a choice of temporarily sacrificing a measure of either redness or expertise, redness is generally seen as less dispensable. The Chinese believe that if the drive to deepen socialist morality is allowed to lapse even for a short period it opens the door to more revisionism and deterioration all around. Therefore, by putting emphasis on redness there will be a greater commitment to socialist construction, which in turn helps to spur on the masses' creative energy that Mao so insistently talks about, thus speeding up the development of their expertise as well. Both revolutionary dedication and technical competence are seen to grow and deepen by stressing redness.

The more highly politically aware people in China, however, do not see the victory of the red and expert line as final. Similar battles have been fought many times on many fronts. The Cultural Revolution, like the struggles before it, achieved tremendous success both in undoing the damage caused by revisionism and in further developing a revolutionary ideology. But revisionist tendencies cannot yet be completely eliminated and are expected to gain strength and adherents time and again in the future; the Chinese say that they must be on guard against it. This does not mean that they see their recent past and their future as an endless swing from revisionism to revolution to ultraleftism and back again without any qualitative changes. With each successful battle, the revolutionary line becomes deeper and stronger; each successive campaign is fought at a higher level.

Part of the reason for the present optimism in China can be found in the care with which problems are approached. The Chinese are not glib, but rather they are pointed and methodical. They ask fundamental questions: who is the enemy? For the student, is it the teacher? For the teacher, is it the student? No, the enemies are those who willfully work to sabotage socialism. Individual teachers or students may be conscious agents, but as groups they would more likely be innocent pawns in such a process. Whom do we serve? Our friends? Our enemies? Ourselves? Obvious. But answers are obvious only when questions get to the nub of an issue. In many schoools they now ask, "For whom do you study?" When students enter Sun Yat-sen Medical College, each one is given a hoe and a straw hat for an answer.

What is the basic job of the schools? Educators in China will tell you that it is "to train young proletarian successors who are instilled with the spirit of serving the people with all their hearts and souls." The Chinese maintain that every ruling class in every society educates its youth to uphold its own class outlook, because only by so doing can it hold on to its class rule. Every ruling class trains successors to perpetuate itself. In China, they say, "the workers and peasants are masters" and "the proletariat should have leadership in everything." The only difference—an enormous one—is that in China the successors are being trained in socialist morality. Tens of millions of young people are learning the attributes and skills that will develop them into "proletarian successors" qualified to replace the older revolutionaries. The Chinese are confident that many skilled leaders will emerge from among them.

This is happening in many ways. There are students all over the country, even at the primary level, who can articulate overall educational objectives, and they will accentuate essentially the same points as their teachers. Because they have already had practice in responsible citizenship, they know what is expected of them now and sense what is ahead in the years to come. A great many of the things that happen in the schools are the result of open discussion and conscious decision on all sides. This kind of practice has developed leadership qualities not only in the "special few," but in many young people who have learned, in their ordinary day-to-day activities, to show initiative and act responsibly. The real legacy of Mao's leadership is, in fact, the preparation of conditions where his individual leadership is unnecessary and where innumerable others are capable of forwarding the revolutionary line which Mao's life and thought have come to symbolize.

One consequence of the consolidation of that legacy is that most young people have a remarkably clear unmuddled sense of direction and purpose in life. There is little in China of the situation so common elsewhere among youth who feel confused, powerless, fatalistic, and often overwhelmed about their futures.

Soon after his arrival in Canada, a young Chinese student was at an informal gathering at which I was present. During his conversations with several Canadian peers, he asked questions about what kind of work they wanted to do when they finished school and what they saw as their purposes in life. It was only due to his deeply bred sense of courtesy that he could conceal his utter shock at their answers—a shrug, a grunt, some half-mumbled comments—"who knows," "we'll see," "you never know," "whatever comes up." These were apparently new to his experience and left a deep impression on him.

Later, during a discussion on educational objectives and individual aspirations in China, he said, perhaps recalling what he had heard from the Canadian students, "The main point as I see it is that if you have a real purpose in your life, a very clear purpose, you will feel energetic; you will see things clearly and handle things correctly. But if you don't have any real purpose, then—how shall I explain it—maybe sometimes you will feel happy, but it's not happiness really; sometimes you will feel very sad; sometimes you will have nothing to do; you will feel that you don't know what your future will be; you will not know what you live for. I think this is very important, at least for the students of China," he added, not wanting to be discourteous or critical since he was, after all, a guest in another country.

"We have a very meaningful education. Every day we are taught to serve the people, to do more for the society, to build our country stronger and stronger, richer and richer, and to do things for the whole world, the whole of mankind. And this makes us feel very happy. We compare things with the old times and we feel deeply that they have changed very much, because people have worked hard to change them. We can see a bright future. Our living standard is not very high—it's not as high as yours here—and we must do a lot of hard work; we must use a great deal of strength to build our country. But from work we get happiness. There is a saying: 'To do more for the people is happiness.'

"So we have a strong belief in our lives; we have a very clear purpose; students know why they study and what they work for. If we meet with difficulties, we try our best to help each other to overcome them, to do things better."[14]

It is not only clarity of purpose that he was expressing, but also

14. This sense of purposefulness has been observed by many non-Chinese as well. One, a New Zealander with long and varied experience in China, has written: "In all, one feels that Chinese children are a wonderful bunch of humanity, knowing where they are going, what they live for, who are their friends and who are their enemies, sane, thoughtful and always with their feet firmly on the ground. Part of the salt of the earth with an immense contribution to make to the development of mankind. They know what their role should be in China, and they know too that two-thirds of the world is still hungry and exploited. Today all have food, clothing, housing and medicines, and they all know very well that their task is to serve the people, and to be one with the working folk of the world. For them the future is like the big lotus flower of summer, opening out into a glorious blossom." (Rewi Alley, *Chinese Children* [Christchurch, New Zealand: Caxton Press, 1972], p. 8.)

mutuality of purpose. What political education in China does as much as anything else is to connect youth to each other and to the community. For many young Chinese, individual fulfillment comes more through the fulfillment of collective needs than at their expense. Training in this attitude begins very young, as illustrated by this incident in a third grade primary class.

Some of the children apparently had difficulty adjusting to the more mundane jobs during a jump-rope contest. "The teacher tried to promote the idea of 'friendship first, competition second,' but found that some pupils thought that only the jumpers were 'heroic,' while those who swung the rope, kept score, and brought drinking water were of a 'lower order.' "[15] This became the occasion for a political lesson, for a discussion of the importance of all activities and their mutual interdependence—the value to everyone of a rational division of labor.

And this lesson deepens with time, even to the point of it often not mattering to young people what their life's work will be. They can be certain that they will have a job, that it will bring a decent wage, and that regardless of what it is, if they do it conscientiously, modestly, and well, they will in all probability earn the esteem of their workmates and community. The same young man who talked about the importance of having a selfless purpose in life had worked in a factory before going abroad to study. He told me that when he left middle school several years before, his classmates all got together. "Everyone made a resolution to work where they were needed. You know, we must not only be expert in our work; we must also be red in our outlook. The students with the most revolutionary consciousness asked to be given the most difficult jobs. They set a good example for the rest of us."

In his region, jobs were assigned through a placement office composed of students and teachers from the schools, and workers and cadres from the enterprises. They discussed job openings and students' skills and interests and then matched up students with jobs.

I asked about job preferences and dissatisfaction with jobs. What choices do the young people have? "When possible, they will try to give students particular jobs if they have preferences. But sometimes a young man or woman wants a certain job, not to serve the people, but because they think it is more important than another job. For instance,

---

15. "Growing Up Healthy in Mind and Body," *China Reconstructs* 22, no. 6 (June 1973), p. 9.

in my factory, some students were assigned to the painting group when they graduated. However, in the old society painters were looked down upon; people thought it was an inferior job; so some of them were dissatisfied because they still carried the burden of the old ideology. When that happened, the factory leaders tried to educate them, to explain the importance of every job. Several of the older workers told them stories of the bitter past and this made them think about their own happiness in the new society. Now they do their jobs very well and they are proud of their work because it is difficult. You know, we always say that though the jobs may be different, the goal is the same; we are all working for the revolution. Workers give us clothes; peasants give us rice. All jobs are important."

YOUTH ORGANIZATIONS

The youth of China don't rely only on adults for their political education but take on a share of the responsibility themselves. Fostering revolutionary political attitudes and behaviors in oneself and others is the job of all youth, but is more pointedly the objective of their organizations—the Little Red Soldiers, the Red Guards, and the Communist Youth League. Unlike many youth organizations in a number of other countries, there is no sex segregation in any of these.

Many foreigners have heard only about the Red Guards, and much of that has been incomplete and at times distorted. Unfortunately, too many of us in North America were told little about the Red Guards other than their excesses—their ultraleftism. "Teenage, slogan-drunk mobs" they were called, and that image has stuck. "Did you see any?" someone asked me when I got back from China, as if they were an aberration. It is certainly true that in some quarters, at some moments, groups of Red Guards did go too far. Some did accuse unjustly, did fight, did destroy, did abuse their new-found strength. But these are seen by the Chinese as incidents peripheral to the main thrust of the Red Guard movement.

A number of us have also been led to the vague notion that the Cultural Revolution was conducted only by the Red Guards and Mao—another misconception. In China, politics and revolutions are supposed to be everybody's business and it is inconceivable that any group would ever imagine that it could go about having its own "private" revolution. Like all revolutions, the Cultural Revolution involved everyone in some way or other, very often quite actively. Other groups besides the Red Guards also took leading roles, most notably the urban workers and the PLA.

While hearing much about the sensational acts, many of us outside of China never heard enough about those aspects which formed the core of the movement. In fact, as I recall, the most crucially significant aspect of the movement—its powerful impact as a political education for the Red Guards themselves and for their elders—was just about completely ignored. Few of us knew that the reason classes were suspended all over the country was so that the schools could become centers for a unique kind of education that focused on political discussion and debate. What is revisionism? What is the two-line struggle? How is it manifested in our school? What ideas do we have for transforming our education, our mentality from feudal and bourgeois to revolutionary? What do all these things we always hear mean—"serve the people," "put proletarian politics in command," "study hard for the revolution?" How have the schools failed to bring these slogans to life? What must be done to correct the situation? On and on, debate, write, study, listen, criticize—millions of youth engaged day and night.

It was the need for youth to address themselves to these very questions that led to the spontaneous sprouting up of hundreds of grass roots organizations early in the Cultural Revolution, organizations that came to be identified under the umbrella name of Red Guards. Students in the middle schools and higher institutions and even some of the older primary school pupils became involved. It was a movement that grew with great speed to huge proportions. The purpose was to criticize and expose revisionism.

The Red Guards traveled around the country to spread their own views and to learn what others were thinking elsewhere. Millions met in the cities, especially Peking, to hear each other out and to continue the debate. Thousands upon thousands of urban students went to the countryside to get the opinions of the peasants. They lived in their homes, shared their simple lives, worked with them in the fields. They brought the peasants news of the great ferment of the Cultural Revolution, introduced them to political ideas that many had never heard before, encouraged them to criticize revisionism in their own brigades and communes. For their part, the peasants taught the city youth about the wretchedness of their past lives and gave them a new respect for the realities of hard work and plain living. The activities of the Red Guards were, in the main, revolutionary both in conduct and consequence; they were also usually well organized, only infrequently rowdy.

The lasting effects are to be found in numerous transformations of outlooks and behaviors in all parts of the society, including the schools where much that was elitist has been dethroned, where the lives of students more fully intermesh with those of the workers and peasants, and where the work of the school now has much more intimate linkage with all facets of community life. That is why Chinese of all ages have nothing but the highest regard for the Red Guard movement of the late 1960s and point to its revolutionary fervor as a source of inspiration from which all can learn. The youth have proved themselves willing and qualified proletarian successors.

The Red Guards today are more subdued, simply because the Cultural Revolution has passed, but they are still looked up to as models of revolutionary enthusiasm. While they continue to involve themselves in community work, their activities also focus on "making revolution in the classrooms."

Red Guard organizations are now found only in middle schools. The younger children in the primary grades may become Little Red Soldiers, while qualified youth between the ages of fifteen and twenty may join the Communist Youth League.[16] All of the youth organizations resemble each other in that members are expected to be exemplary in their dedication to study and work and in their political attitudes and actions toward each other and the people.

Wu Huei Chu, a professor from the Shanghai Teachers' College, gave me a rundown of the youth organizations and how they function in her city. "The Little Red Soldiers take the lead in their primary schools. They should be bold in their thoughts and deeds. They set a good example in everything they do by their honesty, courage, liveliness, and good style of studying. They always work hard to promote unity among their classmates."

The red scarf of the Little Red Soldiers, worn round the neck and symbolizing "a corner of the national flag," is to be seen everywhere.

---

16. There is some overlapping of ages between the Red Guards and the Communist Youth League, and some young people are members of both. The Communist Youth League is not confined only to students; the lower age limit of fifteen enables working youth who have left school early to become members. Leaders in the League retain membership until the age of twenty-five, and occasionally two or three years longer if their services are required.

Little Red Soldiers visit a weather station where they learn to use meteorological instruments.

The majority of primary school pupils belong—70 percent in one school where I inquired, 95 percent in another. Though a high proportion of the children belong, membership is still regarded as an honor. The organization of the Little Red Soldiers differs from the Young Pioneers, its predecessor from before the Cultural Revolution. I spoke to a young woman who had been a member of the Young Pioneers. "At first it was for the politically advanced children to set a good example for the others. But then, in 1964, Liu Shao-ch'i said, 'They are very young; let everyone be a member.' Regardless of a child's behavior or attitude, they all could join; they did not have to work for it, so the purpose was lost. Because of this revisionist outlook, the organization became useless." Care is being taken to make sure that the new organization of Little Red Soldiers retains its meaning and purpose.

The Communist Youth League provides leadership for the Little Red Soldiers, but the latter are remarkably self-reliant and democratic. In each school they are organized first into a brigade which includes all members in the school; then into teams—one in each grade; and groups—one in each classroom. Leaders are elected by the members. Any child may apply for membership to the group in his or her classroom. "The students have a discussion," Wu explained, "where they comment on the child's study and work style and on his political behavior. The teachers can also give their opinions but final say rests with the Little Red Soldiers themselves." The group recommendation is passed on to the "committee of brigade cadres," the Little Red Soldier leaders of the school, for final approval.

Very similar procedures are followed in the middle schools among the Red Guards. Other than age, the main difference is that the Red Guards maintain higher standards of eligibility; consequently the proportion of young people who qualify for membership is lower, ranging from 25 to 40 percent in the schools where I asked. However, there is much variation from one school and locality to the next. In discussing the Red Guards, Wu said, "They have been steeled by the Cultural Revolution so they have become bold in daring to think, to act, and to make revolution. They are the pacesetters. To become a Red Guard, a young person must be very good at serving the people. These girls and boys must have a good political consciousness of the struggle between two lines and of continuing the proletarian revolution. Of course they must also study well and must be very good at uniting all the students. They must also be active in community affairs outside of the school."

The Red Guards organize numerous activities such as political study groups, visits to factories and communes, and sports events. As Wu pointed out, their activities are not only for themselves. Often included in their plans are those classmates who are not members. They also help to organize and lead after-school homework groups and recreational programs for the Little Red Soldiers.

Both the Red Guards and the Communist Youth League are under the leadership of the Chinese Communist Party although they have their own independent recruitment mechanisms and run their daily affairs themselves. Communist Youth League members can be found in middle schools in some places, but usually they are workers, peasants, or students at the higher levels of education. The League works closely with the Red Guards, and in Shanghai membership criteria are the same for both organizations; upon leaving middle school, a Red Guard automatically becomes a member of the League. "This is not necessarily true of all places," said Wu. "The League constitution is being revised, so they are not yet unified across the country on this and some other questions."

League members are sometimes referred to as "the powerful assistants to the Party." Membership in the Communist Party, however, is a completely separate matter, and anyone who wants to join, whether a League member or not, must apply directly to the Party itself. But as an organization that develops leadership qualities in large numbers of young people, the League is a fertile recruiting ground for the Party.

The League engages itself in pursuits similar to those of the Red Guards. It organizes political study sessions and numerous other educational as well as recreational activities at places of work or study and sometimes in centers outside. At one factory its function was explained by an older Party member as "mobilizing the youth and bringing their revolutionary vigor and creativeness into play. The Communist Youth League motivates youth to be like young tigers. But," he added with a grin, "even young tigers must be well organized."

All the youth organizations of today model themselves after the Red Guard movement when it was in its infancy during the Cultural Revolution. "In those days," said a new Red Guard member, "our older brothers and sisters burned the revolutionary fires. We must learn from them and cultivate the same spirit, the spirit of the Red Guards. We must follow their lead in becoming successors to the proletarian cause."

VII: TEACHING THE TEACHERS

> Those who would be teachers of the people must first be students of the people.
>
> MAO TSE-TUNG

THE MAIN PROBLEM

When he was just seven, Mao attended a village primary school which was

run by an old-type teacher, well thought of because he beat his pupils mercilessly. No teacher was reckoned worthy unless he showed severity to the children in his care. Each child, to recite his lessons, would leave his desk, stand in front of the teacher's desk, then promptly turn his back to him and recite. Mao refused to stand up. "If you can hear me well and sit, why should I stand up to recite?" he said. And clung to his desk and stool. The teacher was pale with fury. Never in a thousand years had this custom been challenged. He ordered the seven-year-old to stand before his desk, but Mao dragged his stool with him and sat himself next to the teacher. The teacher then tried to heave him upright. Mao got up and left the school, and lost himself for three days in the hills. His distraught parents were overjoyed when he was found, and after that he was not beaten in school. "The result of my act of protest impressed me. It was a successful 'strike.'" From this episode, Mao would go on; in each school he would attend Mao would lead student revolts, to reform teachers whose conduct he thought unbecoming.[1]

The total authority of the teacher, the submission of youth to their elders, was an unquestioned way of life in China's past. Mao's acts as a student were shockingly audacious. Now, of course, the old ideology rarely manifests itself in such overt and obvious cruelty by teachers, but, if it does, there are a great many more students who would not

---

1. Han Suyin, *The Morning Deluge: Mao Tse-tung and the Chinese Revolution, 1893-1954* (Boston: Little, Brown and Co., 1972), pp. 16–17.

hesitate to challenge it, just as Mao did. The more subtle expressions of teacher authoritarianism, however, are infinitely more stubborn because they are less conscious on the part of the perpetrators and more difficult for the victims to perceive. The reason, for example, why lecturing was a standard teaching method right up to the Cultural Revolution is that it was a still commonly held belief (although many people thought they thought otherwise) that teachers knew everything, and for students to attempt to contribute anything to the learning process would be a presumptuous and costly waste of valuable time.

There were also hangovers from the past of the entrenched overweening pride that compelled people to go to great lengths to avoid what used to be called "losing face." Students were often reluctant even to ask questions of the teacher for fear that it might be interpreted in one of two equally distasteful ways, suggesting either that the students hadn't understood the lecture, bringing loss of face upon themselves; or that the teacher hadn't lectured well, causing loss of face, perhaps accompanied by some sort of reprisal, from the other side of the desk.

China's history during the first half of this century alone created formidable obstacles to the building of a new socialist educational system. In 1949, the revolutionary government was in no position to pick and choose the most ideologically desirable teachers. Only a fraction of the population could even read and write. And many of the things that the more highly educated among them had learned were either stilted and outmoded conceptions from the Chinese classics or "bourgeois ideas" held by those who had studied abroad and had been trained to see the West as the center of all that is modern or of any significance. Although the latter gained some useful knowledge, particularly those who studied science and technology, they often were as much out of touch with conditions and needs in their own country as the classical scholars were with the times.

The impetus to modernize and popularize education that began early in the century had waned considerably by the late 1920s and 1930s as the once progressive Kuomintang government became more corrupt and less interested in reform under Chiang Kai-shek. China was wracked by many years of war: first, a civil war between the Kuomintang and the Communists, which was followed by more than eight years of war (1937-45) against the Japanese who had invaded China, and soon after their defeat, by the resumption of the civil war which lasted until the defeat of the Kuomintang in 1949. By then, the effects of the earlier limited educational reforms were hardly evident and the school system was in shambles.

In 1960, the Vice-Minister of Education summarized conditions and priorities during the period when the Communist Party first came to power:

> Everything from transport to schools was broken down. The nation was bankrupt. Money was useless; we were reduced to a barter system. All schools were closed. Our task was to put teachers back to work, in both public and private—mostly missionary—schools. We did this by appeals to patriotism and promising regular pay—mostly in rice—and full cooperation, without much change in the system.[2]

Millions of teachers were needed very quickly to even begin to work toward universal literacy, to say nothing of those required to train people at advanced levels of science and technology if the country was to pull itself out of its abysmal poverty and backwardness. Where were they to come from? Not everyone in that small portion of the population which was literate could be pressed into teaching; many had limited educations themselves and among those who had more, a high percentage was from the overthrown privileged classes. A good number of that group left China or resisted cooperating with the new government. At any rate, the skills that the educated could offer were also needed to satisfy other equally urgent demands. The situation was desperate. Ideology aside, more teachers, many, many more, were essential if the schools were to attempt to fulfill their objectives. The schools took whoever they could get—those who had been teachers in the past and anyone else who knew more than the students.

Not unexpectedly many of the teachers that the new revolutionary government was able to find saw themselves as an exclusive intelligentsia apart from and far above the ignorant masses of the people. This was a less serious problem at the lower levels of education, where teachers themselves required little schooling and where the drive for mass literacy and general education soon resulted in an infusion of new teachers from the ranks of workers and peasants. At the other end, however, it was quite another matter. Even though student enrollments

---

2. Edgar Snow, *The Other Side of the River: Red China Today* (New York: Random House, 1961), p. 225.

at institutions of higher education increased rapidly during the early years after liberation,[3] university education was still very far beyond possibility for most people. It is therefore no surprise that many teachers continued to hang on to the old ideas that singled them out as an elite.

Even in 1958, of 2,474 professors and assistant professors in 46 institutions of higher education, an absolute majority came from landlord and bourgeois families and more than 90 percent had received their education either abroad or in the old China.[4]

Many attempted to protect their old prestige from the encroachment of the new revolutionary ideology and to pad their futures by making sure that their ranks remained "pure." The tremendous influx of much needed educational assistance from the Soviet Union during the 1950s apparently did not do much to change traditional Chinese attitudes and practices. Russian professors arrived in large numbers to staff the institutes and universities. They brought with them their own tradition of authoritarianism and formalism as well as their own teaching materials that were usually translated and taught unaltered, proving to be hardly more suitable to the changed conditions in China than those already available. The nonrelevant materials and the rigid mechanical teaching style fit well with existing educational practices and served to further feed the self-importance that pervaded the higher reaches of education.

Growing revision of revolutionary principles occurring in all spheres of activity in China lent support to teacher authoritarianism and elitism. Revisionism was becoming so prevalent, and sophisticated revisionists were exerting so much pressure, that even some older, experienced revolutionaries sometimes unwittingly and unknowingly became accomplices.

In *Hundred Day War: The Cultural Revolution at Tsinghua University*, William Hinton relates one such story, the story of Liu Ping who in

---

3. According to U.S. government figures, the total number of students enrolled in institutions of higher learning in China had risen from 130,000 in 1949 to 810,000 ten years later. (See *An Economic Profile of Mainland China, being Studies prepared for the Joint Economic Committee of Congress of the United States* [Washington, D.C.: U.S. Printing Office, 1967], cited in R. F. Price, *Education in Communist China* [London: Routledge & Kegan Paul, 1970], p. 145.) It is also relevant to note that by 1958–59, more than 35 percent of the greatly increased number of university students were in teacher training programs. This was higher than any field, showing again the priority placed on education. (See Snow, *Other Side of the River*, pp. 230–31.)

4. *Hsinhua News Agency*, January 19, 1959. Quoted in Peter Mauger et al., *Education in China*. (London: Anglo-Chinese Educational Institute, 1974), p. 11.

1956 became the vice-secretary of the Party Committee at Tsinghua University, a job that carried with it the main responsibility for the day-to-day work of the University. Liu had a fine revolutionary record; he had joined the Revolution in 1938, had been trained at Resistance University in Yenan,[5] had worked actively to spread mass education in the countryside, and had become a member of the Central Committee representing the Communist Youth League.

Any hopes he may have had about revolutionizing education at Tsinghua, the most highly regarded school of science and engineering in China, were, however, quickly dampened. The revisionist professors at the University claimed that political education and physical work were out of place there, that technical and scientific competence required many years of study (they had developed a post-junior middle school program of eleven years), that reams of material simply had to be memorized, and that therefore only those regarded as highly intelligent were capable of successfully completing the course.

All of this went against Liu Ping's grain, but the revisionists went to great lengths to intimidate him, frequently reminding him that he had not even finished middle school and had no technical knowledge. They made it clear to him that a high-powered science education must be guided by the wisdom of sophisticated urban intellectuals like themselves, and not by the ignorance of "a clod, a country bumpkin" like Liu. "How could a middle school student lead professors?" they asked condescendingly.

In later reviewing what had happened, Liu recalled being told:

" 'That old Resistance University method won't work. This is something new and different. Here we must produce scientists. A little Marxist-Leninist theory, a little study of society, a little military training won't solve the problem.' "

The arguments presented to him were persuasive, and Liu became more uncertain of his positions. He explained:

"When we were at Resistance University Mao Tse-tung told us that the center of our work should be changing the thinking of our students. We

5. Yenan was the location of the revolutionary headquarters established in northern China at the end of the Long March in 1935. Resistance University (resistance to the Japanese who had invaded China) was set up by the revolutionary forces to train cadres. Like other educational endeavors in the Yenan area at the time, Resistance University stressed the integration of theory and practice and of intellectual and manual work. As such, education as practiced in Yenan has come to typify the revolutionary path.

should strive for three things: (1) a staunch political orientation, (2) flexible strategy and tactics, and (3) a good working style.

"But when I came here everyone said the task was just the opposite. We weren't here to change people's thinking but to teach knowledge, science. Here we put technique above all, expertise above all, and organized mountain-climbing teams to scale the peaks of science.

"So I thought, 'Maybe this polytechnical school is different from Resistance University, where the main subjects were politics and social theory.' So I too put technique in command.

"As to teaching methods, Mao Tse-tung advocated the method of enlightenment as opposed to the stuffed-duck method. But we had regulations here that tied the students hand and foot. In Yenan the classes had been lively, we had had debates, discussions. I thought, 'Maybe that is suitable for a training class, but here where there is so much science to learn, perhaps we must cram the facts in.' So I fell for the stuffed-duck method.

"Chairman Mao said all along: 'Cut the school years shorter.' At Resistance University the time was short—at first three months, later a year, then the graduates went out to work. Of course, technical courses needed more time than the social sciences, but they didn't need all the time we argued for. . . .

"I thought, 'I have no experience. I know nothing of technical things. Probably more time really is needed. . . .'

"Then, in 1960, we had drought and flood, the Soviet Union pulled out, tore up their agreements. Suddenly Liu Shao-ch'i stepped forward and said that our students were doing too much labor, that the quality of education had been lowered, and that it wouldn't do to go on like that. So we got the students back from the countryside . . . and set up all sorts of regulations about passing courses: what sort of grade allows you to go on and what sort of grade means you must drop out.

"Although I personally liked to see the students going out to work, when the capitalist-roaders said this was a mess, I thought they were probably correct."[6]

Thus before long Liu Ping was a revisionist, if not by his intentions then certainly by his deeds. Many like him succumbed to the super-professional and careerist educational ideas and practices of the day.

This was hardly the most suitable situation for lively, innovative, and all-rounded education. As could be guessed, the effects on those

---

6. William Hinton, *Hundred Day War: The Cultural Revolution at Tsinghua University* (New York: Monthly Review Press, 1972), pp. 29–32.

students who managed to make it through university were highly detrimental. A significant proportion of them easily took on the coloration of their mentors and became silent but enthusiastic partners to the patronage heaped on them at the expense of the less favored students and could-be students from the nonprivileged classes. In their turn, many of these successful students added their bit to the hardening of inegalitarian practices and outlooks.

It is no mere coincidence, then, that so much of the activity of the Cultural Revolution centered in the schools. Or that in the early months of the Cultural Revolution Mao identified teachers as "the main problem" hindering the transformation of education. Or that several of his conversations during which he urged youth to rebel were widely circulated at the same time.

IDEOLOGICAL REMOLDING

Long before the Cultural Revolution there was an awareness that teachers had to cast off their old retrogressive ideas and imbibe the new revolutionary ones if they were to be fit to teach others. Early in the 1950s, a countrywide movement was launched to transform the ideology of intellectuals. This involved criticism of what at the time was a heavy influence of both Kuomintang and foreign ideas on Chinese education. Teachers participated in numerous other political and economic struggles—the movement for agrarian reform, the movement to wipe out corruption and speculation. In the late 1950s, they were involved in such movements as the development of the People's Communes and the Great Leap Forward, all of which, according to Chinese educators, gave an impetus to educational reform by influencing teachers' outlooks. In many places teachers began to go to communes and factories on a regular basis and their students did likewise. School factories and farms were set up during this period.

"All these activities were carried out in line with Chairman Mao's policies in education," said Li Hua-chieh, a politics professor at Kwangchow Teachers' College. "The changes were consistent with the principles of serving proletarian politics and productive labor. Chairman Mao said that through their education people should develop morally, intellectually, and physically but Liu Shao-ch'i distorted this by removing the head and the tail. That left only intellectual work. He said that students weren't learning enough and that going to factories and farms was just mixing things up. He advocated the line to 'put everything in order,' meaning to concentrate only on intellectual work and to remove ourselves from the masses. It was really an endorsement of feudal, bourgeois, and revisionist education. So, as these ideas gained strength, they seriously affected the advances made in earlier years.''

By the start of the Cultural Revolution, feelings of outrage often ran high, particularly among students. Not all young people, even among those who were doing well in university, had been co-opted. Millions felt themselves victims of oppressive and unreasonable school practices, and, to many, all these had been perpetrated by teachers. While Mao and the rest of the revolutionary leadership made it clear at the outset of the Cultural Revolution that the targets should be the saboteurs of socialism—the conscious and highly placed perpetrators of revisionism—it took time for some students to see the larger picture. Before then they saw their job as a struggle against revisionism wherever it existed and many were convinced that they had found it when they looked to the front of the classroom. Although many teachers thought that what they had been doing was in the best interests of their students and the society, and few among them, as it later turned out, were genuine "capitalist-roaders," criticism was nonetheless sharp, often relentless, and sometimes unjust.

Kuan Chi-yu, head of the Office in Charge of Revolution in Education at Kwangchow Teachers' College, told me: "Many of us were sufferers of the wrong line in education, but we also carried it out and made others suffer from it. So even if the criticism was sometimes severe, it was not entirely mistaken because we did things that had to be criticized. In fact, teachers who were criticized during the Cultural Revolution think that it was really deserved. It has given us encouragement to do better now. It was a hard-learned but necessary lesson. We call it 'paying tuition fees,' paying for what we've learned.''

The criticism unquestionably shook large numbers of teachers from their smugness and self-satisfaction. They were forced to question how they had taught and why; what was wrong with their teaching—and with themselves. The teachers were being educated by their students.

Like the learning that took place during the movements before the Cultural Revolution, however, this was not education as it is usually conceived, the kind of education that implies initial exposure to new experiences and ideas without the prior existence of contradictory ones to obstruct the smooth flow of learning. Teachers did have obstructions in their minds, and they were many and formidable. They were not, after all, children. The process they were undergoing was, more precisely, re-education, and that's what the Chinese call it. To accept the new ideology, they had to rid themselves of the old one, a difficult, elusive, and at times even painful process. These were no "blank sheets" that had simply to be filled; the "sheets" were already full of "erroneous ideas"; they had to be rewritten with fresh ideas while at the same time erasing the old ones.

Perhaps the most difficult part of the re-education process has to do with the content itself—the two sets of ideas, one that needs to be dropped and one that is to be embraced. It's not simply inaccuracy of facts and information, or superficiality of interpretations that create problems. It is a question of ideology, of a person's total world view—the hidden assumptions and attitudes that fully embroider the most seemingly incidental thoughts and actions and color a myriad of responses to the world including ideas of each person's place in it. These have to be dredged up and confronted, examined and understood, criticized and in a great many cases rejected. To create a new world, no less is required than the transformation of the very innards of one's mind, the very foundations of one's conduct. One's total ideology must be remolded.

The Chinese often speak of the need to "rectify erroneous ideas." A foreigner might well want to know who is to say what ideas are erroneous. The Chinese would answer that by erroneous ideas they are referring to those that are a disservice to the people and that, therefore, only the people can decide. They would perhaps point to the Cultural Revolution as a good example of people on a massive scale deciding which ideas were erroneous and waging battle against them.

While phrases like "rectify erroneous ideas" and "re-education" are foreign to most of us and make us at best uncomfortable, "ideological remolding" can be downright frightening. It can easily trigger off images of thought control and brainwashing.[7]

---

7. On the matter of "brainwashing" Premier Chou En-lai, in a light moment during an interview with a visiting delegation of the Committee of Concerned Asian Scholars from the U.S. in 1971, said, "I haven't thought of a way to wash one's brain yet." Then upon reflection added, "In a certain way I would also like to have my brain washed because I also have old ideas in my mind. I have already passed seventy-three; how can it be said that I have no old ideas in my head, because I came over from the old society?" (Committee of Concerned Asian Scholars Friendship Delegation to China, "Interview with Chou En-lai," *Bulletin of Concerned Asian Scholars* 3, no. 3–4 [Summer–Fall 1971], p. 35.)

None of these terms are frightening to the Chinese—which is why they have no hesitation in using them. As they see it, all people, whether they like it or not, are molded in the first place, regardless of whether the molding is consciously and purposefully perpetrated or not. We all develop ideologies, and these are shaped by the economic, social, and political conditions that obtain in whatever society we happen to live in and by our own particular class positions within that society. Our actions as well as our outlooks derive from our experience. To the Chinese, that is a universal fact of human existence.

The only question they would ask is: *what* ideology has been learned—one that is for the interests of the people or against them? For example, the Chinese would undoubtedly frown upon that kind of molding which teaches people to "need" short skirts one year, long skirts the next, and pants the next. They would call that bourgeois because it serves the interests not of the skirt and pants-wearers but of the manufacturers. They would also say that the creation of such "needs" and the means and media through which they are inculcated are instruments used by the capitalists to separate the people from their own real interests by developing in them an individualistic and hence divisive mentality; that such a process is aimed at encouraging people to look upon themselves as special and better than others, and to compete for esteem and status; that the collective interest is sacrificed for the sake of the profit that goes to the few.

The particular example of skirts and pants as aspects of bourgeois ideology is not transferable to China where their history has left them with a different cultural tradition from ours. Regardless of specifics, however, the presence of very powerful antisocialist ideologies, both bourgeois and feudal, is not to be underestimated. The Chinese fully subscribe to the Marxist principle that "the ideas of the ruling class are in every epoch the ruling ideas."[8] Since feudal and bourgeois classes ruled China in the past, those were the ideologies that prevailed. The Chinese are convinced that the classless future will never by attained if the inherited ideologies into which people were initially molded as well as antisocialist ones created by new inequalities in a transitional society are left intact. Hence, remolding is deemed essential.[9]

---

8. Karl Marx and Frederick Engels, *The German Ideology* (Moscow: Progress Publishers, 1968), p. 61.

9. The Chinese say that great care should be exercised in deciding what kind of behavior requires remolding. For example, many old people, especially in the rural areas, still believe in religion which is considered to be ideologically retrogressive. Nevertheless, they are allowed to practice it on the grounds that it is deeply a part of them and it

Urban teachers receive ideological re-education from a production brigade leader.

The students have played and continue to play a role in the ideological re-education of their teachers. But this has not been without its shortcomings. Students by themselves could not be expected to typify and teach the new proletarian ideology when they too were largely cut off from the proletariat as so many of them were before the Cultural Revolution.

Only the working people could remold ideologies in a proletarian direction. With the formation of the school revolutionary committees from 1967 onward, workers and peasants assumed more direct and influential positions in running the schools. When teachers had to sit down with them and thrash out educational problems jointly, many began to see things from a new perspective.

However, ideological remolding is a continuing process. Each new

would be overburdensome, unkind, and unnecessary to expect them to remold themselves in their advanced years. Ideological remolding is conducted primarily among teachers and leaders—those people who are in positions to influence many others. So, in the case of religion, while individuals can continue to practice it, a teacher would be prevented from teaching it in school. This position is reflected in China's new constitution adopted in early 1975. A portion of article 28 stipulates that citizens "enjoy freedom to believe in religion and freedom not to believe in religion and to propagate atheism." By this means it is expected that it will die a natural death.

insight builds on others and they must all become operative. If a teacher agrees with a new idea only intellectually and then persists in conducting his daily affairs in the same old way, the Chinese would consider that his ideology has essentially been untouched. Outlooks are remolded by changed behavior every bit as much as behavior is remolded by changed outlooks.

Therefore, the successful remolding of teachers' ideologies requires appropriate changes in their practice. This is being achieved in large part through their participation in manual work. Work in factories and communes has become an institutionalized part not only of the students' education but also of their teachers' re-education. The arrangements are different in different places, but it is happening all over China. In one kindergarten I visited which is connected to a factory, the teachers work in the factory for one month a year; in a rural primary school they do a few hours of farm work every second week and more during the harvest; in an urban middle school, besides spending some time with their students in the school workshops, teachers are relieved of their teaching responsibilities for six months every three years during which time they go to a factory or commune; in one university, some teachers work in the university factories and farm while others work periodically in nearby factories and farms outside. By such means teachers are increasingly being integrated with the proletariat physically and ideologically.

CADRE SCHOOLS

For concentrated ideological molding and remolding there has developed in China what is undoubtedly one of the most extraordinary, important, and apparently successful educational innovations—the May 7th cadre schools. Also deriving from the Cultural Revolution, these schools, located in the countryside, are specifically for the ideological remolding of cadres.

The term cadre is applied to people who play leadership roles in any organization.[10] Since cadres hold jobs which, on a daily basis, do not

---

10. For a fuller discussion of cadres see Franz Schurmann, *Ideology and Organization in Communist China,* 2d. ed. (Berkeley: University of California Press, 1966), pp. 162-67.

fully connect them to manual work and manual workers, they are considered in need of ideological remolding. In China leaders are expected to be both models and instructors, and the way they conduct their work exerts a great influence on others. Thus many cadres, including those not directly involved in the work of the schools, have important educative functions and are looked to as teachers in the widest sense of the word.

Imagine our nearest counterparts to cadres—bank managers, government administrators, political party leaders, corporation executives, high school principals, and university professors—in the fields digging. Not the symbolic spadeful of soil for an appreciative audience and a bevy of photographers on Arbor Day or in a ground-breaking ceremony for a memorial to someone rich and famous. Not for a picture in the local newspaper the next day. But many spadesful hour after hour and with no glory attached. The cadres really *work*. They are being remolded, and among their teachers are those who work with their hands—the peasants.

It is quite likely, however, considering China's feudal past and the enormous traditional hiatus between physical and intellectual work, that some cadres, even with the best political intentions, still find this kind of work distasteful. The Chinese do not have anything resembling our pioneering tradition that values and often finds great pleasure in strenuous physical labor. But the fact that they nevertheless pitch in, many of them with enthusiasm, undoubtedly goes a long way toward eroding this feudal anachronism.

At the Hsuan Wu District May 7th Cadre School outside of Peking, one of the members of the Revolutionary Committee, a thin, middle-aged, intellectual-looking man explained the dangers inherent in the kind of work that cadres ordinarily do. Many of them have jobs that keep them much of the time in offices, or at meetings, or in classrooms, situations that are potentially harmful to their outlooks since it is all too easy for them to develop a certain amount of distance from both the common laboring people and their labor. The cadre schools are designed to immerse them in both and thereby remold their ideology.

"Our aim is to prevent the servants of the people from becoming their masters. We have three channels or media for training the cadres. The first is the study of Marxism-Leninism." Having held the preconception that when the cadres went to the countryside they did nothing but unpleasant, hard manual work, I was a bit surprised to hear that study was considered a central, in fact the first, aspect of the cadres' re-education. But the Chinese think that practice without theory can mislead people as much as can theory without practice. So while a basic job of the school is to provide the means for the cadres to integrate with the peasants, theory—the study of what that integration and practice mean—is also essential if the appropriate lessons are to be drawn.

As in regular schools at the higher levels, the main method is self-study supplemented by discussions. Unlike other schools, however, there are no teachers in the cadre schools. They are unnecessary since a good number of the students are capable of serving as teachers. As cadres, many of them are already advanced in their political thinking, and if younger or less experienced cadres need help with their studies there are always people to call upon. Peasants, workers, professors, or others who may not be studying at a cadre school are also sometimes asked in to give assistance.

"By their study," continued the explanation, "students can heighten their ability to distinguish genuine Marxism-Leninism from phony Marxism-Leninism and increase their awareness of class struggle."

However, they must be able to do more than just make an intellectual distinction between "genuine" and "phony" Marxism-Leninism. They must eliminate the latter within themselves and develop the former, an objective that the leaders at the cadre school see as achievable largely through practice, especially of the kind provided by the second medium in the school program—physical work.

"The cadres do farm work just like ordinary laborers. They should learn not to put on official airs and be pompous and bureaucratic, but to remain forever as ordinary workers. In this way, they will be better able to prevent the emergence of revisionist ideas."

As he spoke, I could not help but notice the cadres who were serving us tea, particularly the three middle-aged male factory administrators. Perhaps they had assumed official airs at some points in their lives, and maybe some of them still weren't completely beyond it; but here in the cadre school in their simple clothes and plain surroundings, carefully watching the level of tea in our cups and popping up to fill them when they got low, these cadres looked and acted like anything but bureaucrats.

The value of physical work in combatting revisionist ideas was pointed up by an older man who, on another occasion, related a younger friend's experience during his stay at a cadre school. The friend taught English to advanced students who would eventually work in the diplomatic service or as interpreters or teachers. The work entailed language instruction, and the history, geography, and literature of English-speaking countries. The younger man felt that in the past he had carried out Liu Shao-ch'i's revisionist line in education, sacrificing redness for expertise.

The man who told me the story explained what had made his friend change. "When he went to the cadre school in his district the first thing that had to be done was to put up some buildings, which meant that the cadres had to carry logs—baby tree trunks they were practically; they had to carry them from the river bank to the construction site, which was a bit of a distance.

"Well, one morning my friend got up, had a whacking good breakfast, and then went off to the river and started carrying this young tree. But after a short while he felt his legs just turn to jelly. He simply had to put it down; he couldn't go any further. And as he was sitting there he began to think about the people who used to do this sort of work before liberation. He realized that they never had the leisure to sit down and rest whenever they felt like it as he did; they would just have to keep right on going no matter how heavy the load and no matter how tired they were. And now he was teaching their sons and daughters English. So he asked himself, 'Is it really the most important thing in the world to teach these students Jane Austen's *Pride and Prejudice?*' Well, he decided it wasn't!''

His story seemed adequate testimony to the Chinese view that ''the arrogant air of an official disappears by half the moment he carries a hoe on his shoulder.''

The third part of the school's three-pronged program was described as ''learning from the former poor and lower-middle peasants.'' This is done in ways that blend with the rest of the program. On the theory side, the cadres conduct social investigations about the conditions of the peasants' lives and the contours of class struggle in the communes or brigades. They also sometimes hold joint political discussions. Their practical learning from the peasants comes primarily through doing physical work with them. In some cadre schools the students also live in the peasants' homes for a period of time. In addition, there is quite a bit of informal contact; in the evening they might get together for recreational activities or the peasants might give the cadres class education by telling them of their lives before liberation.

The benefits are not all one way. While the peasants are helping to re-educate the cadres, the cadres, with their greater formal education, are also able to assist the peasants by discussing with them the results of their social investigations, reading and interpreting difficult Marxist-Leninist texts with them and informing them about national and international events. They sometimes also help the peasants improve their levels of literacy, or pass on their skills in specialized fields like medicine, accountancy, or engineering.

"This is how we run our cadre schools in an open-door way. Through such close contacts everyone gains; but what we consider most important is the opportunity these contacts provide for the cadres to remold their world outlook. They can learn the peasants' good qualities of hard struggle and they can develop strong proletarian feelings."

The way in which close contact can yield "strong proletarian feelings" was revealed in the diary of a highly regarded engineer and scholar. It was written in 1955, more than a decade before the Cultural Revolution or the establishment of cadre schools, by an old man of privileged family background. Wearied by the years of corruption and uncertainty that marked Kuomintang China, this Western-trained intellectual was certainly not dedicated to socialism like so many students at the cadre schools that were to come later. But, like many others with national feelings, he had stayed on in post-revolutionary China with reluctant optimism. He had always seen himself as an intellectual above the struggle, an observer, not a fashioner of the new society in the making; yet he was nonetheless profoundly influenced by his prolonged contact with a revolutionary peasant. He wrote:

I had a stroke two months before Liberation, and the blood froze in my head and my left side became useless. As I lay on my bed, unable to move, I could see them pack, my wife and my Second Daughter, hastily picking up things all through the house and flinging them into their suitcases. They were going away. I knew they were frightened, frightened because the Communists were coming. But I was not frightened. I had been expecting them for so long, so long . . . in fear and hope, in doubt and wonder, for nothing could be worse than what we had undergone, yet who knew what the new era would bring?

At last they were coming, and because they were coming my wife and my daughter were leaving, and so I was left alone. I was looked after, I became well again, and I have been working. And though I often disagree with them, yet they have treated me well, and certainly many things have been done which needed to be done. Comrade Lu, who is in charge of the Department where I work, has always been respectful to me, though we have argued, each one holding to his own viewpoint, until a few months ago. Because he is a peasant, a soldier of the Eighth Route Army, thus neither an intellectual nor a scholar, and I and my colleagues are classified as high-grade intellectuals, at first we made fun of him secretly, insulted him smoothly in many ways, calling each other loudly 'Comrade' in front of him, aping his talk, his humility. But now I have changed, or has he changed, or have we both changed? The change came when he said to me:

'Comrade Chou, why do you not write down your life in full? It would be precious teaching for us, young ones with no experience. Certainly valuable material to add to our knowledge, and enable us to avoid mistakes, to correct our shortcomings.'

That is their style of speech—self-depreciatory, almost impossibly modest, all the more annoying to someone like myself because it seems to make fun of our own pompous modesty, our own tricks of speech. And people like Comrade Lu have power, which makes their humility all the more galling to us. But Comrade Lu says he wishes to learn from us, he wishes to understand science, to become in a way an engineer. He has had little schooling, being an illiterate boy of fourteen when he joined the Red Army. He has fought twenty years of war and has had five years of administration, looking after the running of our Engineering and Design Department, its finances, our welfare, and our souls. Every night the lamp glows in the small cubby-hole where he sits, without fire in the winter, a muffler round his neck; in his cotton underpants in the summer, fanning himself; poring over the engineering books he borrows. He is studying. He will know as much as we do, we the intellectuals, the engineers, one day.

We all resented him, resented his political lectures, his telling us to read political books; he, the coarse peasant who scarcely knew how to read, now put in charge of us, so many of us graduates of western universities, the élite of China. Our vanity was unbearably hurt, we were humiliated, and prophesied disaster. The Party cadres had no regard for us, for our learning, we the intellectuals. And Lu was so slow, so slow to understand us, so stupid the first two years . . . but in the last three he has begun to know; he follows our work, he put himself to school with us. In the last year he has been particularly zealous to learn from me, and now I am forgetting that I disliked his ways, and we have begun to talk, and I think I must have told him of my dreams, of episodes in the past when I was young, of my life on the railways. . . . Perhaps that is why he suggests that I should write a book about myself. Yet he is younger than my own son. And so, when he suggests my writing down my life, 'I'm busy with some plans for water reservoirs,' I reply.

'Yes, Comrade Chou, I know that. But think about it. We feel that you have so much experience of life which we lack, we need to remember the past in order to be wise for the future.' ...

At the end of each year for the first four years, and after each Great Movement, we have written down our thoughts, held meetings at which we spoke our feelings about our work, voiced our criticisms of the Party, of Comrade Lu, who has pilloried himself for what he calls shortcomings or faults in the Department. To this I have been hostile, calling it an ample waste of time. But being old, and having some achievement behind me, no one has tried to change me, or is it perhaps that they truly value sincerity? We have learnt to re-appraise and criticize our own conduct, and we have also been taught not to backbite or gossip but to criticize each other openly.

This time, I have no feeling of hostility, no reflex at being snared. I suddenly *want* to write down my life, to write down everything that happened. Many of us now have this urge, for we feel we have lived through a great change. For a Revolution is not impersonal events moving helpless human beings about. It is made by man, and it also is an inner process, it changes us. I feel as a pond that has been dredged, mud gone, bottom stone seen. As I left my department that day, spring had begun.

Spring has begun, and spring hurts, for there is Marguerite [his wife, a Belgian] still, though she has left me. And the children. Lu knows about them; therefore he never asks, for his heart is polite even if his manners are coarse. And suddenly he is my friend, thinking of me as a friend, wishing me to release myself into the time to be remembered. And it is so true that now we have peace, and the days have come when memories, reminiscences, can be remembered in tranquillity and stored, for our young generation will need to know the past as it was for us, they will need also to remember the long, long and hard road we have come.

As one looks back after a long and terrible ascent at the slopes left behind; as the embroiderer, having put each stitch into place after hours and days bent upon his frame, rubs his eyes and looks at the whole pattern at last understood; so must I now look at myself, whole, in the clear light of spring that has come back.[11]

What this old man was expressing would be seen in China as the awakening of proletarian consciousness. It is a recognition that the highly educated and the highly placed don't know everything. In fact, many Chinese would say that sometimes they are very ignorant—especially about things having to do with simplicity, honesty, genuineness, modesty, and struggle, "the good qualities of the working

---

11. Han Suyin, *The Crippled Tree* (New York: Bantam Books, 1972), pp. 55-58.

people'' that are so often looked to as lessons for others to learn from. To the Chinese today the measure of wisdom about life and how to live it has very little to do with size or subtlety of vocabulary or sophistication of manners. Instead, richness of experience is more highly valued and it is commonly felt that the experience of intellectuals closed off from life in offices and classrooms with only each other is poor indeed compared to the peasants' wisdom gained by experience in the fields, a kind of experience that has required that they grapple with the realities of life's hardships.

What happened to this old man is in no way unique. It happens to many people in China; the cadre schools are simply a way of regularizing it for many on a wide scale.

The Hsuan Wu District May 7th Cadre School was set up in October 1968, around the same time as many others. They are an implementation of a directive issued by Mao. The May 7th Directive was initially aimed at the PLA, workers, peasants, and students, and to a lesser extent, cadres. It advocated their all-rounded development; they should both study and directly participate in political, military, cultural, industrial, and agricultural affairs. That was on May 7, 1966.

In October of 1968 a section addressed to cadres was added to the Directive: ''Sending the masses of cadres to do manual work gives them an excellent opportunity to study once again; this should be done by all cadres except those who are old, weak, ill, or disabled.''[12]

There are a great many cadre schools in China. In the first few years of the schools' existence it was not uncommon for cadres to attend for as long as two years, and even more. Since then, courses have been shortened and generally run from three months to a year.

The shortening of the courses does not indicate, however, that they

---

12. Outsiders are often taken aback when they hear statements common in China like ''We must follow Chairman Mao's instructions'' or ''directives''; it is easy to assume them to be orders specified down to the last detail, orders that have to be obeyed whether or not people understand or agree with them. These are unfortunate words, at least as they translate into English, since they convey quite misleading meanings. What are called ''Chairman Mao's instructions'' or ''directives'' are, to the Chinese, simply general guidelines. The May 7th Directive, for example, just states the need for a certain kind of education. Mao does not specify that there should be an institution called a cadre school, the length of the program, the details of the curriculum, or any other administrative, organizational, or programmatic arrangements. All this is left to the people concerned. A statement like ''Study hard, make progress every day'' would be called ''Chairman Mao's instruction.'' Such an ''instruction'' is issued with the expectation that it will receive full discussion with mass participation before it is transformed from a general statement into concrete practice.

are coming to be looked upon as unimportant or that the schools will soon disappear. Although they developed out of the Cultural Revolution in response to the sharply felt need to re-educate cadres at the time, that need is apparently still felt and the schools are expected to continue on far into the future. Once all eligible cadres in a particular locality have completed a course they have the opportunity to apply for a second full stint. In the meantime, some cadre schools have provisions that allow those who have already attended once to return for a period of about two to four weeks a year.

"We see the schools as permanent during the period of socialism, but we must work hard to do an even better job in the future," said a member of the Revolutionary Committee at Hsuan Wu. "You know, in a way, these schools are not really new. We have inherited a good revolutionary tradition of training cadres through combining work and study that dates back to the 1920s when the Institute of the Peasant Movement was established in Kwangchow. So while the May 7th schools grew up during the Cultural Revolution, we still use very similar methods for learning."

When we visited the cadre school the student population totaled slightly more than two hundred men and women, a small class since about five thousand cadres had already studied there since the school was founded. Ranging in age from nineteen to middle fifties, they had all entered together and would complete their course at the same time, whereupon they would return to their jobs.

To guard against undue inconvenience for the cadres and their families during the period spent in the cadre school, there is no tuition and the only expense is food. Students receive full pay and benefits from their places of work, including days off. Depending upon the distance of the school from the cadres' homes, the days off might be once a week or they might be together in a four or five-day monthly leave. At Hsuan Wu, the workplaces even provide transportation for the students when they are on holiday. Some other cadre schools have living, educational, and recreational facilities on the school grounds to accommodate the cadres' entire families.

We asked the students at Hsuan Wu what happens at the workplaces while the cadres are away at school. "Perhaps families are not inconvenienced, but what about workmates? How do they manage with such a long absence of their leaders?"

Wang Ye-ming, one of the older students, supplied the answer. "I am a vice-chairman of the Revolutionary Committee of a metallurgical plant. While the chairman was here I took his place, and now that I am here he is taking mine. The leading comrades on the Revolutionary Committee have a division of labor with one of us in charge of one aspect of the work, another in charge of the work in a different field, and so on. So we fill in for each other and keep the work of the factory going as usual. Of course, those who remain must work harder to pick up the responsibilities of the one who is in school. But we think that the extra work is worth it because after studying at the cadre school people come back and do a better job than before. They have made political progress and their style of work has improved."

At the school it was apparent that more than style of work improves. The cadres all looked bronzed and remarkably healthy. Leaving relatively cloistered lives in the city and coming to the open air and the muscle-building activities in the country make an obvious difference, one that they themselves seem to fully appreciate. A quite young woman who taught in middle school, an excellent physical example of just this point, said most enthusiastically, "While we are here, we not only have a bountiful harvest in our minds, but also in our bodies. We get very good exercise, and so we become very strong and healthy."

All work assignments, we were told, are made with the physical condition of individual students as a primary consideration. The same young woman said, "Of course, some people are stronger than others. When we work in the fields we always help each other. The older and weaker comrades do not have difficulties because they do not have to handle any very heavy jobs."

We had a chance to see some of the work that was being done and to hear about other work that had been accomplished in the past. When we walked around the school grounds, we saw some prosperous-looking fields of sorghum and millet and, on the other side of the road, small fish ponds that had recently been stocked with three thousand fish. ("They are not very big yet.") We could see orchards in the distance.

Large platters, piled high with peanuts and peaches, also products of the cadres' labor, filled the long cloth-covered tables back at our meeting room. As we talked, it became clear that the cadres could be credited not only with the crops in the fields, ponds, and orchards, but with virtually everything we had seen on our walk. In 1968 the site where the school is located had been a sandy wasteland. We saw photographs of a completely barren expanse of land, unrecognizable as the same place, except for the river on one side.

In less than five years the cadres had reclaimed 1100 mou of land (about 180 acres), had dug wells and irrigation ditches mostly by hand, had dredged ponds, and had planted tens of thousands of trees. By themselves they had erected all the buildings and had installed the electricity. On the previously uncultivated land they now grew rice, millet, sorghum, apples, peaches, pears, peanuts, and grapes. They also raised fish, pigs, and chickens, and ran a factory.

There is a small exhibition room containing a pictorial history of the school from its founding to the present. This is part of the cadres' education, a way in which they can gain an appreciation of the efforts extended by cadres before them as well as a sense of how they too might contribute to the school's further progress.

The exhibition is not only for the students' ideological education but also points up the importance of the results of production. Near a series of photographs showing cadres digging, planting, and building appears a small sign which reminds them: "We gain not only spiritual sustenance, but also material sustenance." Although cadre schools are primarily concerned with education rather than with production, many of them can boast self-sufficiency in a number of agricultural products.

Hsuan Wu District May 7th Cadre School has a Revolutionary Committee, the same kind of administrative body that is found in all schools. Assisted by a permanent staff of thirty-nine people, the Revolutionary Committee consists of a chairman, three vice-chairmen and seven "ordinary members." These eleven are the cadres who are in charge of the ideological remolding of the cadre-students. Along with the peasants and the students themselves, they are the re-educators. I asked about their own ideological remolding and was told that they have much greater opportunities than other cadres since they are there all the time. Besides their administrative duties, they often take part in study and manual work along with the students. They pointed out that they try to run the school democratically by soliciting student opinion. It was felt that by such means the re-educators' own re-education can stay apace.

The lives of the cadres while they are at the school can most accurately be described as simple and plain. The living quarters looked, from the outside, like they would be more affluent than they turned out to be. They were long low buildings of brick and concrete set around open courtyards with young trees and small benches. Each building had several doors with each one opening into a dormitory room shared by six people.

The interior was quite bare. We entered one room that had six cot-sized beds lining the walls, each one with a quilt, pillow, and towel neatly folded on top. The beds were equipped with long wooden planks underneath on which shoes, clothes, and bowls were carefully arranged—the only visible storage place in the room. In the center of the room was a table with several books, two vacuum bottles, and some teacups. At the far end of the room, washcloths were hanging from a short clothesline. Two bare lightbulbs hung from the ceiling. There were a couple of small mirrors and some fly swatters. On the wall was a reproduction of a painting showing children playing ping pong and a piece of paper on which was written the students' schedule. These were the full contents of the room—not many frills yet apparently all the necessities.

The simplicity of the dormitory reminded me of a brief conversation I had had with a man two weeks earlier at the huge and impressive Industrial Exhibition Hall in Shanghai. Among the many displays there was a large section for textiles—colorful, bright, varied fabrics. They were more representative of the materials produced for export than for internal consumption, which prompted me to ask my guide why there was relatively little variation in the way Chinese adults dress.

"The important thing for us today is that everyone has enough to wear and that the clothes are of good quality. It was not long ago that most people had very little clothing and it was sometimes ragged and not warm enough in winter. We must exercise thrift and economy in everything we do so we do not think too much about color and design. There are many other things the people must be provided with.

"You know, though, even if we become a wealthy country, we should follow this principle of thrift. Before liberation, the rich thought it was very important to have decorative clothes. They tried to place themselves above the common people however they could, and one way was by their clothes. But now there is a new respect for the common people, for the working people; there is respect for their simple style, including their clothing."

So at the cadre school, the unadorned style of life made sense. Even with this in mind, however, it was something of a surprise to enter the library. It was no larger than one of the dormitory rooms that housed six people, which made us wonder how it could possibly service the needs of 250 cadres and staff members.

A single long table filled the center of the narrow room. For seats there were only wooden, sawhorse-style, uncushioned benches about five inches wide. The few small bookcases in the room were almost empty. In fact, the only things about the library that looked at all conducive to any sort of educational activity were the maps on the walls. Only three students were availing themselves of this meager facility when we entered.

I expressed my concerns to one of them and he laughed and said, "Oh, there are more books, but the students have most of them in their rooms. That's where people usually study." I later found out that the students also bring many of their own books from home so that reading material is not as scarce as it first appeared to be. In addition to the classical Marxist-Leninist works there were books by Kim Il Sung, Premier of the Democratic People's Republic of Korea, and other revolutionary leaders. But less expected were some novels and poetry.

Though it is a basic component of the program, even at the cadre school not everything is hard work. Recreation is also deemed important. There is time to read for relaxation, time for morning exercises, for swimming, basketball, and other sports, and for music and performances, often with the peasants from the surrounding villages.

Perhaps the least austere part of the cadre school (looking at it with totally Western eyes) was to be found in the kitchen. No matter what China's critics might say about the Chinese manner of dress, none would have the audacity to apply the "drab-uniformity" stereotype to their food. As one of the cooks, with the help of a rope pulley, proudly lifted the copper cover of a gigantic pot about five feet in diameter, we beheld layer upon layer of the most splendid array of bowls and plates heaped full of mouth-watering delights, as pleasing to see as they were to sample.

We were not the only appreciative ones. In the dining room there was a big-character poster directly above the menu—which, incidentally, contained such items as fried pork, 15 fen (about 8 cents U.S.); beef, 15 fen; fresh tomatoes, 3 fen; etc. in a long list. The poster, which had been written by some cadres, commended the cooks for a job well done.

Every bit as noteworthy as the food was the spirit of enjoyment among those preparing it. Beneath a bamboo shelter just outside the kitchen were small groups of animated men and women on low stools gathered around smoothed down and cleaned tree stumps that served as little tables. All of them seemed to be chatting and laughing at once while they chopped cucumbers, sliced tomatoes, cored green peppers, shelled peanuts, and beat eggs.

The sight of people enjoying themselves at work is not at all uncommon in China. Unfortunately we did not always get to see people working as much as we would have liked. Often when we entered a factory workshop or other workplace a number of the workers would interrupt what they were doing to talk with us, a luxury that could not be afforded in the cadre-school kitchen where the lunch deadline had to be met. Nevertheless, while people may be able to interrupt their work easily they cannot disguise their feelings toward it; and at every workplace we visited there were signs of the same kind of good cheer as in this cadre-school kitchen.

There were several services available to the cadres—a clinic and dispensary, a barber shop, a center for repairs, a small canteen for the purchase of daily necessities, and a broadcasting station. The facilities, however, do not really add up to the totality of what a cadre school is.

There was a painting in the exhibition room that probably told us more about this place than any other single item. It showed an old cadre seated on a log, absorbed in the difficult task of digging and scraping the rust from his shovel with a sharp stone. "He is guarding against his mind also getting rusty," the young woman next to me said softly and admiringly.

Removing the rust from one's mind, remolding one's ideology, is a difficult and demanding undertaking. The unavoidable question is how to get people to actually do it. Considering the weight of tradition and the ease of sitting in an office and perhaps not even questioning any condescending feelings and actions one might exhibit toward others, of conducting affairs bureaucratically and basking in the glory of leadership, it would seem to make sense that cadres would want to keep away from the May 7th schools. Yet from all we could gather, they were eager to attend.

To understand their enthusiasm it is important to recognize that, contrary to what has sometimes been implied by outside observers unfriendly to the Chinese way of life, the schools do not bear resemblance to forced labor camps.[13] The work is not overly taxing nor is attendance compulsory. Procedure for admission into a cadre school is similar to that of other upper level schools, beginning with the voluntary application of the prospective student, and including recommendation by workmates and approval by leaders.

The responses to my own numerous questions about the ideological remolding of counterrevolutionary cadres and well-intentioned but seriously misguided cadres revealed to me that I too had brought with me some misconceptions about the nature and purposes of the cadre schools. It was stressed that cadre schools are not "reformatories" or rehabilitation centers; they are not for those people whom the Chinese call "bad elements" or "class enemies." Those cadres who commit crimes are dealt with by official authority and are not qualified to study at the May 7th schools. "The cadre schools are for the broad masses of the cadres. Ninety-five percent of the cadres are good; they are dedicated to building socialism. Of course, good cadres sometimes make minor mistakes; sometimes they slip back and begin to get rusty. At the cadre schools they are helped by their studies and by integration with the peasants. But the cadres who are not slipping back also benefit by coming to the cadre schools. Here they can develop their understanding of Marxism-Leninism and deepen their proletarian feelings."

This is not to suggest that there is no such thing as the cadre who would prefer to avoid the cadre schools or that there is never any pressure exerted on cadres to attend. There must be some who are reluctant, who feel that it is a waste of their time, or that they are above the need for ideological remolding. There are still cadres who cling to a sense of their own special dignity and would at least privately feel somewhat humiliated mingling with ordinary peasants and doing manual work. The two-line struggle is still alive on this issue and is often expressed in the question, "Are cadres to be the servants of the people or overlords who ride high on their backs?"

The revisionist line is not defeated easily or quickly. It can take very subtle forms that can slowly but surely, and even unconsciously, creep into a person's ideology. A revolutionary ideology begins to erode when a person becomes too attached to his own personal comforts, when a

---

13. It is true that when the cadre schools were first organized in the heat of the Cultural Revolution, there were ultraleft factions which sometimes used the schools for punitive rather than the intended ends, making them unpleasant places to which they sent people in opposition. This problem has since been corrected.

cadre is "too busy" to work alongside those he leads, when a youth who "grew up in a honey jar" starts to take other people's hardships lightly.

The prevailing view at present, however, is simply that no one is beyond improvement. There is nothing terribly unusual (potentially dangerous, but not unusual) about the weaknesses that can so easily develop among cadres. Even those who do not fall prey to these weaknesses recognize that there is still more to be learned. Among the steady stream of cadres returning to work after completing a course at the May 7th schools, many are in high spirits and begin to exercise better leadership, gaining greater admiration from their workmates. For all these reasons, attendance at a cadre school is often considered an excellent opportunity of which cadres are eager to take advantage.

As for pressure, there is also undoubtedly a certain amount of informal social pressure to attend a cadre school, if only in the form of the generally positive feelings toward them that pervade in most places. The more significant fact, however, is that, despite the wide availability of cadre schools, there are often more applicants than accommodations, and a cadre sometimes has to wait two or three terms before being able to secure a space.

Most important of all is that China is a socialist country where growing numbers of people are coming to agree that they learn best by combining their efforts with others. When the Chinese talk about the struggle involved in changing or deepening outlooks, they see it very differently from the way we generally do. Ours is a competitive society that places a high premium on individualism. Most of us have learned to see our own problems as fairly unique, and therefore tend to treat them as private concerns. Some people even resist trying to overcome them, because "unique" problems can become badges of specialness and definitions of individuality. Others, however, sometimes become worried and concerned, fearing that there may be something deeply wrong and even unfixable about them. This debilitating reaction also stems largely from viewing individual problems as unique.

But even when we honestly disrespect traits we see as unworthy or problematic in ourselves, and even when we are not completely overwhelmed by them, we have few alternatives in our attempts to solve them other than prolonged, painful, solitary, and often not very constructive introspection. There are not many social channels that connect us to a common means for their solution. Most of us are on our own to identify and then strive to conquer our weaknesses. But whether alone or not, the approach to problems is often inward-looking and done in an individualized manner. An increasing number of practices are turned to from psychotherapy to drugs, to "communes," to obscure religions and a growing variety of "extra-sensory" and "psychic" sects—all of which serve, among other things, to find solutions in pure individualism and escapist isolation.

On the other hand we also use a different kind of approach to certain problems that more closely resembles standard practice in China. Organizations like Alcoholics Anonymous begin with the premise that anyone can suffer from alcoholism; there is nothing unique or necessarily shameful about it. Treatment consists of bringing together people with this common problem and those close to them to define, discuss, explore, advise, and generally support each other's efforts to overcome it.

In China, a very similar view of problems and how to handle them extends to practically every area of life that is seen as having significant social consequences. The Chinese do not define individual problems as unique, but just the opposite. They foresee the likelihood of certain problems arising in particular circumstances and anticipate that they will be shared by many. Mental habits, they believe, derive from the actual concrete conditions in which people find themselves. Thus it is only to be expected that cadres, many of whom live in cities and spend much of their time in offices, might begin to assume a pattern of anti-socialist attitudes and behaviors. It does not happen because the cadres are necessarily "bad." On the contrary, they presumably got to be cadres precisely because they were exemplary. It is their conditions, which include elements of the still lingering mandarin ideology of the recent past, that can stimulate negative changes.

From regarding their conditions as similar and their shortcomings as more or less common, it is a small step to seeking correction and development through active and systematic linkage with others. Rather than turning inward to themselves, they can look outward toward the world. Two hundred cadres working and studying together can identify and penetrate elusive dimensions of problems so much more fully than a single individual on his own or in consultation with only a few others. And when they merge with peasants—people who hardly have the same problems—the very contrast and example are helpful in bringing new insights into sharp relief. In combination with physical work, this method affords concrete means for the cadres to discover, question, grapple with, and transform their ideological perspectives.[14]

There are many stories in China about the value of collective re-education. There is the one about the doctor who was more involved with his skill as a surgeon than with the curing of sick people until he experienced the concern and patience of the peasants who went to great lengths to help him develop agricultural skills. And the government official who had to stop and reflect on his embarrassment when he was seen carting night soil by an old acquaintance.[15] And the city housing administrator who had no time for complaints about leaking roofs until she shared the simple and hard life of the peasants. "Now my comrades and I work deep among the masses and our work has improved greatly," she remarked, only a variation of what so many returned cadres have to say.

The person from whom I learned the most about ideological remolding was a man well into his sixties with a long uninterrupted history of revolutionary experience dating back to the 1930s. We were discussing the development of the two-line struggle during the Cultural Revolution. Knowing that he was an active participant and hoping to get a clearer picture of the actual dynamics of the struggle, I asked him to relate his own experiences.

He had been subjected to severe criticism by a faction of what

---

14. Even the types of problems that result in extreme mental states or antisocial acts are commonly interpreted and handled in much the same way as any other. The social cohesion based on commonality of purpose in China accounts for the remarkably low incidence of both mental breakdown and criminal behavior. Both kinds of problems are seen as requiring changes in outlooks—re-education. In mental institutions and in prisons, as in society at large, the correction of problems comes in great part through collective effort, political study, and physical activity. Not only are there few who require institutionalization but periods of stay are usually short and readmission rates very low.

15. Another visitor to China, an astute observer, related a similar encounter with an official who had experienced the same feelings of humiliation about collecting garbage. Nevertheless, he stuck with it and gradually began to change as he realized that by doing this work he was held, not in contempt as he had feared, but in esteem by the common people. For someone in his position to come to accept that he is not above such a job is to conquer "the greatest of all petty-bourgeois loathings." She then added by way of contrast with what she had found in China, "Who are the 'untouchables' in India but the people of the lowest caste, who are made to sweep the streets, pick up the garbage, clean the latrines, and so on? In Asia, where sewer systems are almost unknown, people tend to be divided into two classes: a lower class forever fated to clear the ground of the leavings of the upper class." (Maria Antonietta Macciocchi, *Daily Life in Revolutionary China*, trans. Kathy Brown et al. [New York: Monthly Review Press, 1972], p. 97.)

turned out to be ultraleftists and had even suffered a long and solitary term of unjustified imprisonment at their hands. Eventually they were exposed and defeated and he was released and fully exonerated. But he spoke very modestly and with no bitterness about the injustices that had been heaped upon him. When I marveled at his dispassion and selflessness, he assured me that his own personal suffering was not that great. "Chairman Mao has said that 'revolution is not a dinner party'," he stated. His emphasis was on the nature of the struggle and the lessons that he and others had learned, never on his own personal discomforts or privations. Somewhere near the end of the discussion, I remarked that it certainly sounded like he had been remolded.

The next day I saw him again and he said, "You said something yesterday that has been bothering me." Leaning forward, his eyes narrowing, and gazing at me intently, this aging revolutionary spoke slowly and deliberately. "You said that I was remolded, but that is never true. No one is ever completely remolded. We must always, always struggle to improve ourselves."

TEACHER TRAINING

The hospitality that the Chinese extend to visitors was demonstrated as usual on our arrival in Shanghai. Among the small welcoming party that met us at the airport was a woman introduced as Comrade Wu Huei Chu.

After going to our hotel for a brief chat with us, all of them left except for those who would be our interpreters during our stay in Shanghai. Wu remained, but it was several hours before I discovered that she was a professor at the Shanghai Teachers' College who had joined us specifically to answer my questions about education in China.

Wu stayed with us nearly all the time for the duration of our stay in Shanghai. She walked with me on school tours, saved me a seat next to her on the bus, was always ready to answer whatever question I had. I squeezed them in anywhere and everywhere that there was a spare moment—during the intermission at the acrobatics performance as we strolled outside in the cool June air licking popsicles, over lunch as I chased perfectly round and frustratingly slippery mushrooms from one side of my plate to the other with polished chopsticks, and late at night in the hotel room after each full day of activities.

Wu is fortyish, has a round plump face, protruding teeth, and a sunburst for a smile. She had taught in primary school for three years and then gone to university. After completing her university study she did three years of postgraduate work and became a professor at the Teachers' College where her work is now centered on general pedagogy. Once, when I was asking her something about her own education, I began with "When you went for a higher degree..."

She waited until I finished, and before answering the question I had asked, she clarified my wrong assumption. "We don't have degrees, but we have university and postgraduate studies. We study not for degrees but to develop more ability in serving the people."

In further discussion with others on this subject, I was told that there had been a degree system up until 1956. "But this was a revisionist practice learned from the West and the Soviet Union," a professor at another college said. "Knowledge was seen as private property, as a commodity for conducting business. Many intellectuals would do anything for a degree, to go higher up and away from the working people. They wanted degrees so that they could buy and sell knowledge."

Among the numerous facets of education that Wu and I talked about was teacher training. Many of her points were qualified by comments like, "But that is only in Shanghai; other places do it other ways"—a reminder of the great diversity of this enormous country, of the extent to which education is decentralized, and of the possible inaccuracies of generalizations about almost anything having to do with the details of educational practice.

The Shanghai Teachers' College is for the training of middle school teachers. Procedures for admission to the school are the same as for any other higher level institution—a senior or even junior middle school education, a minimum of two years work experience, and recommendation by workmates. "Their ideological and political qualifications are the most important and the masses in their work units are the best judges," Wu very carefully pointed out. "They must also be professionally competent. Our teachers must be both red and expert. These are the general considerations, but since they are going to be teachers, we also must look at some specific factors. For instance, they should be quite good in verbal skills, and they should be in good health."

The period of study at the College is three years during which students specialize in the subjects they will later teach. There are four compulsory subjects for all students: politics, pedagogy, physical culture, and a foreign language. "In the politics class we examine Chairman Mao's revolutionary line in education and then analyze how specific policies in the schools serve to implement the revolutionary line—the teaching methods, the relationship between teachers and students, questions like that. Another aspect is to look at the history of education in China and in foreign countries. We also consider it very important to study contemporary educational practices in foreign countries, but in this field we are weak. Our knowledge is limited, but we introduce whatever we can to the students. We should learn as much as possible from other countries. By talking to you, I can learn more to tell our students." (This comment, made with only the best of intentions, was a bit embarrassing as I recalled how I had been pumping her with questions without letup, hardly giving her a chance to ask any of me.)

As would be anticipated, combining practice with theory is a central feature in the training of teachers. The study of pedagogy begins in the second year in conjunction with practice teaching in the middle schools of Shanghai. Students spend a minimum of eight weeks in the field during which they participate in all aspects of the schools' work.

In some teacher training institutions students go to the schools part-time every day for the entire period of their training program. In line with the principle of learning through practice, it is generally felt that the best way for prospective teachers to acquire effective teaching methods is by observing other teachers in action and trying out different approaches themselves. In some places advanced students work with their professors in offering short-term courses to less experienced prospective teachers or in helping to set up programs in factory colleges. Such projects not only lend practical significance to educational theory but also link varied educational undertakings.

In their practice teaching, students are usually supervised by teachers from the college or institute and the school, "but they are treated like regular teachers," a member of the faculty at Kwangchow Teachers' College pointed out. Appraisals of their work in the schools are written by the individual students themselves after conferring with fellow students and supervisors. Any problems or disagreements in judgment are discussed before the self-appraisal is approved and signed. "In the old days, teachers could write down their remarks without showing the students. That kept the students under their thumb."

The professors at the teachers' colleges also follow schedules that blend practice with theory. Wu's year, for example, is divided equally among the tasks of teaching, research, and physical work. "All of us do them in rotation; while a third of us are teaching, another third are working, sometimes in cadre schools, and the last third are doing research. We call it a three-one-third system."

Each segment of her schedule, not just the physical work, was heavily infused with practice. The teaching involved only six hours of classroom instruction a week and more time in practical activities such as working with students who were practice teaching in the secondary schools. The practical bent of the research, however, was less expected. "When we conduct research we often go to factories and people's communes," she said, "because in order to combine practice with our theory we should go among the masses. It also helps us to receive ideological re-education at the same time."

During the time we spent together Wu was in the research phase of the cycle. Discussions with a foreigner about education in China and in the foreigner's country were apparently considered justifiable research. "Besides," said Wu smiling warmly and leaning over to gently touch my arm, "I am very happy to have the chance to be your companion."

People who will teach in the primary schools follow a program similar to those preparing to be middle school teachers insofar as the prominence of ideological education and practical application are concerned. There are several differences, however, in the specifics of their training. They usually have less education than their counterparts who are headed for the secondary schools and because of this some of the courses they take resemble those taught in the middle schools. They will usually be expected to teach several of the primary school subjects, so there is less specialization than at the middle school teacher training institutions and the course of study includes music and art. The period of training is also shorter, generally two years.

As for the training of kindergarten teachers, Wu said, "Before the Cultural Revolution we had normal schools in Shanghai especially for kindergarten education, but during the Cultural Revolution they closed and have not yet started again." She speculated that it would probably not be long before they resumed operations, but, for the time being, most kindergarten teacher training was done on the job. This was not the case all over. In a factory kindergarten I visited in Tsinan, all three of the teachers had completed a three-year, post-junior middle school training program at a municipal district institute. The large staff of thirty-two assistants was receiving short-term training courses in rotation.

Besides the regular full-term courses, teachers' colleges and institutes often arrange special teacher training programs. At the Kwangchow Teachers' College, there were under 4,000 students enrolled in the regular program to become middle school teachers while an additional 6,000 were availing themselves of special short-term courses, some of which were offered at the College, others through correspondence, and still others by the mobile teaching teams that traveled to remote areas. It was explained that "in the past we stressed standardization, but now we walk on two legs."

A picture of teacher training in China would be incomplete without including the continuing education of practicing teachers. A wide variety of arrangements have been instituted to upgrade teachers' qualifications; as usual, these arrangements differ from place to place.

At one particular primary school in the south each new teacher was attached to an experienced one and served a period of apprenticeship— observing, assisting, and learning. The teachers at the school organized themselves into spare-time study groups to exchange experiences and discuss problems that arose in their teaching. They commonly sat in on each other's classes and later offered suggestions.

Sometimes teachers are given time off for in-service projects, like the kindergarten teacher I met who was taking piano lessons during school hours. Some schools arrange for teachers to spend time at job sites with workers engaged in practical work related to their subject areas. For example, the chemistry teachers in one school went to a petrochemical factory. Foreign language teachers in a Shanghai school paid frequent visits to the dockyards where they held discussions with the dockers "to learn from their international spirit."

In addition to the in-service activities provided by the schools, teacher training centers—in some places called Red and Expert Colleges—take a share of the responsibility for the continuing education and training of teachers. They might organize meetings for teachers in a particular subject area, disseminate information about new methods that have been shown to be effective, or help to arrange teacher exchanges. An English teacher at a language institute in Peking told me about the in-service work of her department. A group had been dispatched from the institute to poll the middle schools in the district to discover the shortcomings in English language instruction. On the basis of the group's findings, several English teachers designed two programs and prepared the necessary teaching materials. One was a four-month crash course given at the institute; the other took place in the middle schools, with the teachers from the institute working directly with the middle school teachers in their classrooms. Reminding me that this was the open-door way of running a school, she said, "It isn't just our students who go out into the society; our institute goes out too, and so we can all give our services."

Judging from the descriptions I heard of the pre-service and in-service training activities, there seems to be continuity between educational methods as narrowly defined and education as a more total social process. For instance, when professors from the teacher training colleges visit the schools, whether in their own localities or the ones more distant which they reach with their mobile teams, they often concern themselves with school administration as well as pedagogy. They sometimes arrange discussions with the teachers, students, parents, and others in the community. In the instances that I heard described, they seemed to see their job as helping to train, inform, and advise all those in any way connected with the work of the schools.

In 1973 there were 127 million children in China's primary schools alone,[16] an indication of the problems involved in staffing the schools. I remembered hearing somewhere that housewives were commonly recruited into teaching and asked Wu about it. She began with the correction, "You mean *former* housewives. It's very hard to find women just idle at home. But to answer your question—yes, in the nursery schools and kindergartens some of the teachers are from among the former housewives. Also a few in the primary schools, but not in the middle schools. You see, before liberation most of the working women and housewives were illiterate. Only a very few women ever received middle or higher education; so it is much harder to train them to teach in the secondary schools."

Perhaps the best answer to the more general question of where teachers come from is, all segments of society in China. And, because any education whatsoever is new to nearly every segment, teachers can

---

16. William Kessen, ed., *Childhood in China* (New Haven: Yale University Press, 1975), p. ix.

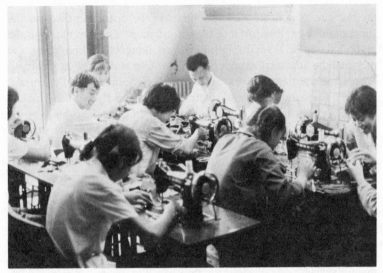

Teachers in training develop their "ideological qualifications" by continuing to do physical work. These future middle school teachers are making canvas shoes.

be found who do not have much by way of formal teacher training qualifications. This is true not only of teachers. A dentist I met on a commune had only a middle school education and a few months of medical training; yet he did all the regular dentistry work along with another more formally educated dentist. A doctor practicing in the same small medical complex had learned most of what he knew through self-study and from his father who had been a practitioner of traditional medicine and whose own training had consisted only of his apprenticeship with doctors from the preceding generation. Only recently had the son begun to receive any formal training though he had been practicing for some time.

Wu's sentiment that "the ideological qualification is the most important one" is widely shared in China. As far as a prospective teacher's own level of education is concerned, or the number of methods courses taken, there apparently is flexibility, but "the ideological qualification" seems to be less negotiable. So long as redness—the ideology of serving the people that is the overriding consideration in China—has been deeply internalized the expertise can be expected to develop through conscientious and persistent practice. So, for example, there are teachers like the young man we met who taught politics at Shanghai's Pai Kwang Middle School after only one year of teacher training. His experience working on a commune had been judged sufficient to provide "the most important qualification."

Furthermore, it is the responsibility of those who know more than others to share their knowledge. This means that ordinary workers and peasants with no teacher training background and perhaps even limited formal education are sometimes asked to come to the schools (at all levels including the highest) to make their contributions, which can encompass subjects outside of their regular fields of technical competence. An example of this was reported by a Dutch visitor to China who toured a primary school and discovered that the English teacher was a former factory worker who had learned the language from a radio course. Trying to get more information about her teaching qualifications, the visitor asked if she had written an exam to test her fluency in English or her suitability to teach, questions which provoked only laughter. The teacher explained that her comrades at the factory had recommended her for the job and that was guarantee enough.[17]

THE EMERGING TEACHER

The Chinese see an intrinsic (what they would call a dialectical) relationship between teaching and learning. Teachers obviously have as their first task to teach students, but good teachers maintain that to do their job well they must also learn from their students.

This applies not just to new and inexperienced teachers. I spoke to a university teacher who, after nearly twenty-five years of teaching, was asked to suspend all of his university activities for a couple of years to work full-time on an important research project. It was interesting work, a job that needed doing, and one which he was highly qualified to handle. He agreed and started to work on the project.

"The work was going really well and I enjoyed doing it but after a few months of being cooped up in an office I began to miss the students. Those young people are so invigorating and have such fresh ideas! While I was working in that office I felt as if I wasn't learning anything.

17. Loes Schenk-Sandbergen, "Chinese kinderen maken hun eigen school schoon, doen boodschappen voor ouden van dagen en helpen bij de oogst" ("Chinese Children Clean their own School, Do the Shopping for Old People and Help with the Harvest"), *De Groene Amsterdammer* [Amsterdam] (June 26, 1974), p. 20.

You know, it is very unhealthy for people's minds to stagnate, no matter what their age. So I put in an application to resume my old teaching responsibilities part-time and this request was granted. Now I teach only a couple of hours a week and devote the bulk of my time to the research work but I feel stimulated from my contact with the students and don't mind being in an office any more. I think that even the research is improving because the students have made my mind more alive again."

Another example was in a letter I received from Wu upon my return home about her plans for the coming term at the Teachers' College. "This term at school, apart from teaching and learning, I will bring the students to middle school for an experience in middle school education." For Wu to include learning in that little phrase—"apart from teaching and learning"—was as automatic and essential as it was for her to say teaching. It doesn't matter that she is among the most highly educated in China. If it ever happens that she stops learning (and not necessarily from those as well educated as herself; when she mentioned learning she was referring to what she would learn from her students)— if that day ever comes, as Wu sees it, she will no longer be fit to teach.

What is coming to be widely accepted as the proper attitude toward teaching and learning was formulated by Mao in 1938 when he wrote:

> Complacency is the enemy of study. We cannot really learn anything until we rid ourselves of complacency. Our attitude towards ourselves should be "to be insatiable in learning" and towards others "to be tireless in teaching."[18]

The progressive triumph over complacency—that smugness and self-satisfaction that has characterized the tenacious literati tradition—is bringing with it a new respect for teachers. In old China teachers at the higher levels were held in awe and fear and, by those just a peg or two beneath them, in envy as well—powerful emotions that were often mistaken for respect.

Things were different for primary school teachers in the past. Although their pupils feared them, others looked down upon them. "Their

---

18. Mao Tse-tung, "The Role of the Chinese Communist Party in the National War," *Selected Works of Mao Tse-tung*, 4 vols. (Peking: Foreign Languages Press, 1961–65), vol. 2, p. 210.

pay was very low,'' said Wu, ''and it only reflected their low position in society. There was a saying in the old days that 'If my family has sixty kilos of rice then I won't be in charge of those kids!' That means that even if a person is poor he would not want to be a teacher.''[19]

The genuine respect that is now given to teachers derives from their new relationship with the people. Though not all teachers have been to cadre schools, and, among those who have, there is no guarantee against getting rusty, they are generally integrated with the workers and peasants on an ongoing basis. Their regular participation in productive labor is an important in-service activity to upgrade ''the ideological qualification.''

A Peking University professor observed that material as well as ideological measures were taken. At this institution they consisted of a wage range of 56 to 345 yuan a month. He agreed that the range is still considerable and explained that less than one percent of the teaching staff receives the very high pay, and that the wide range is seen as temporary. ''Our policy is to reduce the gap by gradually increasing the lower wages,'' exactly the same policy that had earlier been described to us in a factory in Shanghai. The rationale given then was that the highest wages go to the veteran workers, and that while it is desirable to lessen the gap between the two ends of the scale this should not be done at the expense of the old workers who have given long and invaluable service, it being better to slowly raise the bottom rather than to penalize the top. More significant perhaps than the extremes is the average wage at the University, which is 70 to 80 yuan a month, not much higher than that received by the workers in most of the factories we visited.

As for overall changes in teachers' outlooks, Wu thought that things had much improved in the last few years as a result of these practices and the freer flow of criticism between students and teachers. ''Most teachers are conscious that they must serve the people. But,'' she cautioned, ''you must not think that the problem is fully solved. There are still many who have bourgeois and petty bourgeois ideas from the old society.'' I was to hear several other teachers make the same observation during my stay in China, which indicates that it is indeed a vital issue.

---

19. In North America we have an analogous saying that shows the lack of esteem reserved for our teachers: ''Those who can, do; those who can't, teach.''

To the visitor, however, the leftover "bourgeois and petty bourgeois ideas" are not very visible. In their place, what is strikingly clear is the positive quality of the relationship between teachers and students. There seem to be a great many teachers who no longer think that their work is done when the bell rings. They do individual and group tutoring, sometimes even going to the dormitories to help the students, have discussions with parents, students, and each other about their own and their students' progress, do preparations for future work in their own classrooms, in the school, and in the community, and other such jobs that appear to be taken very seriously. Students are often active in these undertakings; many of them now count themselves as partners with those who not long ago struck terror in them.

The growing social concerns of teachers are perhaps a good measure of their diminishing distance from ordinary people. Wu inadvertently drove this point home for me not long before I was due to leave Shanghai. We had both started to feel a bit uneasy about my pending departure, because we still had so many questions, and time was so short. We had tucked quick questions and partial answers in at scattered moments; they were not systematic or thorough enough to satisfy either of us. To ensure a better job of it we decided to compile a short list of questions for each other of those areas we wanted to be certain to cover in what little time remained.

Looking through some papers recently, I came across Wu's list. Settled back again at home with 9,000 miles separating me from China, I re-read the questions which at the time had seemed to be perfectly "natural" and not at all unusual. Reading them here, however, I realized that the questions themselves reveal a great deal about the new social conscience of Chinese teachers.

Here is what Wu wanted to know about American education:

What is the participation of teachers in the mass movement?

What is the relationship between teachers and workers? farmers?

How do the schools integrate theory and practice?

How do young people participate in politics?

As teachers come to see themselves less as the superiors of others and more as their equals they not only gain respect but also, according to Wu, develop a new self-respect. "All of society has the job of training the young generations to be revolutionary successors, but the teachers are particularly responsible for this task." It was clear from the

Teachers at the lower levels of education enjoy new respect.

look on her face that she considered this to be one of the most noble of occupations.

And the primary school teachers who before had been at the opposite end of the superiority-inferiority scale—what about their status now? As far as I could judge, the old distinctions are receding.[20] The teachers at all levels of education seem to take great pride in their vocation, sometimes reminding foreign guests that "after all, Chairman Mao was a schoolteacher, too."

It is not merely the fact of Mao's having been a teacher that is such a boost to their morale, but also the esteem in which he holds that profession. Edgar Snow's report of his conversation with Mao shows that respect as unequivocal.

Of course the personality cult had been overdone [during the 1960s].
Today, things were different. It was hard, the Chairman said, for people

20. The changing position of teachers at this level and in the preschools is indicated by their wages. At The East Is Red Kindergarten, the average wage falls between 50 and 60 yuan, 20 less than the average for professors at Peking University.

to overcome the habits of 3,000 years of emperor-worshiping tradition. The so-called "Four Greats"—those epithets applied to Mao himself: "Great Teacher, Great Leader, Great Supreme Commander, Great Helmsman"—what a nuisance. They would all be eliminated sooner or later. Only the word "teacher" would be retained—that is, simply schoolteacher. Mao had always been a schoolteacher and still was one. He was a primary schoolteacher in Changsha even before he was a Communist. All the rest of the titles would be declined.[21]

———
21. Edgar Snow, *The Long Revolution* (New York: Vintage Books, 1973), p. 169.

VIII: EVERY FACTORY A SCHOOL

Learn the simplest things. For you
whose time has already come
it is never too late!
Learn your A B C's, it is not enough,
but learn them! Do not let it discourage you,
begin! You must know everything!
You must take over the leadership!

. . .

Don't be afraid of asking, brother!
Don't be won over,
see for yourself!
What you don't know yourself,
you don't know.
Add up the reckoning.
It's you who must pay it.
Put your finger on each item,
ask: how did this get here?
You must take over the leadership.[1]

BERTOLT BRECHT

Arguing in favor of spare-time colleges for workers, an editorial that appeared in China in 1960 stated: "The cultural level varies a great deal from worker to worker. Some workers need to cease to be illiterate, while others need to receive higher or secondary education. It is thus necessary to educate the workers in accordance with their differing cultural levels."[2]

---

1. Bertolt Brecht, "Praise of Learning," in Alan Bold, ed., *The Penguin Book of Socialist Verse* (Harmondsworth, Middlesex: Penguin Books, 1970), p. 236.

2. "Extend the Work of the Young Communist League to the Spare-Time Universities." Quoted in Stewart Fraser, ed., *Chinese Communist Education: Records of the First Decade* (Nashville: Vanderbilt University Press, 1965), p. 350. Originally published in *Chung-Kuo Ch'ing-Nien Pao* (March 5, 1960).

In China, such a statement is not a mere truism or an expression of good will. In virtually every village, concrete expressions of adult education in various forms are to be found. Everywhere you look—workplace or residential neighborhood—there is some type of adult educational program and just about everyone you run across, whether an old peasant or a Party functionary, is studying something.

Everyone everywhere is reading, studying, questioning, probing, and perhaps more than anything else, discussing. All this makes for a vigorous and involved citizenry. One of the most striking impressions on a visitor to China is the enthusiasm people have for learning. "We are building a new future," remarked an energetic woman nearing sixty years of age, "so we all like to study and learn. If we don't, how can we conquer our problems? How can we progress?"

Hundreds of millions of people are "at school." The proliferation of mass educational activities in China into spheres hitherto unknown in their variety and scope makes the subject worthy of volumes. For now, however, a sketch of the origins and principles and a few samples of mass education will have to suffice.

THE MASS LINE

It was from Yenan that the revolutionary leadership directed military operations in the war of resistance against Japan, and it was in Yenan that a number of social, economic, and political policies were worked out and put into practice—policies which would later lay the foundation for the development of socialism in China.

Many of the educational theories and practices which were revitalized during the Cultural Revolution had been earlier set forth in Yenan: decentralization of education and grass roots control; flexible educational forms evolving from people's conditions; curricula based on the principles of "fewer and better" and of serving the immediate requirements of the students; methods of firsthand investigation and self-study; extension of education to adults; and, most importantly, the integration of theory and practice, the breakdown of the status distinctions that fell to mental work as compared to manual work, and the emphasis on redness as well as expertise.[3]

3. See Peter J. Seybolt, "The Yenan Revolution in Mass Education," *China Quarterly*, no. 48 (October–December 1971), pp. 641–69.

All of these revolutionary changes in education were part of the overall objective of making the common people masters of their own fate. This could be done only by eliminating China's deeply entrenched elitist educational system and eventually—some day in the future—making meaningful education available to every single child and adult. To even embark upon such an ambitious venture was by no means an easy matter. The peasants were illiterate, superstitious, and closed-minded. Their time and energy had always been consumed by their efforts, often unsuccessful, to eke out a bare existence. Education hardly figured in their calculations as a "necessity."

"How," asked one Westerner who observed the living conditions and plumbed the consciousness of the peasant,

teach this ignorant human beast of burden anything? How teach him, for example, those terribly complex Chinese characters that the scholars and the wealthy had monopolized for centuries so that they dominated the political and social life of the empire? How drive into the head of a manure-stinking, ghost-believing peasant a bunch of Chinese characters that he did not want to learn and that hitherto he had got along without? . . .

The Communist solution was both simple and typical. They combined education with life. Instead of drilling the peasant in school (except in winter), the Communists began teaching him how to read by showing him characters connected with his daily life and occupation. Thus a shepherd would be taught the characters for sheep, dog, stick, grass and so on. A farmer would learn the characters for field, millet, wheat, mule and the like. The methods of teaching were also as ingenious as they were pleasant. A school child would go around at the noon recess to the homes of five or six housewives and paste on the front door, the living room table, and the kitchen stove the characters for each of those objects . . . Or, as I saw, a farmer plowing in his field would put up one character on a big board at each end of the field. Thus, going back and forth all day, even his primitive mind could grasp the complex convolutions.

In village after village I have seen these clods of the soil, hitherto barred from any education, poring over lessons, trooping to the winter schools, watching rural dramatic teams perform on the threshing ground, listening to newscasts broadcast through hand megaphones, and studying the slogans painted on the walls, spelling them out in their tortured but patient way.[4]

---

4. Jack Belden, *China Shakes the World* (New York: Monthly Review Press, 1970), pp. 116-17.

This early commitment to the wide dissemination of useful knowledge which emanated from Yenan was based on a belief that knowledge is not something to be monopolized, patented, hoarded, or accredited. It is to be spread around, enriched through sharing and application to real life conditions. Any technique that worked was used—an evening class, an impromptu discussion during a work break, or a traveling theatrical group. "Everyone learning and everyone teaching at the same time. It was 'do-it-yourself' and collective education."[5]

A mere cataloguing of content and methods dating back to the Yenan days is insufficient to fully appreciate mass education in China today. The techniques developed and the themes emphasized have largely been the result of trial and error experimentation, but they have not been simply fortuitous. They derive from a very definite and consistent world view articulated repeatedly by Mao, and embraced by the great majority throughout China as the only appropriate orientation for building socialism.

This view sees the proletariat (the industrial workers) as the most progressive force in developing socialism and in creating the conditions for eventual communism, the future classless society. To succeed in this task, leaders are required. They are to be the most highly conscious elements in society, those who, in theory, best comprehend the class nature of society and who, in practice, are most selfless and dedicated to the interests of the working people. They are the members of the Communist Party, "the vanguard of the proletariat."

The Party is thus expected to lead the proletariat in all struggles. Mao has often stressed that the Party must be at the forefront of the masses yet always integrated with them. "We Communists are like seeds and the people are like the soil. Wherever we go, we must unite with the people, take root, and blossom among them."[6]

The proper relationship of the leaders to the led, of the Communist Party to the people, is referred to in China as "the mass line" which rests on the principle "from the masses, to the masses." Mao frequently reminds the Party that it can do its job only if it proceeds in all

5. "1949–1974: The Revolution in the Concept of the Chinese Scholar," *Broadsheet* 11, no. 10 (October 1974), p. 2.

6. Mao Tse-tung, "On the Chungking Negotiations," *Selected Works of Mao Tse-tung*, 4 vols. (Peking: Foreign Languages Press, 1961-65), vol. 4, p. 58.

cases from the interests of the people, then develops the "correct political line" (the one that will best further those interests), and then brings
it back to the people where it is translated into action. This interaction
constitutes "an endless spiral, with the ideas becoming more correct,
more vital, and richer each time."[7] This can happen only if the relationship between the leaders and the led is as "seeds to the soil," "fish to
water."

In education, the mass line has meant devising programs that begin
with the cultural and ideological levels of large numbers of people and
that gradually but consistently raise those levels. For example, the
leadership initially dealt with feudal ideas about the place of women in
society by stimulating widespread discussion, especially among
women, on those practices which were among the most oppressive and
were of first importance in moving toward their liberation. In old China,
a woman could not go beyond her own yard unaccompanied without the
risk of being considered a "broken shoe."[8] Women could expect to be
beaten regularly and mercilessly by their husbands and parents-in-law
with little or no cause and with no protection from anyone. Such humili-
ating and oppressive but almost universally practiced customs had to be
challenged first if women's horizons were ever to expand beyond their
own households and families. Discussions revolved around an analysis
of the injustices of these practices, why they existed, whom they
served, how they limited women's possibilities, what alternatives were
available, and the like.

Basic to the mass line is that new ideas must live through new and
appropriate action; talk alone is never sufficient to create change. Therefore, women were encouraged to form local organizations to deal with
the problems they encountered in their villages and neighborhoods. This
meant leaving the house to go to meetings—an act which many people
considered scandalous and which in some cases increased the frequency
and severity of beatings instead of eliminating them. In handling this
problem, women sometimes reasoned that if an irate husband could not
be rationally convinced of the irrationality of his behavior (and many
couldn't; after all, wives were property which their families had paid

7. Mao Tse-tung, "Some Questions Concerning Methods of Leadership," *Selected Works*, vol. 3, p. 119.
8. A prostitute.

good money or grain to purchase), perhaps he himself needed a beating by the more emancipated women among them.[9] This kind of action did not have to be repeated many times before husbands got the idea and grudgingly let their wives out of the house. Emboldened by success, their concern about their lot led them, over time, to challenge their role as breeders and servers. Footbinding, prostitution, concubinage, arranged marriages, restrictions against women owning property, against divorce—discrimination of every sort that had been meted out against girls from the moment of birth on has, in its turn, since been challenged.

These changes have not come about by themselves or in response to orders issued from above. They are largely the result of constant and persistent mass education and re-education often initiated by leaders at the grass roots level.[10] Nor has everything been dealt with at once. The most immediate and pressing problems come first, and with their solution, other problems take their place as the most urgent. In fact, the very solution of one problem can create other problems. Before women could work in jobs outside their homes there was no need for alternative day-care provisions for their children. Before the elimination of infant diseases which had caused millions of deaths every year there was no need for a birth-control program.

According, then, to the mass line as the approach to solving problems, leadership must be ever alert to the real needs of the people at any particular time. They must demonstrate their leadership first by finding out from the people what these needs are (educating themselves), and then by bringing back to the people a more concentrated analysis of the the situation and possible concrete solutions (educating the people). Through this cycle, the people become more conscious of some of the more complex dimensions of their own conditions and gain a greater measure of control in shaping their lives. This is seen as the proper method to be used for education of all kinds—be it ideological or

---

9. See "Half of China," in William Hinton, *Fanshen: A Documentary of Revolution in a Chinese Village* (New York: Monthly Review Press, 1966), pp. 157-60, and "Gold Flower's Story," in Belden, *China Shakes the World*, pp. 275-307.

10. Even the Marriage Law of 1950, which made illegal many of the practices which had oppressed women for centuries, was the result of widespread discussion and consultation. "It was the fruit of years of struggle, the experience of the 90,000,000 people in the Liberated Areas [liberated by the Communist forces during the wars against Japan and the Kuomintang prior to 1949], of thorough discussion and study of relevant data by a wide cross-section of the population and by official and popular bodies." (Maud Russell, "Chinese Women: Liberated," *Far East Reporter*, p. 9.)

political, basic literacy skills or "cultural knowledge," technical proficiency or artistic enrichment.

Of course there have been problems and reversals. The fact is that the mass line has not always been followed; leaders within the Communist Party have sometimes *mis*led the proletariat. That the "seed" at times has not been firmly planted in the soil, that the "fish" has occasionally removed itself from the water is taken as one of the reflections of the continuing class struggle.

The Chinese often say that good things sometimes come from bad. So while revisionism is seen as bad, it nevertheless resulted in the Cultural Revolution which brought many good and enduring consequences. Millions of ordinary people came to perceive more clearly their own class interests and to deepen their commitment to struggle against any forces that would divert them from satisfying those interests.

There is no question, for example, that the same women who had fought so many of the earlier battles to achieve their remarkable degree of liberation would, along with their daughters, vehemently oppose anyone who would seek to undo their gains. Over the years the revisionists, through subtle means cloaked in high-sounding language, had maneuvered for women to return to the home, to be removed from production and political study, and from participation in the great social currents of the day—what in essence amounted to a return to stagnation. Women had everything to lose and nothing to gain from revisionism. They could be counted on as staunch supporters of the mass line—once they saw it.

The same was true for most other people on innumerable other issues. An egalitarian educational system or an elitist one? Other questions arose in agriculture, industry, the arts—nearly everywhere. The mass line or the revisionist line? The great majority of people would choose the mass line, but only after they discovered which was which.

The very fact that these problems were handled through a revolution directly involving millions of people rather than being dealt with quietly in the upper reaches of the Party out of sight from the common people is one of the most revealing examples of the workings of the mass line. It provides ample testimony to the trust of the revolutionary leadership in the potential of the masses, an indispensable prerequisite for any application of the mass line.

Certainly the people relied on the leadership during the Cultural

Revolution as at other times, but they were also forced to rely more than usual on their own judgments since there were in effect two leaderships at the time—a revisionist one and a revolutionary one. To disentangle one from the other, to not be taken in by the "wolves in sheep's clothing" demanded increased participation and greater strain toward sound and more independent analysis.

Thus the mass line entails many things. It means that the people's actual needs and their awareness of their needs form the starting point of all social endeavors, educational and otherwise. It facilitates the possibility of many people learning many things very rapidly. It allows more and more people to become more fully engaged in controlling their collective futures; their growing control, in turn, empowers them with greater creativity and capacity to assume their own leadership.

However, before the mass line can be practiced the possibility must exist for a leadership to gain the confidence of the masses. To take root and grow the seed requires the soil. In the decades just prior to liberation the Communists had access to the masses only in certain areas of the country, but their skillful development and application of the mass line resulted in the phenomenal growth of mass support, which accounted for their eventual sweep to power. At this point only could the mass line be practiced on a countrywide scale. The Chinese consider that the conquest of power involves not only a quantitative implementation of the mass line, but also a qualitative change in its educative effectiveness. To gain clear and authoritative control over the means of education is to institutionalize a continuing and more stable basis for the development and consolidation of a mass line.

If, as the Chinese claim, the Communist Party represents the interests of the masses, then when it took control of governmental power, it did so to further those interests. It established what the Chinese call a dictatorship of the proletariat. The phrase should not frighten us.

It will be recalled[11] that Marxists contend that the most basic and significant characteristic of all class societies is class struggle which stems from the conflicting and antagonistic interests between the possessing and the dispossessed classes. Those who own the means of production hold economic power, which also enables them to wield political power. Such two-pronged power constitutes them as a ruling class.

By holding political power, Marxists mean organizing and control-

---

11. See pp. 87-88.

ling the machinery of the state, such as the executive and legislative bodies, courts, police, and armies as well as exercising control over ideological spheres such as educational institutions, the communication media, and the arts. All ruling classes construct and use this machinery to safeguard and further their own interests, and, obversely, to suppress the interests of classes not in power. Marxists maintain that the furtherance of ruling class interests and the thwarting of the interests of classes not in power are two sides of a coin. Any ruling class will go to great lengths to maintain political control, because only in this way can it protect its economic control.

It was this analysis which led Mao, as the leader of the dispossessed classes in China, to say that "political power grows out of the barrel of a gun,"[12] a statement that has often been quoted in the West as evidence that communism is no different from fascism and that the leader of the Chinese Revolution is no more than a bloodthirsty lunatic. What Mao is saying, however, is that those who hold economic power also hold political power, meaning that they control the repressive instruments of the state apparatus—the most important being the armies and the police—and that they can and will marshal these instruments if their class rule is seriously threatened. Their political power, then, ultimately resides in the barrels of the guns at their command. This analysis accords with the realities of violent suppression during China's centuries of feudal rule as well as during the imposed control by foreigners in the nineteenth and first half of the twentieth centuries.

Mao's statement also means that the only way that the dispossessed classes can realize their interests is by gaining power, and, in order to do so, they must be prepared ultimately to resort to force. This position is based on an acceptance of Marx's and Lenin's analysis that fundamental economic, political, and social transformation is necessary if the exploited classes are to cease being exploited, and that such transformation can come about only through revolutionary means in which the dispossessed take up arms against the already armed ruling class. This is precisely what happened in China during the 1920s, 1930s, and 1940s.

To guard against its own overthrow, any class in power really has no choice but to suppress the interests of the opposing class or classes which either are or else eventually will be out to replace it as a ruling class. This suppression, for Marxists, constitutes a dictatorship.

For the Chinese, the word dictatorship is not fraught with horror.

---

12. Mao Tse-tung, "Problems of War and Strategy," *Selected Works*, vol. 2, p. 224.

We are accustomed to applying the word only to those situations where suppression is imposed through the most extreme, inhuman, and blatant methods, as in overtly tyrannical regimes. For the Chinese, however, dictatorship is not identified by the severity of the methods used by a ruling class. It refers instead to *class power* which, under all circumstances, must necessarily suppress other classes. That the suppression can be gentle or violent, open or hidden does not change the fact for them that it is suppression and therefore a dictatorship.

Dictatorship does not depend upon which class is in power. The Chinese say that every ruling class exercises a dictatorship. Thus, for example, in China before 1949 there was a dictatorship of the feudal landlords and the comprador bourgeoisie who, in alliance with foreign capitalists, shared power. Today there is a dictatorship of the proletariat.

The Chinese claim that a dictatorship of the proletariat is a great historical advancement over a dictatorship of the bourgeoisie or any other prior dictatorships in that it rules for the benefit, not of a privileged minority but of the great majority of people and means to eventually do away with all forms of privilege. Since the proletariat and its allies own the means of production collectively, the Chinese consider that the precondition is now present for developing a society where everyone will share equitably in the bountiful products of cooperative labor, and where exploitation will become impossible.[13]

Strange as it may sound, another objective of the dictatorship of the proletariat is to one day eliminate itself, to make its own class rule, its own dictatorship unnecessary. One of the tasks of the proletariat is to work, through the implementation of the mass line, for the proletarianization of everyone so that at some future time all people will have compatible economic, and, hence, social-political interests. At that time, but not before, class struggle will end, because if there is only one class there are, in effect, no classes. The future classless (communist) society, they maintain, will have no further need for any repressive apparatus—a state—since there will be no classes to repress. Once all

---

13. This development, however, is seen as a long, hard process whose success is not guaranteed. Lenin, who elaborated and first successfully applied the concept of the dictatorship of the proletariat, cautioned: "The dictatorship of the proletariat means a persistent struggle—bloody and bloodless, violent and peaceful, military and economic, educational and administrative—against the forces and traditions of the old society." (V. I. Lenin, " 'Left-Wing' Communism—An Infantile Disorder," *Collected Works,* 45 vols. [Moscow: Progress Publishers, 1961-70], vol. 31, p. 44.)

people share common interests, both the state machinery used to suppress counter-interests, and the dictatorship that controlled it will lose their functions and "wither away." The final victory of the proletariat's class rule will be the elimination of all classes and all dictatorships, which the Chinese say is wholly unlike other dictatorships, as there can be no final victory for a dictatorship of the exploiting classes. Their objective can be only to retain their class power as long as possible, a power which, by the nature of class struggle, will eventually and inevitably be challenged and overthrown by those who are exploited.

Three months before the Communist Party came to power, Mao wrote:

Like a man, a political party has its childhood, youth, manhood and old age. The Communist Party of China is no longer a child or a lad in his teens but has become an adult. When a man reaches old age, he will die; the same is true of a party. When classes disappear, all instruments of class struggle—parties and the state machinery—will lose their function, cease to be necessary, therefore gradually wither away and end their historical mission; and human society will move to a higher stage. We are the opposite of the political parties of the bourgeoisie. They are afraid to speak of the extinction of classes, state power and parties. We, on the contrary, declare openly that we are striving hard to create the very conditions which will bring about their extinction.[14]

The increasing proletarianization of more and more people, the thrust toward broadening the ranks of this new ruling class lends greater significance to the mass line. Educational efforts should appeal to the masses; they should reiterate and strengthen the commonality of their interests.

An important arm of the state machinery in any class society includes the means through which people are educated. In China, the mass line in education has the potential to flourish because the proletariat's official dictatorship gives it a firm base in the masses. It can therefore dictate those educational policies which at once undermine the interests of its enemies while serving most of the people. When the Chinese urge each other to "serve the people," they do not mean that they should serve every single human being in their country, but rather the great majority who make up the ranks of the working people.

14. Mao Tse-tung, "On the People's Democratic Dictatorship," *Selected Works,* vol. 4, p. 411.

It is to the dictatorship of the proletariat that the Chinese attribute much of their success in education. This is what they say accounts for the growing egalitarianism in education, the greater respect for manual work, and the grass roots control of education in its many forms. They view these changes as an embodiment of a developing socialist ideology resulting not simply from everyone getting some rudiments of an education (this already happens in capitalist countries), but from everyone getting a concentrated and systematically proletarian education—and one that continues throughout life.

THE SPIRIT OF MASS EDUCATION

Something of a definition of what the Chinese include in their usage of the term mass education is perhaps called for, because they bring conceptions to it which differ markedly from our own. Our usual ideas of who qualifies for mass education, how it's conducted, where it takes place, what its underlying principles are, and what it includes need to be considerably expanded if we are to gain an appreciation of mass education in China and its enduring and encompassing nature. For example, we tend to restrict the meaning to widespread or universal education for children and youth. Adult education is usually a separate category for us and generally refers to courses for adults offered by local high schools and universities, or educational programs set up by local organizations. Mass education in China is more than just the sum of these two conceptions in two respects: quantitatively—everyone, adults as well as children and youth, is included in some kind of educational activity; and qualitatively—the content of these activities is proletarian and their purpose is the deepening of proletarian consciousness.

Another major distinction between our idea of mass education and theirs is to be found in the underlying assumptions about the proper functions of the forms and instruments through which it is consciously communicated. In all societies, the mass media and the arts—whether popular or "highbrow"—convey definite values and expectations. As such, they exert a tremendous influence on how people think, feel, and act; they are powerful mass educators. However, in many societies, including ours, those who create what others consume seldom conceive of their work as explicitly and deliberately educational. By the same token, their creations are generally not looked upon as educational experiences by their audiences. It is only the occasional film, play, or television program, only some of the things we read in newspapers and popular magazines, and only the very rare painting or song that we would consider to be primarily "educational." (The very delineation of what is called educational television illustrates this point.) Even though learning of some kind is a result of all of them, it is not usually intended or recognized. A great many of our exposures of these types are meant to divert more than to educate.[15]

The difference in China lies in the fact that all institutions in society are seen as having educational responsibilities. So, to use the same example, while the media and the arts may serve recreational purposes they almost always also contain consciously included educational ingredients—usually very prominent ones. Their fundamental aims are stated explicitly, "to educate and inspire." They are to contribute to the shaping of well educated working people imbued with "socialist consciousness and culture." Anything else in society capable of making this kind of contribution also qualifies as a means of education.

As for the locus of education, we generally place it squarely and almost exclusively inside of school buildings and therefore tend to regard things of an educational nature that happen elsewhere as "special" programs—in a sense bonuses which are somehow above and beyond the normal responsibility of educators and leaders in other spheres of activity. In contrast, the Chinese, who define education as a normal and regular feature of everyone's life and as a process that encompasses a whole spectrum of activities that educate, would not think of questioning that education could and should take place in a cowshed, a movie theater, a threshing ground, a clinic, or a living room just as well as in school.

The greatest difference, however, besides the actual content, is to be found in the underlying principles of mass education in China. Of the many that could be identified, one of the most striking is the building of social cohesion and unity of purpose. Very largely through education millions upon millions of people gain a deeper understanding of their commonality of interests. This is often facilitated by an intermeshing of the vehicles of mass education. By way of example, we can look at how

---

15. Critics of our mass media and the popular arts complain that we are fed a constant diet of pap and sensationalism that alienates people and encourages passivity. Therefore, if we think of education in the more positive and active sense of developing people's critical powers, their abilities to analyze, comprehend, and control their world, such exposures could be seen as antieducational.

newspaper editorials are sometimes used. *People's Daily* is one among many newspapers in China, but, as a very important one, it is made available all over the country. The most significant single item within it is the editorial, or, on days when there is none, the main news story. The Chinese seem to have a different newspaper reading style from ours. While many of us tend to treat a newspaper like a smorgasbord to be surveyed rather superficially, dipping to taste here and there until satiated, in China, where the papers are much shorter, most people seem to read them rather thoroughly, paying particular attention to the editorial. If the editorial is of special importance, it might be posted at places of work and on bulletin boards in the streets. It may very well be read during "prime time" on the radio.

The same editorial might be the subject for discussion at the next meeting of many political study groups. These are groups organized at the grass roots level. Nearly every workplace and neighborhood has several and almost all adults belong to one. They meet regularly—perhaps two or three times a week—to discuss current affairs, new policies, theoretical works, or problems encountered among themselves.

To get an idea of what might take place in these study groups, we can recall the case of the young man who had entered university through the back door, criticized his selfishness and subsequently left school to go to work, a case which became the subject for news stories and editorials in *People's Daily*.[16] This was not just a small scandal to provide food for petty gossip. Nor was it an out-of-the-way illustration of some high-flown, abstract principle with little relevance to the lives of ordinary people. It is a concrete example of the two-line struggle between seeking privilege for oneself versus combatting that tendency and working for the common good.

Such a newspaper item might stimulate a discussion on how the problem applies locally. Back doors are not confined to universities; they can be erected anywhere. Pulling strings, going after and giving out favors, abusing authority, being selfish—all are dangers that can exist in any quarter, dangers that can spread and conceivably develop in anyone anywhere in the country. What might look to outsiders like a simple, relatively insignificant newspaper article can become an issue of great concern with which people all over China become directly involved. "Have we been guilty of such practices? Do some of us look for

16. See pp. 85–86.

a soft life without caring if others work hard? Do you remember how bitter life was before liberation? How shall we follow the good example set by this young man in correcting his mistakes?'' Such are the kinds of questions that people in their study groups in widely scattered parts of the country might ask of themselves and each other. The questions themselves draw people closer together; the answers they are prepared to give define their very existence.

Interest in the issue that was initially brought to light by the news stories and editorials in *People's Daily* might find several other forms of expression. Broadcasts emanating from some of the small commune radio stations might focus on local variations of the same issue. Workers in factories might write poems and short stories on their workshop blackboards about the manifestations of the problem in their workplaces. Any issue receiving such widespread interest is almost bound to find its way onto innumerable big-character posters tacked up on walls and bulletin boards. China is a newly literate society where the written word is taken especially seriously. When a poster appears, people are likely to gather around to read and discuss it and, if it is sufficiently controversial, possibly add their own big-character posters in support or opposition to a position taken. Such are some of the spontaneous and democratic forms of grass roots expression that link people to common goals. It becomes difficult for people to remain aloof.

The newspaper written in far-off Peking becomes to the peasant a thousand or two thousand miles away not merely an interesting pastime or even just a useful bit of learning material, but ammunition for waging the class struggle and a tool for furthering socialism. Though *People's Daily* is a large and powerful organ produced in huge quantities by people he has never seen, in a place geographically distant from him, the peasant nevertheless has a kind of real connection to it, and through it, to his countrymen.

The result is that the Chinese do not feel estranged from their surroundings. They tend not to be wary of bigness—big government, big institutions, the big media of communication. Institutions, for the Chinese, do not appear to be regarded as remote, imposing, impersonal, and all-powerful. Most often there seems to be a high degree of clarity and consistency of purpose internal to each of the big institutions as well as among them, which is generally made evident to ordinary people. This makes for continuity between them and the people; it is in keeping with the mass line. Since the Chinese from all appearances are neither mistrustful nor hostile toward their institutions one does not get the feeling that they see themselves victims of a system which is there to be beaten.

It is often difficult for foreigners who have a totally different relationship to their own institutions to imagine the cohesion and integration of the Chinese with theirs, to understand the outlook of the Chinese peasant, and to accept that he does not feel alienated or manipulated. That he finds a big, powerful, distant newspaper responsive to the realities of his existence. That a centralized organ like *People's Daily* can link up directly and in unbroken continuity with his small production team study group. That it can and does help to equip him and his neighbors with whom he studies to discover their own problems and to grasp their complexities and subtleties. That through the newspaper the peasants can become more conscious of their own collective interests and more dedicated to facing the difficulties they will encounter in fulfilling them. That it can help them to enhance their capabilities, increase their self-reliance, feel greater affinity, not only with each other, but with many tens of millions like themselves, and gain more power over their lives. That through such means as the newspapers the Chinese are being educated in a consistent and meaningful way.

A second principle that guides mass educational practice is the developing of self-reliance. This is accomplished in large part through the emphasis on problem-solving. The Chinese do not seem to indulge in idle speculation or to go in for playing with ideas. For them, knowledge becomes meaningful when put in the service of practical needs. Therefore, the reason to pose a problem is to solve it. An extraordinary example of this is to be found in the new outlook on philosophy. A factory worker told me, "Chairman Mao teaches us that we should liberate philosophy from the classrooms and textbooks and that we should turn it into a sharp weapon to be used by the masses."

Philosophy! Perhaps the last thing that working people or even university students (and maybe some professional philosophers themselves) in most parts of the world would look to for help in tackling their problems. Much the same could be said of the Chinese in the past when philosophy, as the exclusive domain of scholars, would have been awesome and intimidating to ordinary people, assuming that they had ever heard of it. Yet today the study and application of philosophy is not considered beyond the reach of workers and peasants. It is not uncommon for them to get together and analyze their own immediate group problems by using principles of philosophy.

While in the West many schools of philosophy at best have a tenuous relationship to the everyday world and to practice, philosophy in China is rooted in both. Philosophy here begins with wonder; there it begins with a task.[17] Mao's assertion that philosophy should become a weapon in the hands of the masses is but a paraphrasing of the Marxist contention that philosophy must be used not merely to explain the world but also to transform it. It is seen as a tool that enables people to discover insights into their problems and how to solve them so that they can rely more on themselves and less on "experts."

When peasants on a commune say that they have increased their crop yield or athletes say they have improved their ping pong skills using Mao Tse-tung Thought, it may sound to unfamiliar ears like a lot of hocus-pocus, like no more than a religious ritual. Upon closer inspection, however, it will be evident that in actuality, Mao's Thoughts opt for just the opposite—to "do away with all fetishes and superstitions and liberate the mind." To the Chinese, Mao Tse-tung Thought comprises a body of principles and a method of analysis that lend themselves to the solution of just such problems as these.[18]

The Chinese today subscribe to the Marxist philosophy of dialectical materialism which sees the world and everything in it as an objective process that is materially grounded and can be scientifically known. The dialectical side of this philosphy emphasizes that change, both social and natural, takes place through the struggle and resolution of contradictions. This is the normal and essential characteristic of everything in the world.[19] Ordinary working people have been learning to look at things scientifically, using the principles of dialectical materialism to

17. See K. T. Fann, "Philosophy in the Chinese Cultural Revolution," *Far East Reporter* (September 1974), p. 15.

18. William Hinton has observed that "Mao Tse-tung Thought refers to the whole body of Mao Tse-tung's writings, which are considered by Mao's followers to be a development of Marxism-Leninism in the middle decades of the twentieth century. The Red Book contains some highlights of Mao Tse-tung Thought. Mao's *Selected Works* contain much more. ... To say 'Mao Tse-tung Thought' instead of 'Maoism' is an expression of modesty because it quite clearly places Mao on a level below Marx and Lenin as a developer of basic theory." (William Hinton, *Hundred Day War: The Cultural Revolution at Tsinghua University* [New York: Monthly Review Press, 1972], p. 35n.)

19. See Maurice Cornforth, *Materialism and the Dialectical Method*, 4th ed. rev. (New York: International Publishers, 1971), and Mao Tse-tung, "On Contradiction," *Selected Works*, vol. 1, pp. 311–47.

define, analyze, and solve problems. Mao's works are read and studied largely for this purpose.

When we get down to specific cases, however, it is still not always easy to find profound philosophic implications in the application of Mao Tse-tung Thought as commonly practiced. Because highly abstract postulates are applied to mundane and apparently small problems, it might well seem to us as if people aren't really deepening philosophic awareness, but are rather applying a recipe, cookbook style. At first glance, Mao's principles as applied to concrete problems appear to be no more than organized common sense. Unfortunately, single examples by themselves cannot convey the deepening theoretical awareness of the world (which, after all, is what philosophy is all about) that is involved when the Chinese comprehend and apply Mao's thought. What would seem more ordinary and common-sensical than the following case reported by a Canadian visitor to China?

At the Number Two Electrical Fixtures Factory in Shanghai a veteran worker and factory leader, a blind man, related the history of the factory from its beginnings as a small workshop for the handicapped to its present operations as a full-fledged factory. The visitor writes:

> It had always been assumed that blind workers should use only hand tools, that electric lathes, drills, or saws were too dangerous for them. Through the study of the statement, "Dare to struggle, dare to win," the workers in this shop came to the conclusion that they were not approaching their problems in a creative way, but were limited by prejudices about what handicapped workers could do. They therefore decided to install power machinery. In this process, the problems were immense, for none of the blind had any experience on such machines, and they were easily persuaded that it was impossible for blind people to handle them. The group studied Mao's statement that "it is people, not things, that are decisive," which was written about the nature of people's war. Through applying this statement to their specific problems, the handicapped workers decided that since they had the labour force eager to participate in production, they could certainly overcome the problems presented by the new machines.
>
> From study of Mao's "On Practice," they realized that knowledge is gained through experience, so with the help of veteran workers from a normal factory they began to install the machines and then to analyze the production process as they went along. Through their experience, they devised ways to simplify each operation until it could be handled by a handicapped person. The deaf worked in the bakelite-casting department

because the hot ovens were too dangerous for the blind; the blind workers ran the machines which performed the various operations of drilling, tapping, slotting, and machining the brass fittings; then the deaf workers assembled the various components into the finished plugs.

In operating the electric machines, the blind workers were at first extremely fearful: the noise of the machines frightened them, as did the danger of injury and the probability of failure. In turning to Mao for philosophic guidance, they studied the proposition that "one divides into two." . . . In particular, they were inspired by this quotation from Mao: "Just as there is not a simple thing in the world without a dual nature . . . so imperialism and all reactionaries have a dual nature—they are real tigers and paper tigers at the same time." When they examined their own problems in the light of this proposition, they came to realize that their machines were like "reactionaries": they were "real tigers" in the sense that they were dangerous, but they were also "paper tigers" in the sense that their loud noises and fast-moving parts were harmless once one understood the machine and knew its rules of operation. The leaders encouraged the other workers to grasp this "dual nature" of the machines, and under the tutelage of normal workers, the blind learned to recognize by its noises exactly what the machine was doing and whether it was running well or something was wrong. In brief . . . because they were convinced that they could win in the long run, they were able to overcome their problems one by one.[20]

The accumulation of cases like this in all their rich variety engenders a deepening and creative application of the philosophic principles which in one case can only appear piecemeal and exaggerated. Yet this accumulation leads practical life to be theoretically organized at the same time that it leads philosophy to be concretely grounded. For life to be theoretically comprehended and for theory to be a conscious part of the very living of life is what the Chinese mean by dialectical materialism properly understood and properly applied. Undoubtedly China is a long way from the full realization of the marriage between philosophy and daily life, but the Chinese consider that they have begun the process which can lead in that direction. For the time being, it can safely be said

---

20. Bill Willmott, "Education in the Factory: The Study of Mao Tse-tung Thought," *CCFA [Canada-China Friendship Association] Newsletter* 3, no. 3 (August 1972), pp. 5–6. For more examples of how ordinary working people in China use philosophy, the reader is directed to two short publications put out by the Chinese themselves: *Serving the People with Dialectics: Essays on the Study of Philosophy by Workers and Peasants* (Peking: Foreign Languages Press, 1972), and *Philosophy is No Mystery: Peasants Put Their Study to Work* (Peking: Foreign Languages Press, 1972).

that the emphasis on this kind of combined theoretical and practical self-reliance certainly figures as a key factor in the speed and success of China's recent development.

Less tangible perhaps is a third foundation of mass education—inspiration. Education should be a means not only for people to become informed, but also uplifted and encouraged. Thus, press, radio, and television stress content that is informative and optimistic. A substantial portion is given to international, national, and local news. Usually about one-fourth to one-third of the space in the newspapers is devoted to international news. Since China identifies itself as a Third World country, the media deal rather extensively with news from other parts of the Third World. The optimism about international affairs is expressed largely in terms of the progress of revolutionary movements in other countries. The most important message is that China is not alone, that socialist revolution and eventually communism are on the agenda for all of humankind. This persistent theme heightens the audience's sense of international solidarity and inspires a greater commitment to "carrying the revolution through to the end" at home.

There are also documentaries about the achievements, inventions, and breakthroughs of people in different fields of endeavor and in different parts of the country. Nearly every group will be represented at one time or another—workers, peasants, soldiers, youth, the aged, women, minorities. Like the news, this kind of coverage is uplifting as well as instructive. Failures are portrayed as temporary setbacks, as part of the process of struggle which, with persistence, will eventuate in success.

There is no sensationalism or gossip. A deformed child, a robbery, a scandal—none of these would be considered newsworthy in and of itself. They would become news items or subjects of documentaries only as problems that must be or have been resolved and as encouragement to the audience to likewise struggle to overcome their own problems. Those things which either have no social significance—like an idiosyncratic quirk of someone well known—or have the kind of social significance that would be in opposition to socialist values—such as advertisements—are totally absent from the media.

Artistic endeavors—dramas, films, operas, ballets, music, literature, art—are to serve the same ends. They ought, according to an American with twenty-six years of experience working in the mass media and the arts in China, "to reflect the life of the workers and peasants and soldiers, and through this to educate people about the struggles they're in and to inspire them to strive for the highest or the best so that the country can make progress faster.'[21]

Commenting on the content, he notes that what may seem to be overly political to an American audience makes sense to most Chinese.

The ordinary worker or peasant feels rather more comfortable seeing that [an artistic production with explicit political content] than he would seeing some cultural thing that's esoteric and has no connection with his life and his struggles. This was done before, for example, in China the first ballets were like "Swan Lake." Well, the ordinary worker-peasant just couldn't identify with that at all. It was out of his world and he couldn't see what use it was to him. So he just didn't go to see it. The intellectuals went to see it but the workers and peasants—which means 95 percent of the people in China—didn't particularly like it. However, something like "The Red Detachment of Women," they could very much identify with that and very much appreciate the story of the slave girl who became a staunch revolutionary.[22]

Working people cannot only identify with and appreciate a revolutionary ballet such as this. As the story is historically based, they also become better informed. As it depicts heroic triumph through struggle and sacrifice in the face of great odds, they are inspired.

Another cornerstone on which mass education is built is the conviction that people have mutual responsibility for each other's development. Those with advanced knowledge or skills must teach others. Adults in their political study meetings generally select from among their own numbers those who are more politically aware to be their discussion leaders. Newly literate retired people often become teachers for their neighbors who can read and write fewer characters. Technical skills are passed on from more experienced to less experienced workers.

Everyone should be as conscientious in learning from others as in teaching them. There are no "special" people who should be exempted. No one should view himself as "above the struggle." This is true even of artists, a noteworthy example since in many societies they in particular are seldom expected to take on such social responsibilities. "Cultural workers" should not only educate their audiences and in-

21. Gerald Tannebaum, "The Role of the Mass Media in China." Taped interview conducted by Arlene Posner (New York: National Committee on United States-China Relations, 1972).
22. Ibid.

Taking responsibility for each other's education. Here electronics workers in a technical cooperation group exchange experiences.

struct amateurs in artistic skills. They should also learn from those they want to portray. Thus, they solicit opinions, criticisms, and suggestions about their work from ordinary working people. They also often spend extended periods of time sharing the lives of the people by living and working with them. In a discussion with some cultural workers, an actress said, "How can we act the part of workers, peasants, or soldiers if we don't know how they think or feel? If we are a world apart from the laboring people, we might be clothed in their clothing, but our minds are still bourgeois. Cultural work is part of the whole revolutionary machinery. To act the part of a hero you must first be heroic yourself. It's not just our thoughts that must be remolded; our behavior and our very sentiments must also be transformed. We can learn these lessons only from the people themselves."

The very sensible practice of having those who know more in any field teach those who know less helps to explain another related principle that is basic to mass education, perhaps the most important one. That is the conviction that everyone has potential. In situation after situation one encounters manifestations of this conviction. Peasants are seen as capable of mastering philosophy. Ordinary workers are encouraged to improve their machinery. The young people who work in the hotel where I stayed in Shanghai attend service training classes given by the veteran workers one afternoon a week where they learn about the habits and tastes of foreigners so that they can serve them well; they get up early in the morning to catch the English-language instruction course on the radio. When I visited the workers' cultural park in Canton, which is open 365 evenings a year, there were thousands of people of all ages availing themselves of the numerous recreational and educational facilities which, to name but a very few, range from an outdoor roller skating rink to several theaters for amateur performances, storytelling, and films to eight exhibition centers that, at the time, carried large and impressive displays such as children's art and the life of Norman Bethune. Whether in the Convalescent Home for Workers on the shores of the quiet and beautiful lake in Wusih, or the Home for Respect of the Aged on the commune near Peking, people get together to watch films and live performances, and to visit historic sites. They meet regularly to discuss current events and government policies, and to read newspapers. Some of the sixty, seventy, and eighty-year-old men and women in the old age home are even learning to read for the first time in their lives.

Potential is seen to exist in everyone. It simply requires cultivation.

THE PRACTICE OF MASS EDUCATION

The arrangements for mass education programs seem to be as varied as the particular situations in which people find themselves. There are study groups at workplaces and in neighborhoods that focus on the immediate problems of the group and on political issues. There are spare-time courses, part-work, part-study courses, correspondence and radio courses, and full-time workers' colleges and peasants' colleges offering programs in general "cultural knowledge" and technical skills. The programs differ because they are set up locally by appropriate organizations in response to the varied needs of the people concerned, their only relation to each other being the principles that guide their practice.

The educational experiences of five young working men and women as they related them to me during two lengthy and lively discussions provide a glimpse into mass educational practices in China today. These five workers and peasants, all in their twenties, were well educated, fluent in English, and obviously committed to the new China. Chen worked in a machine tools factory in Shanghai. Compared to some of the other factories in Shanghai, it is not very large, employing about five hundred workers and running only one shift. Chen's face wore a perpetual smile; he was modest and always the last to speak up.

The other factory worker in the group, Wang, was from Peking. Her factory was started by seventeen housewives in 1958 during the Great Leap Forward. They began by making buckets. "Those women had such energy and daring. They just started from nothing. They took the light bulbs and windows from their own houses to equip their shop." Since then the factory has grown in all respects—to a state factory employing three hundred and fifty women and men who produce sophisticated electronics equipment.

Yuan, a shy and easily embarrassed young woman, looked more like an office worker or teacher than a peasant. She worked on a densely populated commune with about forty thousand inhabitants not far from Shanghai in "a very rich and flat plain." It was difficult to imagine this slight quiet woman doing heavy work in the fields.

Another peasant, Lu, was from the Northwest, not far from Yenan. Tall, thin, with a sprinkling of prematurely grey hair, Lu with his serious demeanor and his rimless glasses also did not look suited to farm work. He had the appearance of an intellectual, but when he spoke it was clear that he was no stranger to hard work. His commune, quite unlike Yuan's, is located in rugged mountainous country and, although it covers a large geographic area, it contains fewer than six thousand people in widely scattered villages.

The fifth, Chang, was a city woman who had been countrified. Born and raised in Peking, she was among the several million urban youth who have "gone down to the countryside" since the Cultural Revolution.[23] "Moving to the countryside is part of our education. It's

---

23. The policy of having educated urban youth settle in rural areas was recommended in the mid-1950s by Mao as a means of developing greater revolutionary fortitude among young city people and of lessening the gap between town and country. Although many youth did go to the countryside, this policy, like others, was seriously affected by the revisionist influence. In many quarters it came to be looked upon as punishment, a kind of forced labor, since life in the countryside entailed numerous hardships never before experienced by the more privileged urbanites. Some youth treated their stay as temporary, viewing it as a stepping stone in their careers, a way of building up credits that would testify to their revolutionary fervor.

Even after the Cultural Revolution, when the call to settle in the countryside was

another school. Just like Chairman Mao says: the whole world is our school. And it's true. I have learned so much from the peasants. They are generous and warm. My commune is in Honan Province, in the middle between the North and the South. We grow water plants, like the South does and wheat, beans, and sweet potatoes, as in the North. The people say, 'We're very lucky in our commune because we have everything in the world.'"

Rugged in appearance, Chang did not look like she had grown up in Peking; she looked like she had dug the soil, planted crops, and hauled manure since she was a tot. Despite this impression, her health was rather frail and she did more work in the brigade accounting office and the kindergarten than she did in the fields.

I asked if they all belonged to some kind of political study group in their various places of work. They did. "In fact," Wang pointed out, "everyone in China belongs to an organization where they work or live, and the organizations take care of certain things like study. Even children have political study in their schools. In one way or another, just about everyone in China from primary school on does political study."

"How does it work in the factories?" I asked, turning toward Chen.

"In my factory we have two kinds of study groups. Once a week the whole factory has a big meeting. The Revolutionary Committee will sum up the production targets and the tasks for the workers to discuss. Or if they have some information to pass on to the workers, it will come up at the big meeting, but usually information is exchanged on the bulletin boards or through the loud speakers. Some of the big factories have their study meetings during their work time, but our factory is not very big and we can't afford to let everyone stop work unless something very important comes up. The other kind of study that we have is among

---

reissued, not all problems had been solved. "It has been a gradual process to educate youth in the revolutionary spirit," I was told. Two types of problems were identified— ideological and practical. The latter includes such difficulties as poor health or a single parent left alone at home. Youth who are in such circumstances are urged to remain in the city. However, no one, including those whose reluctance is ideological, is forced to go. From all that I could gather, the old revisionist ideas are diminishing and more and more youth are willingly volunteering to leave the cities. The Chinese with whom I spoke felt that the improving attitudes of youth were the result of continued ideological education, better organization on the communes to accommodate the youth and integrate them more efficiently into work and study programs, and the growing and more obvious revolutionary enthusiasm of many others who had already fully adopted rural life for themselves. "Now many young people have done more than just settle down physically in the countryside. Their minds have settled there permanently."

the workshop members. In my group there are twenty-five of us and we also meet once a week for an hour."

"What do you talk about?"

"Oh, the content changes. Sometimes we discuss problems of production in the shop, or we read newspaper articles. We might discuss foreign news. Sometimes we study some theoretical works. It depends."

"What kind of theoretical works would you study?"

"The factory leaders set out a study plan for the workers based on self-study. We read some works on our own and then we get together to discuss them. They encouraged everyone to read through Chairman Mao's four volumes—not intensively, just read through them. Then together we studied some of the basic articles, especially his articles on philosophy. We try to apply the principles we study to our work at the factory. We also have studied several works by Marx, Engels, and Lenin—*The Communist Manifesto, The State and Revolution, Critique of the Gotha Program, Anti-Dühring,* and *The Civil War in France*. But we didn't study the whole thing, just excerpts drawn out by the Party. I think that *Anti-Dühring* is very difficult."

I observed that none of them could really be called easy reading and asked if the workers had understood them.

"Oh, I think so. You see, the groups are organized so that some people who understand better can help the others. There are some young workers and some veteran workers in the group. Often the young workers can read better than the old ones and old workers have rich experiences to pass on to us. In this way, we can help each other and that makes our study more meaningful. Also the cadres and Party members study more and understand more so they can also help with the difficult passages. If the leaders study well, it helps the masses study well. We are interested in getting the most important concepts, not every single detail. We also collect articles from newspapers and other reference materials about the subject we are studying. Though the reading is sometimes difficult, I think the study is successful."

Wang's experiences in her factory were very different. "When I first went to work there, we would study an hour every day after work, but later it changed. At first we discussed what was going on in the factory and did criticism and self-criticism."

"What was the criticism like?"

"I will give you an example. There was a man we criticized who wanted to move to another factory. He was a very skilled worker and even though we really needed him, he insisted on changing factories and didn't do his work well."

"Why did he want to change?"

"They were personal reasons; the factory was not near his house and other reasons like that. He was not really thinking about the needs of our factory."

"He was selfish?" I ventured.

"No, I don't think he was selfish. We must be sensitive to other people and discover their problems. His group met with him and asked him why he was not doing his work well. He said that he wanted to go to another factory and told us why. Then we criticized him and explained why he was wrong. 'You are a skilled worker and this is an important time for our factory. We are trying to build up our factory and we need you. If we can help you, then we will, but now is not the time to leave us.' The problem in this case was that his political consciousness was not high. He hadn't understood that sometimes your country needs you for a certain job and you can't always go according to your own desires because everyone has to work as part of a team. With this kind of criticism we convinced him. So I don't think he was selfish because he changed totally. He worked hard and contributed what he could, using his head and his hands to help our factory. About a year later we found a replacement and he changed jobs. But during that year he worked very well."

"You said that when you first went to this factory the study periods were for an hour a day, but that they changed. What was the change?"

"After I was there for almost a year, we began to study the Chinese Communist Party's history. It was very hard on the workers because we met every single day for two-and-a-half hours after work. Even though it was difficult, the people really liked it for the first four months. But then everyone started complaining. People were exhausted; after working eight hours, two-and-a-half hours of study every day was just too much. We would begin to work at seven in the morning and not get home until after six in the evening. Most of the workers had children. They still had a lot of things to do in the family. I was very moved because many of the workers' children took over all of the family responsibilities during that time. But it was too much work for the children and they sometimes had to neglect their studies. So of course the parents worried. And it was summertime, extremely hot. People couldn't just sit on stools all that time to study, and after a while some of the workers began to skip the meetings.

"By this time—we had been doing this kind of study for almost six months—the workers started criticizing the leaders. They said, 'You want us to study to raise our consciousness, but we can't even think because we are so tired.' The leaders realized that they had been wrong, and we changed it immediately. We discontinued study of the Party's history and went back to our regular study groups, but this time we met three times a week for one hour each time."

"Do other factories have as much study as yours did before it was changed back?"

"No, I don't think any others did. This was a kind of experiment that was tried in our factory to see if it would work out in other places. It was really an ultraleft experiment. There were some PLA men who came and organized this in our factory. They had the wrong idea; they thought that study was the most important thing; they forgot about our workers' health and our workers' welfare. I think it's very important for the people to know about the Party's history, but that is not the way to do it. That is why ultraleftism is so dangerous. It takes a healthy thing and turns it into the opposite. It made people hate to study. What Chairman Mao wants to do is a hundred years' task; it can't be done in a few months. People should study year after year as part of their lives, and they should enjoy it."

"Were there many ultraleft leaders in your factory?"

"No. Actually, it was mainly one of the PLA men. He was not really a bad man. He cared very much for the factory. He would stay for hours after everyone had left, dreaming of ways he could help the factory develop, but he didn't realize that he should rely on the masses. He was trying to do all the work in his own mind, thinking of all kinds of things, criticizing all kinds of things, and making people think they should study for so many hours a day. He was sincere in trying to help the factory but he was following the wrong line."

"Some people who are ultraleft are really very arrogant," offered Chang. "They think that heroes make history, but the masses are much smarter or else we wouldn't be here. Don't you think so?" she asked the assemblage, who did not hesitate to agree.

"I think so, too," Wang concluded, "but I also think that it is very important for us to have this kind of experience. Struggle educates people. We have had experience with revisionism and with ultraleftism. We will still make a lot of mistakes, but because we went through these things we will understand more in the future."

"How do these educational experiences in the factory study groups compare with the work you do in your study groups?" I asked the commune members.

Both Lu and Yuan described the study groups to which they belonged—his in a small far-off mountain village and hers in a bustling town on the fertile plains near Shanghai. As different as their situations were, the descriptions of their study groups were similar in many respects. In both cases, study was conducted primarily at the production team level. The frequency of their meetings was largely dependent upon nature. Ordinarily they met two or three times a week, in a public building in the evening, in the fields during a work break, or in a clearing early in the morning, but during harvest times they met less often. "The peasants do not work eight hours a day like workers in the factories," commented Lu. "Sometimes we are very busy, and we must attend to production first. So then we have less time for study. But in the North when it is cold and there is less work to do, the peasants study quite a lot."

In the smaller village there was a deliberate policy of combining old and young in the same study groups so that the more highly educated could assist the less literate older people with the reading. The sessions were most often led by the production team leaders or those with more formal education than the others, but there was flexibility. "When we are discussing an editorial or essay, whoever volunteers to read will be the leader that day."

In the larger village, where there were more study groups, there was still some rotation of leadership, but the groups themselves were organized "according to the different levels of the peasants."

Their study consisted of discussing current affairs and theoretical issues using newspapers and Mao's works as main sources. Both agreed, however, that the urban factory workers are probably more advanced in their study of theory. In the countryside study is down-to-earth and practical. "We try to draw lessons from the readings so that we will be able to sum up our own work better," Lu said. "For example, I live in the mountains and in my production team we study a lot about Tachai to learn how to change the face of the mountain."[24]

The most informative insights into the practicality of the peasants' approach to study came from Chang when she described her first impressions of the peasant study groups, seeing them as she did through the eyes of a more worldly urbanite. "When we arrived in the countryside we were shocked because we thought that the way they studied was not perfect. We were used to school life in the city where meetings were disciplined and orderly, but in the commune people just gather around at meetings. They even bring their babies, and they chat; they talk; they laugh. We thought they were too undisciplined. But gradually we began to realize that they are much more practical than we are. When they read the newspaper, they analyze the articles in relation to their situation today in the commune. They discuss it very informally, but that is the way people work out contradictions.

"I was really surprised. The first few times when they discussed newspaper articles, I thought, 'How silly they are!' They would read articles that were about some problem in the cities or about production in large factories. I thought, 'Those things have nothing to do with them.' But they would talk and talk and would always find the main idea and apply it to themselves."

"Can you recall a particular instance of this?"

"One time—I think it was the very first meeting I went to—they were reading an article about how one of the big cities had developed a program to take better care of public property. It described the whole plan and the way it was carried out by all the neighborhood organizations, certain ways that the people in each block had worked it out so that they look after things. It was very detailed. But a city is so different from a commune. They have different organizations; the people live close together; their daily lives are different; so are their problems. On the commune there are tiny villages with maybe only a hundred people and sometimes the next village is quite a distance away. Everything about it is different. I thought, 'How can they apply this city plan?'

"But, when I heard them talk, I realized that I was the one who was narrow-minded; I was arrogant for looking down on them. They get the

---

24. Tachai is a model production brigade known for its tremendous achievements under difficult natural conditions; the achievements include "changing the face of the mountain" by constructing terraced fields. It is looked to as an example of what can be accomplished through self-reliance, hard work, and revolutionary commitment.

main idea and then they apply it creatively. They can forget the details if they don't apply to their own lives. One peasant stood up and said, 'This kind of plan is good, and we can learn from it, too.' So they discussed the things that were happening in their own village and that sometimes things got lost or damaged. Then someone else said that if the brigade loses something we all lose something, but if everybody takes care of the brigade property just like their own household belongings nothing will get lost and we will all benefit. Then they figured out ways to implement their ideas by organizing the people to be more responsible, educating the children, things like that. It taught us students from the city a lot."

Chang's admiration for the peasants needed no prompting. She just went on and on praising the qualitites she had discovered in them. The two young peasants in our little group were delighted and at several points found her amazement at things that were commonplace to them quite funny. The other two, who were city people and had never dug roots in the countryside like Chang, their experience of commune life having been limited mainly to their travels during the Cultural Revolution as Red Guards, sat forward in their chairs listening intently and appreciatively.

Chang continued uninterrupted. "Oh, yes, the peasants are very practical people. In the springtime they discuss their plans for the next crop. The study groups get together and people say, 'We have this much land. This kind of soil is good; that kind is not very good. What shall we plant?' Many, many questions like that. Later they have another meeting—how to divide the work, who should go where, how much can each one do, what other responsibilities does each one have. Or another time they might discuss the cooperative medical plan. Everyone will come and they will evaluate last year's medical care and raise criticisms. They figure out how much it will cost to run the medical service, how much the collective should pay, and how much each person should pay. Should they each pay one yuan for the year? They go into each detail very carefully because they want to be sure that it is fair. The best part is that there is no one telling them what they should do. The people decide together. Of course there are many contradictions, but they usually get solved because the people have a common interest. They just sit and talk and talk and talk until they agree."

"But surely they must have serious disagreements sometimes," I interjected.

"Oh, you mustn't think that everything always goes smoothly. At first I was surprised, because the peasants are gentle and good-natured, but they also make sharp criticisms sometimes, like one time when some men were criticizing the women saying that they left the fields too early to take care of the babies and to cook the meals. Well, one of the old women—she is the main leader among the women, sixty years old, strong, white hair; she used to have bound feet, but now she moves very fast and works very hard; she has as much energy as a lot of the young people—she just jumped to her feet and criticized them. She said, 'You young men, you don't appreciate what other people do. You should be concerned about other people's problems. Why don't you help the women with the household jobs? How can they stay in the fields if you don't share the work with them?'

"Some of the men didn't like to hear that and they tried to make excuses. But then some of the other women got up to support what the old woman was saying. She is a good influence on the women because she gives them encouragement. Finally, after a lot of discussion and criticism, most of the men agreed that they should do more of the household chores.

"So you can see that the peasants really get along very well. Even when they get into a quarrel they can usually settle it because they care about the same things—how to improve their lives in the village. Their concerns are always practical. It is very different from the city and the intellectuals who sometimes get involved in abstract questions. Ideas are clear to the peasants; either they help production and improve their welfare or the don't. For instance, if you said, 'Let's not work today; let's all study Chairman Mao,' they would think you were crazy. If someone is doing intellectual work—translating a book or something like that—then he can take a day off and go and study Chairman Mao. But if you are working in the fields, then you can't just take a day off, because production would suffer. That is why I don't think the peasants make as many ultraleft mistakes. They simply would not study for two-and-a-half hours every day and neglect their other work."

The young peasants, workers, and I were so thoroughly enjoying Chang's enthusiastic monologue that when she paused for some tea, we all started to ask her questions at the same time. Laughing over our collision, they insisted that my question take precedence. Her reference to the ultraleftism of the leader in Wang's factory made me wonder how important she considered the leaders in her village to be for stimulating the healthy attitudes of the peasants that she had been describing. As we expected, she had a story to accompany her answer.

"The leaders are very, very important. When I first arrived there the production team was actually quite backward in many ways. We had a big struggle in the village. During the first half-year I was there our production team leader was an old man who was sort of conservative. What you need in a poor village like ours is a strong leader with the correct ideology, but sometimes he came to work late and he didn't like to work in the fields. So he would do some small jobs in the village. It was not really his fault, because he was too old to be very active. But the team suffered because he was not involved in the most important part of production, and therefore he couldn't see the problems clearly. He always had to get a secondhand idea of what was going on. The whole village was like this old man—slow, take your time, don't get excited. And many contradictions were not solved.

"But then another man came, younger and full of energy. This was his village, but he had gone away to middle school in the city before the Cultural Revolution; after he finished school he said he wanted to return to the village. But when he got back, he was raised to the job of a brigade leader and so he stayed in another village. That happened a lot before the Cultural Revolution. Many of the educated youth were given higher jobs and the villages would lose some of their best leaders. He was a sort of small bureaucrat, always organizing meetings and things like that. He was not happy; that was not his motive in coming back to the countryside—not to sit in an office.

"Finally he insisted on returning to his village. Well, within two weeks the whole village began to change to his spirit. It was so encouraging. Everyone began to work harder; everyone began to be more concerned about production problems. At the meetings people became more active; they were eager to study; they dared to speak up just like him.

"He took the lead in everything. He would find the hardest jobs, working in the rice fields in the water and mud for hours and hours. Whenever there were problems, he would go to investigate. He was always cheerful and kind to everyone, and this influenced all the peasants. He lifted their morale. At the meetings of our study groups he would bring up all kinds of questions that had never been talked about before. For example, one time he said, 'This afternoon my wife got an IUD,' and he explained what it was and why it was important to have good birth control. At first some people giggled, and it made his wife blush, but he treated it as something everyone should know about, as scientific and serious. Gradually the people overcame their embarrassment and started to ask questions, and his wife told them how she felt.

"It made me learn that people are really good anyplace. Correct ideology will rouse them and give them energy. When people are happy they can work harder and they will enjoy it. These two leaderships made me see the two lines: with the masses or not with the masses. I also have gained a better appreciation of the creativity of the masses since I have been working in the countryside. By working together, studying together, and struggling together the political consciousness and the general cultural knowledge of the ordinary working people have been very much raised."

It was mentioned several times during our discussion that the heightened political and cultural levels are not only the result of the work done directly in the study groups. Self-study is apparently encouraged among the population at large, as it is among students. Each one of these young workers and peasants said that there were libraries at their places of work. In two cases in the countryside, they were maintained at the brigade level and in one at the commune level. They indicated that the libraries were modest, all of them containing mainly newspapers and a few books. Chen's Shanghai factory had the best equipped library— newspapers, books on Marxist theory and practice, technical subjects, and general literature.

Simple, illustrated books were also available in some of the libraries and were used for literacy training. The arrangements for upgrading the literacy skills of older people with little or no formal schooling ranged from informal tutoring—of individuals and small groups of old people sometimes conducted by Little Red Soldiers and sometimes by adults— to regularized formal classes. This work was organized by neighborhoods rather than work units, presumably because most of the people who lack literacy skills are older retired or semiretired people whose activities center mainly around their immediate neighborhoods.

We moved on to technical education. Where did people learn the theoretical and practical aspects of the technical skills necessary to keep up with China's rapid industrialization? From what I could learn, it seems that these are more often than not learned on the job in a variety of ways. New young workers are often paired off with older experienced ones and serve a kind of apprenticeship.

If there is a complex process to be mastered, courses might be set up, sometimes on the premises, depending on conditions. For example, two of the three communes use tractors, one—Yuan's highly productive commune near Shanghai—quite extensively. Members had been chosen from each production team in her commune to attend short training courses for operating and repairing tractors at a special school in the commune center. There were a number of other special courses offered at her commune: for accountants (to keep the records of work points for the production team), electricians, and machine operators. The commune also ran several factories. Yuan's sister, who worked in one that recycled waste cotton, had received all her training on the job, but some of the other factories requiring more sophisticated techniques had special classes for the peasants-turned-workers.

The communes, however, are not always self-sufficient in providing their own technical training. They apparently quite often arrange exchanges. "A while ago we started planting a new crop we had never grown before," Yuan commented. "A few peasants went to another commune to learn the technique and then they came back and taught the others. We also have some people who are learning to run cranes. They go to a state-owned factory near our brigade and get training from the workers there."

Chen, a very down-to-earth and unassuming man despite the fact that he had always lived in the city and despite his relatively high level of education (he had attended university before the Cultural Revolution), was pleased to hear about the cooperation between workers and peasants. When he heard that peasants were learning to operate cranes from factory workers, he noted, flashing his usual smile, "In my factory we say, 'The peasants are the close allies of the workers. We are brothers.' "

Another example of that alliance was in evidence in the tractor factory I visited in the mountainous region not too far from Lu's commune. It was run by the county and took on the responsibility not only of supplying tractors to all the communes in the area but also of training the peasants in their use and upkeep. The leaders at the factory considered this a normal and reasonable extension of production. "What good are our tractors if the peasants don't know how to use them? Producing tractors is not just a technical problem. We must take the lead and not crawl along at a snail's pace. To do our job well, we try to have a deep feeling for the real conditions of the peasants by doing firsthand investigations. This motivates us to help them and to innovate according to their needs."

On this basis, the factory had set up a two-part training program. It dispatched a number of its technicians and workers to the communes to look into local conditions and problems. When necessary they also supplied repair equipment and spare parts. This aspect of the training was continuous and went on before and after the tractors were delivered. The same people also gave short-term courses to selected peasants on the factory grounds.

Lu's and Chang's communes, being less mechanized and diversified than Yuan's, required fewer specialists. The limited number of tractor drivers at the one other commune that used tractors had been trained in a larger center outside of the commune, and the accountants at both communes were young middle school graduates who learned their trade from the veteran accountants. "They mainly improve their technique through practice," said Lu. "And also self-reliance is very important. We are still a backward country, you know, and we must very often educate ourselves."

In the factories the technical training programs are generally more advanced than on the communes since more highly specialized skills are required. When Wang was an apprentice, she had attended classes at her factory given by the skilled veteran workers. "They taught us about electricity, how to read blueprints, geometry, chemistry, all kinds of things that we needed to know to do our job well. I think that by having the actual experience of working in the factory combined with theory in the classes, we learned much quicker, and we did not slow down production." The classes were held during work hours and the apprentices received full pay whether they were studying in class or working on the shop floor.

To learn one of the more difficult processes in her factory, ten workers had been selected to attend a technical college where they took a three month course. "It was really very similar to the training of the apprentices in our factory," Wang explained. "The technical college also has its own factories. The workers who took the course studied in the classes and then they went to the school's factories to practice. The workers are their teachers just like here, and they learn by integrating practice with theory, also just like here. When the ten workers finished the course they came back and set up their own course in our factory to teach the other workers."

When I asked if this was a common method for upgrading skills, Wang looked a little surprised. "Oh, yes; that's the only way you can do it. How else can we develop if we don't learn from others who know more than we do? When my factory was first started by the housewives in 1958 two workers came to help for two months. If we have any problems there are always other people we can go to for help. We are connected to other factories that are doing similar work. When one factory conducts experiments they tell all the others about it so we can all benefit from each other's progress.

"My brother's friend works in a very big factory which does the same kind of work as my factory. Since it is much bigger than ours, they understand the problems better. When we have a problem I tell him, 'You are just the person we want. Why don't you come to our factory and see what the problem is?' And then he comes and we show him what's wrong. Maybe he can help us but maybe he can't. If he can't he will go back to his factory and get some more experienced veteran workers to help us. We all learn from each other."

Chen reinforced Wang's descriptions with examples of similar arrangements in his factory. However, his factory had gone one step further by setting up their own ongoing spare-time school in conjunction with other factories nearby. The school offered several short-term technical courses, lasting about two months. Most of them met twice a week in the evenings for two hours each session. The courses, which were all voluntary, were apparently quite popular, with workers signing up for them in rotation.

This more stable type of educational program is apparently becoming quite widespread in the urban factories, particularly the large ones, but appropriate variations are also being instituted on some communes. Chang's brigade had recently set up a spare-time school for the peasants which had a three-part program: political study, scientific farming, and literacy.

Both Chen's factory school and Chang's brigade school are small-scale versions of a recent innovation in worker-peasant education known as workers' colleges and peasants' colleges. In Shanghai, the city best known for workers' colleges, I visited a diesel engine factory that ran a full-time July 21st Workers' College, the name deriving from a directive issued by Mao in 1968.[25] Their program, which is two-and-a-half years in length, includes technical courses related to the factory's production, such as mathematics, mechanics, drafting, diesel engine

---

25. The July 21st Directive states: "It is still necessary to have universities; here I refer mainly to colleges of science and engineering. However, it is essential to shorten the length of schooling, revolutionize education, put proletarian politics in command and take the road of the Shanghai Machine-Tools Plant in training technicians from among the workers. Students should be selected from among workers and peasants with practical experience, and they should return to production after a few years' study."

A textile worker explains a new process to students in a spare-time factory school.

design, machinery manufacturing technology, hydraulic press transmission, and computer techniques. The curriculum also includes politics and English.

The College's connection to the needs and work of the factory is, we were told, always close. By participating in production while they study, the worker-students lend practical significance to the theory learned in the classroom as well as helping to fill the factory's production quotas. The factory workers, including those who are not students, can pass on their suggestions and refer their technical problems to the College for study and solution by the students and teachers. This arrangement enables the ordinary workers to have a direct voice in the College curriculum.

The students, who are selected from among the factory work force by essentially the same criteria and procedures as are used by other upper level educational institutions, return to their own workshops after "graduation" so that they can "share their knowledge with their workmates." One of the central qualifications for a prospective student is a background that is "rich in practical experience." The same qualification is applied to their teachers who come primarily from the ranks of the model veteran workers, worker-technicians, and teachers with experience in factory schools and technical institutes. Consistent with this emphasis on practical experience, instruction rests on the principle of "practice, knowledge, again practice, again knowledge," the idea being that the learning of theoretical principles should be based solidly on the students' own experience which, in turn, should lead to practical application again, but at a more sophisticated level, and so on.

As a significant means of educating workers, the July 21st colleges are quite new. They have realized a tremendous expansion in recent years. For example, between 1973 and 1975, their numbers grew from 40 to 360 in Shanghai and from 6 to 100 in Canton. Sometimes smaller factories pool their resources and collectively establish a college. The larger factories which have their own colleges often admit workers from smaller factories which do not have them but which are engaged in related work. Their programs run from several months to three years. In all cases, during the period of study the worker-students receive their full regular pay and benefits.

In questioning one of the worker-students at the diesel engine factory's July 21st Workers' College, I asked about the advantages he would gain from his study. "The advantages are social, not personal. We don't want diplomas, titles, or raises. We try to narrow the gap between mental work and manual work and become good intellectuals who can also do useful work with our hands. Our purpose is to serve the people better."

Varied and cooperative educational programs through study groups, mutual assistance, and technical training are in operation in virtually all parts of the country. They are momentous both in their scope and in their results. In China, it is said that "life is education; all of society is our classroom." Every school *is* a factory and every factory *is* a school. Education does not stop when a youngster leaves primary or middle school. Wherever there are people in this vast and exciting country there is educational activity of some sort. Precisely what sort depends upon the particular conditions of the locality and the commitment of the people to improve those conditions for the collectivity. It also depends upon the imaginations of the people who, since their liberation, have brought their creativity into play as they have successfully grappled with one problem after another. The workers in each factory, the peasants in each village, the students and teachers in each schoolhouse must assess their own conditions and analyze their own problems. Their solutions are as varied as the problems they face and as the imaginations they bring to them.

For this very reason, a book on education in China can no more come to a neat and final conclusion than the process of Chinese education itself. For now, it can be said that the curiosity and vitality of the Chinese people of all ages are products of their profound and even joyous engagement with each other and their surroundings and of their direct, day-by-day participation in struggling with common problems as they discover together how to make the decisions that will shape their collective destinies.

Perhaps Yuan best summed it up when she said in her quiet way, "Our education never really ends. Everyone is a part-time student in one way or another. All of us need to educate ourselves to transform ourselves and our society."

EPILOGUE

Back home, a young woman, a disarmingly ingenuous first year university student, asked me if I had experienced culture shock when I went to China. Culture shock? I've never quite understood what that's supposed to mean. It has always struck me as one of those fuzzy ideas that students have to memorize out of introductory anthropology textbooks. But if my vague notion of what people who use the term mean is anywhere near the mark—no, there was no culture shock.

When you enter China, you feel the almost physical dropping off of weights that you hadn't even realized you were carrying around, you had become so used to being laden down by them. In a matter of hours (literally) you've stopped checking your purse to make sure your wallet hadn't somehow disappeared. You've become accustomed to having no key for your door; it doesn't occur to you that one might be necessary.

You wake up in the morning to a chorus of children's voices wafting from a radio of a nearby resident or the chanting of a group of workers on an early morning jog. If you get up early and roam the streets, you see old people doing *tai chi chuan,* the traditional Chinese exercise. Some teenagers and young workers standing a bit behind and apart are learning to master the art by watching the elderly with fixed attention and duplicating their intricate movements. You might even come upon a track and field meet of the city's clerical workers as I did one morning in Peking. Hundreds of workers gathered for a tournament before work were doing feats of skill and running relay races. Some of the events were serious, others very funny like the one where some middle-aged men were running a race while at the same time trying to balance ping pong balls on extended badminton rackets, the kind of fun we generally restrict to eight-year-olds. Everyone seemed relaxed and good-humored, but I also got the feeling that they had important and meaningful things to do that day.

You're greeted with smiles and applause wherever you go. You're invited into people's homes, served tea, and encouraged to ask any questions you want. You might walk down the streets of Shanghai alone late at night, also as I did—Shanghai, one of the world's largest cities, and a mere quarter century ago probably its ugliest. But you won't need to check nervously over your shoulder, you won't have to avoid the glance of passing strangers. You look at each other—and even smile. Man or woman, you dare smile. But in Shanghai today it's not so bold. How else would you show each other the friendship you both feel? What better way for you to express your profound appreciation of their almost unbelievable achievements?

Culture shock? It's no shock for those burdensome weights to melt away. It's a kind of liberation.

If there is such a thing as culture shock, it comes when you cross the border *leaving* China. Yes, it's a shock when those weights suddenly impose themselves again. They were so easy to forget. But in an instant you are their slave again. Is my wallet still there? How many bags was I carrying? One, two, three, four, yes, they're all here. Why must that poor, ragged old woman in the train station carry that healthy young man's parcels on the carrying pole suspended on her bent shoulder, the baskets sagging low and hardly swaying from the heaviness? Why is that child crying, and why is that hysterical-looking woman screaming at him? Why must those painted, mini-skirted women hang around waiting for customers? Why is that man muttering to himself? One, two, three, four, they're still all there.

"Diamonds are Forever," "You've come a long way baby!" "For those who think young," "Fly me," "Will he kiss you again?" "He knows what I like; I don't have to tell him." Where's "Serve the People"? "Study hard; make progress every day"? Yes, it's a shock.

Why is that man lying in the hallway drunk in his own vomit? Why is everyone in that line pushing and grabbing? Why must that old woman sit on the sidewalk and plead with people she doesn't know for a few cents to feed the withering child in her arms? Why is the music so grating? Why are people afraid to smile at each other? Why? One, two, three, four.

Yes, I guess you could say I experienced "culture shock."

INDEX